JOCK PETERS | *Architecture and Design*
The Varieties of Modernism

CHRISTOPHER LONG

JOCK PETERS | *Architecture and Design*
The Varieties of Modernism

Bauer and Dean Publishers | New York

To the memory of my father, Harry Long

CONTENTS

- 9   Preface
- 13   Prologue
- 17 | Chapter 1
  - **JARRENWISCH AND HAMBURG**
- 25 | Chapter 2
  - **AN ARCHITECTURAL APPRENTICESHIP**
- 47 | Chapter 3
  - **OF LIGHT AND DARKNESS**
- 67 | Chapter 4
  - **EXPERIMENTS IN STYLE**
- 89 | Chapter 5
  - **AMERIKA**
- 101 | Chapter 6
  - **FAMOUS PLAYERS-LASKY**
- 123 | Chapter 7
  - **PETERS BROTHERS**
- 153 | Chapter 8
  - **BULLOCK'S WILSHIRE**
- 193 | Chapter 9
  - **HOLLANDER**
- 237 | Chapter 10
  - **CALIFORNIA MODERN**
- 271 Epilogue
- 275 Works by Jock Peters
- 279 Notes
- 291 Selected Bibliography
- 299 Index

PREFACE

This book has its beginnings in another project. While doing research for my monograph on Kem Weber at the Architecture and Design Collection at the University of California, Santa Barbara, I kept encountering references to Jock Peters in Weber's correspondence. I knew a little about Peters's design for Bullock's Wilshire—the great Los Angeles department store that opened in 1929—and I was aware that he had worked for a time as an assistant art director in the Hollywood film industry, but not more than that. Intrigued, I made a quick pass through the Jock Peters papers held at the archive.

After examining the small cache of drawings and making a thorough study of the other papers in the collection, I realized that what I had found was not sufficient for a book-length study. Speaking with Jocelyn Gibbs, then the archive's director, I discovered that the bulk of Peters's papers were still in family hands. Jocelyn had the contact information for Peters's grandson, Jock de Swart, and after returning home to Austin, I called him.

I learned that he and his partner, Louise Garnett, were living atop a mesa overlooking the Animas River, just south of Durango, Colorado. He invited me to visit and go through the drawings, photographs, and other documents in the collection. In June 2015, my wife, Gia, and I flew to Albuquerque and made the drive to the Four Corners region. Jock and Louise were perfect hosts, and we spent three very full but pleasant days examining and scanning the materials. Over the next several weeks, I read everything, learning to decipher Peters's crabbed handwriting and trying to fill in what were still very evident gaps.

Over the following two years, I conducted additional research in California and Germany. What emerged was the story of a singular American designer. I learned of his early years as the son of a farmer in north Germany, his extended education in Hamburg and Düsseldorf, and his budding career in the last years of Wilhelmine Germany. I found Peters's military records, detailing his service during World War I and the onset of the tuberculosis infection that would eventually lead to his early death. There were other papers concerning his life in Hamburg after the war, his directorship of the School

Jock Peters, top of a display table from the Sportswear Department, Bullock's Wilshire, Los Angeles, 1929. Mahogany, zebrawood, sycamore, and other woods. Gift Decorative Arts and Design Council Fund in honor of Rose Tarlow and others receiving the 2010 Design Leadership Award. Los Angeles County Museum of Art.

of Applied Arts in Altona, and his immigration to the United States. But, most remarkably, there were many drawings and stacks of correspondence offering insight into his years in Los Angeles and his progress as an independent architect and designer. What emerged was a key part of the story of early modernism in Southern California. The following pages tell that story.

I have, I must confess, another aspiration. It is bound up with our conventions for studying history. I recall many years ago, when I attended university in Munich, hearing the great German historian Thomas Nipperdey. He exhorted his students to allow history to be, in his eloquent phrase, "as complex as it is"—to render it with all its embedded convolutions and contradictions. He stressed the need for an openness to the problems and dilemmas faced by those in the past. Nipperdey spoke, too, of the importance of avoiding condescension, underscoring the "otherness" of earlier attitudes and perceptions. I remember once he told us how the German bourgeoisie had come to modernism, how in a secular age art had become a substitute for religion. The process he described, though, was hardly straightforward. He spoke with wonderful fluency about why that was the case: that the dislocations brought on by the new industrial age had compelled the search for alternative beliefs—though not in a way that was "linear" or predictable. The course of and reasons for change were inevitably muddled.

I hope that this book—the study of a figure whose work embodies such historical untidiness—will restore some of that vital ambiguity and uncertainty to the larger account of early modernism.

This book has been an ongoing project for me for almost eight years, and I want to thank the many people who have aided me. Several months after our return from the research trip to Durango, I began writing the book. Other projects interrupted, but from time to time, I was able to send off draft chapters to Jock de Swart. In August 2016, while I was in San Francisco on vacation, he called to tell me that he was dying of cancer. He passed away a short time later. It is one of my great regrets that he was not able to see the completed book. I am deeply grateful to him and to Louise Garnett, who were its gracious and caring midwives.

Other members of the Peters family have also been generous in their support. I thank Elizabeth DeSwart, Cecile Peters, Sabrina Enright, and, especially, Dierk Peters, Jock Peters's son, who, in the last days of his life, shared with me memories of his father.

Many other people have assisted me with this work. I wish to acknowledge Alexandra Adler (Architecture and Design Collection, UCSB), Eric Evavold (Los Angeles), Janine Henri (University of California, Los Angeles, Special Collections), Laura McGuire (Honolulu), Megan and Rick Prelinger (Prelinger Library, San Francisco), Wendy Kaplan and Staci Steinberger (Los Angeles County Museum of Art), and Jewel Stern (Miami) for helping me gather photographs, texts, and other documents. I was especially fortunate to receive support for my archival research into Peters's early life in Germany: Birgit Nelissen, Eberhard Pook, and Katharina Weresch in Hamburg helped uncover aspects of that story. The Hamburg architectural historian Roland Jaeger, who wrote an early and important article on Peters and his work, shared with me a number of documents and insights. I also thank Katrin Peter-Bösenberg for her help. Eva Maria Hölzl at the Technische Universität München-Archiv kindly assisted me with obtaining the student records of Hans Dreier, art director at Famous Players-Lasky and Paramount, where Peters worked intermittently. I also wish to acknowledge Maddie and David Sadofski, owners of Thanks for the Memories in Los Angeles, for generously sharing with me photographs of several pieces from Bullock's Wilshire, and Andrew

B. Hurvitz (Los Angeles), for allowing me to reproduce his photograph of the house Peters designed for the developer and art publicist William Lingenbrink.

I owe a special debt of gratitude to Monika Isler Binz, who shared with me many documents and insights concerning Peters's time in Hamburg, and whose help and generosity made this book a great deal better. Copenhagen architect Adrian Täckman, who has done extensive research on the Danish architect and designer Knud Lönberg-Holm, kindly provided materials and insights into Peters's collaboration with Lönberg-Holm in 1922. I also thank Ulrike Unterweger, who helped me read Herta Peters's very difficult handwriting and made useful suggestions for improving the manuscript.

Donald Albrecht, Monika Isler Binz, Deborah and David Bourke, John Crosse, Marilyn Friedman, Stephen Gee, R. Scott Gill, Michelle Jackson-Beckett, Michael Kathrens, Steven Keylon, Peter McCourt, Monica Penick, Maria Poldson, Robert Richard, Ethel Rompilla, Maddie and David Sadofski, Ronnie Self, and Mark Thayler all kindly took the time to read all or parts of the manuscript and offer thoughtful and useful comments. I also acknowledge my very able research assistant, S. Edith Ware.

I am grateful to Frederick Steiner, former dean of the School of Architecture at the University of Texas at Austin, for his support over the years. Funds from the Martin S. Kermacy Centennial Professorship in Architecture and the Martin S. and Evelyn S. Kermacy Collection Endowment helped to offset the costs of photographs and travel for this project. Martin, whom I came to know well in the last years of his life, was a lover of all things related to architecture and design in Central Europe. It is especially appropriate for his legacy to have fostered this book.

I am also grateful to all those who worked to make this book a reality. I thank Florence Grant, for her splendid editing of the manuscript. Her cuts and suggestions greatly improved the text. Thanks, too, to Jiří Příhoda, for his lovely book design and his support. And I especially acknowledge Beth Daugherty of Bauer and Dean Publishers, for taking this project on and gracefully shepherding it through the publication process.

Finally, I thank my wife, Gia Marie Houck, for her unceasing love, help, insight, and encouragement.

PROLOGUE |

Jock Peters (1889–1934) is mostly remembered today for the lavish interiors he designed for Bullock's Wilshire department store in Los Angeles. That is right and fitting, for Bullock's was one of the landmarks of its era. It was a tour de force of what, in late 1929, when the store opened its doors, was called "modernistic" and what some observers afterward (Philip Johnson perhaps most noisily and speciously) would deem "not yet fully modern" architecture and design. Bullock's and its remarkable interiors epitomized the modern style of America in those years, its design language a triumphant expression of an autochthonous modernism. It was *of* its place—Southern California—and it was American through and through, even if its maker and a considerable portion of its aesthetic voice had come from Europe.

That Peters's star later faded was due in part to his early death, in 1934, when he was only forty-five years old. He was then just beginning to create works that might have cemented his reputation. His first breakthrough, the Bullock's interiors, had come only five years before. The Great Depression, which arrived at the very moment when the store was completed and opened, greatly slowed—though it did not fully arrest—his progress.

Surely another reason—a central one—why Peters has been mostly forgotten is that much of his extensive archive remains in private hands, unseen and unstudied. Only a portion of his papers is housed in the Architecture and Design Collection at the University of California, Santa Barbara, donated more than three decades ago by his eldest daughter, Ursula (Ursel) de Swart. She retained the remainder—many of the documents crucial for making a thoroughgoing narrative and interpretation. They were inherited and kept, until recently, by Peters's grandson, Jock de Swart. This material is presented here for the first time.

Peters's long eclipse also had much to do with the unfortunate fate of his works. Most of his important commercial interiors—the Hollander store in New York City, the Maddux Air Lines ticket office in Los Angeles, the shop of the couturière Irene near Hollywood, and the modern storefronts for William Lingenbrink's Silver Strand Beach development—were all destroyed. Significant portions of the sumptuous Bullock's interiors are preserved in what is now Southwestern Law School, which notably carried out a meticulous and extensive restoration of the interiors in the 1990s. The law school rehabilitated the artwork and the

Jock Peters, 1930. Photograph by Brett Weston. Collection Jock de Swart.

few original furnishings that remained, including Peters's displays in the grand concourse and some of his designs from the menswear department. Regrettably, most of the remarkable furnishings and other freestanding installations have been disbursed or lost. With regard to the Hollander store, Maddux building, Irene studio, and Silver Strand Beach properties, nothing survives in its original form, if at all. All we have are a handful of period photographs and, in the case of Hollander, a small cache of drawings. The same is true of Peters's houses, which, in almost every instance, have seen their interiors significantly altered or destroyed. Equally sad, many of the Famous Players-Lasky and Paramount films for which Peters created sets are now lost or were never produced. And of the films that do survive, only a few can be attributed to him; like all assistant art directors of those days, he almost always went uncredited.

Such a set of circumstances would normally relegate a designer to obscurity. But there is more: Peters's fading from view had to—above all—do with his reluctance to develop a signature style. He became known for a single work, Bullock's Wilshire, in great measure because it was so accomplished and it remains intact to a degree; all the same, it would be difficult to define him otherwise.

Peters did what he did with style—or, more to the point, with styles. He constantly altered his stylistic approach, as often as not experimenting with multiple styles, blending them to produce a novel amalgam. At times, he unashamedly appropriated ideas from others: Frank Lloyd Wright and Erich Mendelsohn were among the most prominent of his "sources." But he could also be extraordinarily inventive, devising his own distinctive means for articulating modernity or remaking the styles of others—either individuals or groups—to forge new forms of expression. What makes Peters a compelling figure in the story of early modern design in his native Germany and, later, in Southern California, has to do precisely with his propensity toward stylistic indiscrimination, his manifold readings of what modernism could and should be.

If this is among the features that make Peters an attractive subject for study, it also presents a historiographic problem. How should we portray his irregular career and work, and, even more, how should we evaluate them? How do we regard a designer whose work is so variegated?

There is a tacit assumption in the art historical world that an artist's style should have an evident consistency, or, at least, that it should undergo certain, and mostly predictable, shifts over the course of his or her lifetime. Thus, we can describe Francesco Borromini as a Baroque architect (if an idiosyncratic one), or Jacques-Louis David as a quintessential neoclassical painter. Most artists and designers in the past worked in more or less the same fashion—the same style—for their entire lives. Indeed, their shared and personal stylistic traits have become their identifiers. This is the basis of all connoisseurship. Yet, what if an artist, architect, or designer constantly shifted styles, week to week, month to month, or even day to day? Instances of such figures in the history of art (other than forgers!) are rare. It is not until the early period of modernism that a rapid flux of stylistic ideas was even a possibility. Starting from the later 1880s, an accelerated parade of styles defined the art scene: Art Nouveau, Symbolism, Decadence, Futurism, Cubism, Expressionism, Vorticism, Constructivism, Surrealism. Many other "isms" marched in step or followed. It is true that some figures worked their way through more than one of these shifts; yet to name a leading modernist of the first decades of the last century is nearly always to summon up a particular image or set of images that are in some way stylistically consistent. At a minimum, we can speak of the "mature style" of most modernists.

With Jock Peters, we encounter a stylistic chameleon, changing guises with surprising swiftness and ease. It is one of the marks—the most conspicuous one—of his oeuvre.

Peters's strategy of constant stylistic experimentation was not always successful. Some of his designs are decidedly derivative, or simply bad. Yet, on his good days—and he had quite a few of them—Peters was making objects and buildings that rivaled the best work of his more renowned contemporaries. His film sets, furnishings, and houses stand out for their imaginativeness; his interiors for retail stores, especially Bullock's and Hollander, were powerful and pathbreaking.

Still, there is no escaping the fact that Peters's time as an active designer, first in Germany and later in Los Angeles, was short, his output small and uneven. The First World War and its tumultuous aftermath interrupted his early efforts—as it did for so many of his fellow modernists. His career in the United States spanned fewer than a dozen years, and, during the first three or four, he was simply trying to find his footing in a strange new country. It was only after 1927 that he began to have a visible part in shaping the modernist culture of Southern California. The achievements of those last seven or so years constitute nearly the entirety of his best work as a designer and architect.

With Peters, more than most of his contemporaries, a discussion of style is unavoidable: the essence of what he did and what concerned him is rooted in it. Seen broadly, Peters's particular importance also rests with style in another way: his story traces the wider history of modernism in its early years. His many designs tell us something about the course of modernism in his native Germany and, even more, in Southern California. It is a story about the progress of modernist ideas, about the emergence of modern modes of expression, of *modern styles*. Peters was working in Berlin and Hamburg when the German avant-garde was making its way from the late Jugendstil to the first glimmers of the new language of Expressionism and the astringent purity of the *Neue Sachlichkeit*. He arrived in Los Angeles just as the new architecture and design were first making their appearance there. He died at the time when a more or less cohesive idea—and face—of California modernism was in the offing.

What lay in between for him were times of intense stylistic probing. Peters would leave his most evident mark on the story of the rise of modernism in Los Angeles, and, again, it is his manner of working that stands out. Some on the local scene, like Richard Neutra, came to their characteristic idioms quickly; others, like R. M. Schindler, Kem Weber, and J. R. Davidson, experimented longer and more freely. But no one in the front ranks of the Southern California modernists tried out quite as many possibilities as Peters did. In his realized creations and many projects, first as a Hollywood assistant art director, then as architect and designer, he tested numerous variants and borrowed here and there, combining and recombining an almost disconcerting assortment of styles and forms. His collected work is like an inventory of those first years of Southern California modernism, and, equally, what it would become. For if, at times, Peters looked to the past or to contemporary design, he could also be remarkably prescient, his works often presaging what would emerge afterward, in the 1940s and 1950s and later.

In telling Peters's full story here for the first time, I hope to cast a fresh light on a forgotten figure in the quest for new modes of expression and the headlong, if not always direct, path to modernism.

Chapter 1 |
JARRENWISCH AND HAMBURG

Jock Peters was born Jakob Detlef Peters on March 16, 1889, in Jarrenwisch, a small farming community near the market town of Wesselburen, in the northernmost reaches of Germany.[1] His family was typical for the region: large, Lutheran, upright, and traditionalist. His father, Georg Fritz Peters, was a descendant of a long-established local line of yeoman farmers; his mother, Anna Marie Friederike (née Kruse), grew up on a farm close by.[2] Jakob Detlef was the couple's first child. Six more children followed in swift succession: a brother, Georg (later George); two sisters, Annemarie and Matilda; and three more sons, Karl, Detlef, and Fritz (whose twin brother was stillborn) (fig. 1).[3]

The Peters farm, in Jarrenwisch, was situated in Dithmarschen, a region of expansive plains, fens, and wetlands along the North Sea coast, near the Danish border.[4] Georg Peters was the owner of an ample freehold there, and the Peters family lived in a sturdy brick farmhouse, with a large barn set to one side (fig. 2).

In the first of several short autobiographies he wrote later in life, Jock Peters refers with pride to his family's deep roots there and the fact that they had not been tenants but had owned their land.[5] His memories of his early life on the fruitful lowlands stayed with him long after he left the farm. Years afterward, he made a small linoleum cut of a Dithmarschian barn, with its distinctive proportions and hip-on-gable roof (fig. 3).

What distinguished Dithmarschian life was its separateness, its longstanding cultural distinctiveness and isolation. Well into the nineteenth century, locals lived almost as they had since medieval times, wresting a livelihood from farming small-to-middling plots amid the wetlands.[6] It was only with the completion of the Kiel Canal connecting the Baltic and North Seas in the 1890s—and the subsequent draining of many of the bogs and marshes—that agricultural reform and development slowly came. In custom and outlook, however, the Dithmarschians remained apart. Most people continued to speak a variant of Plattdeutsch, the Low German dialect derived from Old Saxon, and they willfully resisted outside influence.

Jakob Detlef was a sickly infant, and throughout his life he was never robust. In the 1930s, he told an unnamed

---

1. Peters family, c. 1901. Front row, from left to right: Matilda, Georg Peters, Fritz, Anna, and Detlef. Standing behind, Annemarie, Jakob (Jock), Georg (George), and Karl. Collection Jock de Swart.

reporter in California that as a youth he had "feared the electrical storms and the power of the ocean as it pounded against the dikes." He had hated "the constant battle with the sea."[7]

In other ways, his early life was nearly idyllic. His daughter Ursel (later Ursula) recorded what she had heard as a girl: Georg Peters, like his father, worked great wheat fields. He "was prosperous and happy, and drove his family to church each Sunday in a carriage drawn by six matched horses."[8] His firstborn son had the full run of the farmstead, with its broad, flat fields extending to the horizon.

As he grew, the boy's circumstances changed. His father hired a tutor, so that schooling would not interfere with work: helping to run the farm became his primary focus. And little about that was ever supposed to change. The eldest sons of Dithmarschen were obliged to labor for their fathers, but the youngest sons usually inherited the land.

Young Jakob, as his family called him, detested "the drudgery of farm life."[9] As a boy of eight or nine he began drawing in his spare time. He showed early promise, and his mother tried to foster his talent. His father, however, discouraged his son's artistic tendencies, exasperated by what he saw as his effete habits.[10]

Georg Peters's intolerance doubtless issued in part from his mounting worry about money. "One year a plague of rats destroyed the wheat. The next year drought ruined the grain. In the third year, there was a disastrous flood."[11] So wrote his granddaughter Ursel. Peters remembered it differently: the decline was due to his father's attempts to put into practice "modern agricultural methods" that proved to be "unsuccessful."[12]

It was an all too common story in those years. As modernization came to Dithmarschen and connections to the outside world intensified, the local landowners faced rising competition. The small and middle-sized farms—in spite of their abundantly fertile soil—could not compete with the inexpensive grain pouring in from the great estates of East Prussia or the vast plains of Russia, the United States, and Canada. Georg Peters pursued what he thought was the only sensible course: he bought a steam-powered tractor, a mechanical thresher, and other modern machinery. But the debt he incurred as a consequence served only to compound his woes. Three years of bad harvests forced him into bankruptcy. His only choice was to sell the farm.[13]

Without land, the Peters family was compelled to take the path of legions of country folk in the nineteenth century: they moved to the city. Georg Peters set his sights on the nearby metropolis of Hamburg.

In 1897, the year of the family's arrival, Hamburg was a flourishing place of some seven hundred thousand inhabitants (fig. 4). Over the previous century, it had seen very rapid growth, and in the decade after the Peters family moved there, another two hundred thousand people would arrive. Hamburg became the commercial and cultural center of northwestern Germany and the third busiest port in Europe. Albert Ballin's Hamburg-Amerika Line (HAPAG), headquartered there, was the largest transatlantic shipping company in the world. The greater share of Germans and eastern Europeans who emigrated from the Continent in this period passed through its port.

The city had overcome two calamities: the Great Fire of 1842, which destroyed nearly a quarter of its structures, including the town hall and several churches, and a major outbreak of cholera in 1892, which took more than eight thousand lives. The Peters family found a city in the process of remaking itself: the old, "unsanitary" quarters were being demolished, and whole swaths of modern buildings were being constructed in their place.[14]

Jakob, alone among his family members, rejoiced in his new life in the city. Liberated from the drudgery of farmwork, he spent his free time exploring the streets and neighborhoods, taking in the hum of everything around him. He also pursued his new interest in drawing. Whenever he could, he made sketches, finding ever-mounting delight in the act of putting pencil to paper. Sometimes, in his search for scenes to draw, he undertook day trips into the surrounding countryside.[15] A surviving sketch from his later teens, a landscape, testifies to his growing facility (fig. 5). It is finely rendered, deft and sure—impressive for a boy without formal training. The young Peters decided he wanted to be an artist.

He told the reporter in California what happened next:

Such an idea did not suit his father, who wanted his child to engage in practical employment. [He] kept on with his drawing, and showing his pictures to anyone who would take time to look. He had faith in his artistic abilities and strangely enough the family milkman was the first to encourage him by exchanging a huge bowl of whipped cream for a picture of a dog. However, even this proof of the sales value of [his] work was not enough to convince his father.

[He] then wanted to become an architect, but his father would not agree to this. He finally compromised on sculpture which partially satisfied the boy; it was an art through which he could express himself, and his father

2. Peters farm, Jarrenwisch, Germany, n.d.
Collection Jock de Swart.

3. Jock Peters, *Barn in Dithmarschen*, c. 1913.
Linoleum cut on paper. Collection Jock de Swart.

4. View of the Hamburg Alsterarkaden, late nineteenth century. Photochrom print. Library of Congress Prints and Photographs Division, Washington, DC.

was satisfied because his son would learn the stone-cutting trade and when finished with his apprenticeship wold [sic] be capable of establishing a tomb-stone shop adjacent to some grave-yard.[16]

It was a decision made out of necessity. Georg Peters was bringing in barely enough money to cover the family's basic needs; arranging for his eldest son to learn a trade seemed an entirely sensible course. He had already made—or would soon do so—hard decisions about his other children. His second son, Georg, was packed off to relatives in Heilbronn; he would eventually go to the United States and take up work as a builder. Annemarie, the next in line, was sent to live with an aunt in Hannover; and young Fritz and Detlef were shipped off to England to learn, respectively, the printing and tailoring trades.[17]

Georg Peters made inquiries and decided to send his eldest son to a local master stonemason named Johann Reimer, so that young Jakob could be trained in the craft.

Reimer was unquestionably a fitting choice. He was a renowned practitioner, respected by his peers. Born in 1847, he, too, had come to Hamburg from the provinces. He took up residence and established a practice in the Karolinenviertel, a district of small houses and factories close to the old city. By the time young Peters came to work for him, Reimer was a leader in the local stonemasons' guild, and in 1892, he had been elected to the Hamburgische Bürgerschaft, the self-governing city's parliament.[18]

In late spring of 1903, when Peters came under his tutelage, Reimer's practice was at its height. He had a half dozen apprentices and journeymen in his workshop, and his commissions ran from gravestones and larger funerary monuments to intricate architectural details for new buildings. On occasion, he even made portrait busts for wealthy clients.

Reimer's own portrait bust, executed in white marble by another Hamburg master mason, is housed today in the stairwell of the city's guildhall. It shows a powerfully built man, assured and composed. His dress—tuxedo jacket and tie, not overalls and cap—are signs of his wealth and status within the city's new political elite. In an era when Hamburg was enlarging at a prodigious pace, a stonemason who supplied fine stonework detailing for buildings—this before the age of steel and glass structures—was in a position to profit mightily. And so he did. His busy atelier needed many hands; Reimer was pleased to take on a boy who knew how to work hard.

Nothing in Peters's previous life, not even the constant plod of laboring on the farm, had prepared him for the rigors of his new situation. The lot of a stonemason's apprentice in those years was grueling. Often it involved moving large stones and wielding a heavy mallet and chisel for hours, roughing out a block before the finish work could begin. As the youngest apprentice, he was charged with the most menial tasks, sometimes working more than ten hours a day, six days a week.

Reimer was an exacting teacher and also an excellent one. Gradually, the young boy learned about the different types of stone, how to cut them, how to avoid their flaws, and how to polish them. He learned where stones were quarried, and what to pay for them. The masters of those years gave their young assistants instruction in drawing, as well as the rudiments of design and the attributes of the historical styles. Apprentices also spent hours learning and applying the particulars of lettering in sundry fonts. Peters acquired the fundamentals of architectural construction—a necessary step to understand how to form building elements—and how to produce exact pieces from architectural renderings. And he gained a knowledge of how to deal with clients, basic accounting, and business practices.

Aside from all this, Peters learned an approach to design that was essentially flexible and workmanlike. A monument, a bust, a chimneypiece, a building—each had its own requirements; styles could be picked up and set aside as the job demanded. This stance, fostered within a traditional setting, would eventually evolve, in very different contexts, into the affirmation of stylistic plurality in Peters's later work.

From Peters himself, we have only a few words about his experience with Reimer. He told the reporter in California that he had been "apprenticed to a severe master."[19] That was no doubt true: Reimer was certainly demanding, as most German masters were in those days. But Reimer was also known to be kindly and generous. He is remembered today for one great act of magnanimity: in his will, he left the bulk of his fortune, some six hundred thousand marks, to build a retirement home for independent artisans. Two hundred elderly craftspeople still live in the Seniorenpark der Handwerkskammer in Hamburg.[20]

In his 1920 autobiography, Peters recorded one other notable act of kindness on Reimer's part: "[M]y master gifted me two half years in winter during my apprenticeship."[21] Peters also tells us the reason: the leave was to allow him to attend the local *Baugewerkschule*—the building trades school. Peters was still intent on becoming an architect; Reimer granted him time away to begin his education.[22]

There was one overriding flaw with this plan. The German Baugewerkschulen were not intended to educate architects—at any rate, not directly.²³ Established in the early nineteenth century, the schools were set up to instruct students in the building trades, to provide them with the training to become master builders, not architects. The schools' curricula stressed basic knowledge in construction technology, materials, and management, as well as a general education in writing, history, and mathematics. In the 1840s and 1850s, many added instruction in model making, natural sciences, and descriptive geometry. Over the course of the following two decades, they expanded to teach *Entwerfen*—architectural design.

At first, this idea of "design" was understood narrowly: how to adapt the historical revival styles in a direct fashion to present-day needs and building types. Eventually, by the latter years of the century, the Baugewerkschulen came closer to the idea that design involved finding new formal solutions for functional and technical requirements, a definition adopted in the architecture departments of the new polytechnic universities, which were becoming the main conduits for aspiring architects.²⁴ A diploma from one of the Baugewerkschulen did entitle its holders to admission in a polytechnic, where they could formally study architecture, but the overwhelming majority of the schools' graduates went on to careers as builders.

Founded in 1865, the Staatliche Baugewerkschule zu Hamburg was a late addition to the roster of these schools.²⁵ With the flurry of building in the city after mid-century, it educated many of those who were charged with constructing the new urban landscape. Peters chose the school because it was almost the only place he could go. Without a leaving certificate—*Abitur*—from a secondary school, the polytechnic universities were closed to him, and an apprenticeship to an architect was out of the question, because he was already obligated to Reimer.

How well Peters performed at the school is not known: its records were destroyed in the cataclysmic bombing of Hamburg during World War II. He must have done at least passably well, for he was able to complete the full course in less than the usual time.

In April 1907, after nearly four years of training with Reimer, Peters received his *Lehrbrief*, the credential attesting to the successful completion of his apprenticeship. By then, he had already made the decision not to continue on as a journeyman. He wanted no part of being a master stonemason. He had set his sights instead on becoming an architect. After leaving Reimer's employ, he spent one more year at the Baugewerkschule, passing his final examination in the fall of 1908.²⁶

It almost had not come to that. Peters was a keen student, but he was also a rebellious one. He described to the reporter in California how he had vexed his teachers with his stubbornness and his progressive aesthetic ideas:

It was not long before he began to revolt against period design, and created his work according to his own conception of beauty, combined with present-day needs. In this he received no encouragement from his instructors, and his work was held up to fellow students as a horrible example. The professor believed Peters absolutely incapable of understanding the principles and history of architecture.²⁷

In the end, Peters rallied, driven more by determination than any form of conversion. "To his surprise and chagrin, [he] passed his examination with the most classic and perfectly executed design," he remembered.²⁸

The compromise must have been difficult for him, but it marked the first real success of his young life. He could hardly have foreseen at that moment that it would take him six more years of work and sacrifice to become a full-fledged architect.

5. Jock Peters, landscape sketch, c. 1906. Pencil on paper. Collection Jock de Swart.

Chapter 2 |
AN ARCHITECTURAL APPRENTICESHIP

With his diploma from the Baugewerkschule tucked safely into his pocket, Jakob Peters could have studied architecture at any of the German polytechnic universities. But he simply lacked the means. His father was still barely eking out a living, and young Peters had no other resources to fall back on. He was instead compelled to find work, hopeful that he might someday go on with his education.

Over the next four years, from 1908 to 1912, Peters was employed as an ordinary draftsman, first in the offices of the Hamburg municipal rail office—the Hoch- und Untergrundbahn—and, later, for the architecture firm of Jacob and Ameis (fig. 6).[29] He learned much in the process, though he often found the jobs dull and unsatisfying. His work for the rail office was purely technical; and the architecture of Jacob and Ameis was characteristic of the time, traditional in form and construction, while employing a faintly modernized version of late historicism.

Slowly, Peters began to forge connections in the Hamburg arts scene, connections that would eventually help him move on with his career. In a brief autobiography, written in 1920, he describes his breakthrough: "Herr Prof. Lichtwark and Herr Baurat Vivie [sic] made great efforts to make it possible for me to attend a technical university."[30]

Peters could hardly have wished for more august patrons. Both men were intimately coupled with the worlds of art and architecture in the city. Wilhelm Daniel Vivié was a respected figure in local architectural circles and a visible presence in the development of Hamburg in the decade before World War I.[31] His close friend Alfred Lichtwark was then one of the leading personalities in the German art world.[32] An esteemed art historian and educator, Lichtwark was the director of the Kunsthalle Hamburg, the city's foremost art museum. In the 1880s and 1890s, he had built up the Kunsthalle's collections from almost nothing, gathering Hamburg's medieval art and assembling one of the first and finest collections of early modern painting in Germany.[33]

What drew the two men's interest to Peters were his obvious sincerity and his desire to find a new way in architecture. Vivié knew Peters well; he had been one of Peters's professors at the Baugewerkschule. Over time, he had come to appreciate the (admittedly stubborn) young man. That Lichtwark sought to aid an up-and-coming architecture student of little means was perfectly in keeping with his

6. Jock Peters, Christmas 1909. Collection Jock de Swart.

temperament. He, too, had come from a modest background, and after he found success, he campaigned to open up the city's cultural life to working-class Hamburgers.[34]

Nonetheless, as Peters wrote in his autobiography, "There were insufficient private funds and the [available] scholarships were already committed for years to come."[35] He told the California reporter what happened next:

> Peters was by this time intent upon becoming a student of the best architecture of the revolutionary school of design. In 1912 he decided to go to Amsterdam for six months of study, and thence to America to size up the opportunities for a budding young architect. At the suggestion of his old professor, he went first to Düsseldorf to receive introductions to famous architects in Amsterdam. The man from whom he was to receive these introductions was behind with his work, and, impressed with Peters, asked him to remain a short while to assist in doing some very urgent work.[36]

Missing in this account are two important details. The unnamed Amsterdam architects Peters wanted to meet were Hendrik Petrus Berlage and Eduard Cuypers, the leading Dutch modernists of the day. Of even greater consequence for Peters and his future was the name of the Düsseldorf architect: Carl Gustav Bensel (fig. 7).

Vivié was closely acquainted with Bensel: the young architect was his son-in-law.[37] He sent Peters to Bensel because Bensel had previously spent time in the Netherlands and had visited Berlage's and Cuypers's ateliers.

Bensel was then just coming into his own as an architect. After completing his studies, he had worked for the directorate of Prussian railroads in Cologne. Bensel spent nearly four years there, during which time he designed a number of railroad terminals. Some, including the ones in Mönchengladbach and Rheydt, were executed in robust brick in the manner of Berlage.[38] A private commission from the Crefeld railroad company allowed him to leave government employ and open up his own practice in Düsseldorf.[39]

On Vivié's recommendation, Peters traveled there in the late spring of 1912. He spent a few days in Bensel's office, and, impressed with the projects he saw and with Bensel himself—and encouraged by an offer from Bensel to work in his practice—he decided to stay. "The idea of study in Amsterdam and the trip to America was abandoned," as he put it.[40]

Peters remained with Bensel in Düsseldorf through the late summer. Finally, in September, he took time off for a month-long tour of the Netherlands.

Despite Peters's claim that he made the trip to see the works of the great Dutch modernists, he filled his surviving sketchbooks with renderings of generic scenes and old buildings in Nijmegen, Alkmaar, and other small towns. The new Dutch architecture is entirely absent. Perhaps he made other drawings, now lost. Yet it may also be that those scenes of everyday life interested him more.[41] Nothing in the sketchbooks suggests that he met Berlage or Cuypers or that he made any effort to study the newest trends.

By the time his trip was nearing its end, Peters had already resolved to return to Düsseldorf and continue his work for Bensel. It was unquestionably the right decision for him. Bensel was an ideal employer. He patiently taught Peters new skills and gradually gave him greater responsibility. At first, Peters did ordinary drafting; as time passed, Bensel allowed him to become more and more involved in the design process. Peters's ultimate reason for staying, though, was bound up with another offer: Bensel promised to help him study architecture at the Kunstgewerbeschule (School of Applied Arts) in Düsseldorf, and allow him to work part-time in order to do so.[42]

The Düsseldorf Kunstgewerbeschule was a relatively new institution, founded only in 1883. It was one of a group of related schools established by the various German provincial governments in the nineteenth century to elevate the design standards of the country's handcrafted and machine-made products.[43] Its first director, Hermann Stiller, was an architect of some importance. When he departed, in 1903, he was replaced by a figure soon to become even more prominent in the world of German architecture: Peter Behrens.

Behrens was then still young, freshly arrived from a several-year-long stint at the Darmstadt *Künstlerkolonie*, the artists' group headed by Austrian architect and designer Joseph Maria Olbrich. Behrens had started his career as a painter, illustrator, and book designer. But the experience of building his own house in Darmstadt—and designing everything contained within—marked a turning point that led him into architecture. During his four-year tenure at the school, he transformed its curriculum, reorganizing the studio structure and introducing more modern teaching methods. By the time he departed in 1907, the Düsseldorf Kunstgewerbeschule had become one of the most progressive architecture faculties in Germany.[44]

Wilhelm Kreis, another pioneering modernist, followed Behrens as director. He was still in the post when Peters began his studies in 1912.[45] Kreis would go on to earn a certain ignominy: during the Nazi period, he worked with Albert

7. Photograph of Carl Gustav Bensel presented to Peters, c. 1914. The inscription reads, "As a reminder of our time in Düsseldorf." Jock Peters Archive, Architectural Drawings Collection, Art, Design, and Architecture Museum, University of California, Santa Barbara (hereafter UCSB).

Speer on Adolf Hitler's megalomaniacal plans for the rebuilding of Berlin. In the 1910s, though, he was known for his role as a founding member of the German Werkbund and for his designs for the massive Tietz department stores in Elberfeld and Cologne, for which Kreis employed the latest in construction methods and materials.

Kreis, however, was less insistently progressive than Behrens. After assuming the directorship, he modified the school's curriculum, undermining some of his predecessor's more radical reforms (a move that, not coincidently, aided him in finding his own commissions in Düsseldorf, where some had viewed Behrens's radical ideas with misgivings).

One of the few surviving drawings Peters produced in this period, a form and motion study in shades of red, shows what had remained of Behrens's curricular reforms (fig. 8). It was typical of the experiments arising out of the Jugendstil, an exercise intended to impart lessons about movement and fluidity. Drawing exercises like this were then common in the most advanced art and design schools of Central Europe. They borrowed from the ideas of educators like the Viennese Franz Čížek, an early proponent of children's art education, who developed a series of basic visual exercises for his students. (Johannes Itten, the Swiss painter who later instituted the renowned preliminary course at the Bauhaus, was among those he influenced.)

The practical instruction that Peters and the other students received in architecture itself was less advanced, relying mostly on older historicist practices. Peters, though, was absorbing a great deal about the newest architecture while jobbing for Bensel. In 1912, just at the time Peters began his studies, Bensel was involved in a competition to design the new Düsseldorf Kunstakademie (Art Academy). Peters made one of the early renderings for the project (fig. 9).[46] It is a version of the neo-Biedermeier—very much in vogue at the time. The drawing is also—patently—the work of a young architecture student with limited experience, unsure and awkward.

Peters was also learning from another member of Bensel's office staff. In 1912, Bensel formed what would turn out to be a short-lived partnership with Fritz August Breuhaus (or, as he would later fashion himself, Breuhaus de Groot). A recent graduate of the Düsseldorf Kunstgewerbeschule, Breuhaus was already an accomplished practitioner; he took the younger man under his wing, and Peters's skills, as a result, developed rapidly.[47]

Throughout this time, Bensel was involved with the design of several large commercial buildings—the so-called Kontorhausneubauten—for Hamburg's inner city. In 1908,

8. Jock Peters, form and motion study in red, c. 1912.
Tempura paint on paper. Collection Jock de Swart.

9. Jock Peters, competition project for
the Düsseldorf Kunstakademie (Art Academy), 1912.
Pencil and pen and ink on paper. UCSB.

10. Carl Gustav Bensel and Jock Peters,
competition project for a department store in Nuremberg, 1912.
Black line print. Collection Jock de Swart.

AN ARCHITECTURAL APPRENTICESHIP 29

in the ongoing effort on the part of the authorities to reduce the density of the oldest area of the city after the 1892 cholera epidemic, many older structures were torn down, and a broad new avenue, the Mönckebergstraße, was laid out, connecting the city hall and the main train station.[48] Alfred Lichtwark, who was close to Bensel (through his friendship to Vivié), encouraged Bensel to submit entries to the competitions for the new structures. Beginning in 1910, Bensel did so, and he won a first prize for a building called the Rappolthaus, for a local textile firm.[49]

After much political wrangling, the contract to design and construct the Rappolthaus went to another up-and-coming architect, Fritz Höger.[50] The publicity Bensel had attracted with his entry, however, drew the notice of a local architect and developer named Franz Bach. Bach had designed and erected the first building for the Mönckebergstraße. He met with heavy criticism at the time, in large measure because those in local art and preservation circles deemed it insufficiently sensitive to Hamburg traditions. Beginning in 1911, encouraged by Lichtwark, Bach turned to Bensel for assistance, asking him to devise the façades for two new buildings, the Rolandhaus and the Südseehaus.[51]

Bensel worked on the two buildings over the following year. Peters, by this time, was spending the greater portion of his time at the Düsseldorf Kunstgewerbeschule, but he assisted on several of Bensel's subsequent Mönckebergstraße projects.[52] He also aided Bensel with a competition project for a department store in Nuremberg. Some of the preliminary drawings and the final competition entry are in his hand. The latter shows how much his skills had developed (fig. 10). The large rendering is forthright and sure, its lines all put down without the aid of a straightedge, conveying a strong sense of purposiveness.

In the early summer of 1912, not long after his arrival in Düsseldorf, Peters met Hertha Boeger, who would become his wife (fig. 11). They encountered each other by chance during a doubles game of tennis. Each had come with a partner—in Boeger's case, with her fiancé, in Peters's, a girlfriend. Over the course of the match, the two fell in love.[53]

Herta, as she became known, was very nearly the same age as her future husband, born just nine days after him, in March 1889.[54] Her father, Friedrich Boeger, a local tobacco and pipe shop owner, was passionately committed to vegetarianism, nude sunbathing, and vigorous exercise—practices then all the rage in some German progressive circles. Peters's daughter Ursel recalls in her memoir that he "taught his children to take cold baths, eat raw foods, and walk a great deal in every kind of weather."[55] His enthusiasm would carry over to Herta, who became devoted to her own health regime and to the nurturing of others.

Herta was energetic, animated, and intellectually curious. She had gone to a local Volkschule in Düsseldorf, but as was usual in those years for girls from petite-bourgeois backgrounds, she had only briefly attended secondary school. She spent a year at a finishing school "for artistic needlework and women's work," and when she met Peters, she had a job in a factory nursery school.[56]

To judge from the letters they exchanged, the relationship between the promising architect and the young woman was ardent and also, at times, stormy.[57] The main trouble was that Peters was often unavailable. He spent long hours at the school and in Bensel's atelier. He was also away from Düsseldorf for much of the late summer and fall of 1912, and, as it would turn out, for most of 1913, as well.

His absences had everything to do with his budding career, which was then branching out into teaching. Among those Peters encountered during his studies at the Düsseldorf Kunstgewerbeschule was the young architect Alfred Fischer, then teaching at the school. Fischer had been a student of famed educator Theodor Fischer (no relation) in Stuttgart and had worked briefly in the atelier of Paul Schultze-Naumburg in Berlin.[58] He was a rising star: in the 1920s and 1930s, Fischer would become one of the most important modern architects of the Ruhrgebiet. Toward the end of Peters's first year of studies, Fischer was called to head the Kunstgewerbeschule in nearby Essen. Impressed with Peters, he hired him to work as a *Dozent*, or adjunct instructor.

Peters received word confirming his appointment in early August 1913.[59] He began teaching in Essen that fall, working closely with his young mentor to revamp the course of studies and raise the quality of the students' work. According to an employment application Peters filled out in 1920, he also claimed to have worked in Fischer's private office, but no record of what he might have done there remains.[60]

While teaching in Essen, Peters continued to work for Bensel, and so he found himself continuously traveling back and forth between the two cities. On the days when he was in Bensel's office, Peters was helping to design another building for the Mönckebergstraße, the Levantehaus. Bach had once more approached Bensel to assist him with the project, to come up with an appropriate façade; this time, Bach requested a more modern design.[61] Bensel turned the task over to Peters, and it was his rendering—and to a large extent his design, as he gleefully reported in a letter to Herta—that won them the job (fig. 12).[62]

11. Herta (Hertha) Boeger, c. 1912. Collection Jock de Swart.

Bensel was also collaborating with Bach on the nearby Karstadt department store. Peters produced the final façade drawings—once more, it seems, inserting some of his own ideas (fig. 13).

Both buildings, the Levantehaus and the Karstadt store, feature vertically articulated pilasters and mullions, which stand out all the more because the windows and spandrels are deeply recessed. With its rhythmic quality and pronounced lucidity, the Karstadt store, in particular, bears a certain kinship to Alfred Messel's Wertheim department store in Berlin (1896–1904), one of the signal German designs of those years. Even more than the Levantehaus, the Karstadt store pointed to a new and more modern conception. When completed, the two structures were instrumental in shaping a new chapter in Hamburg's architecture.[63] Despite their vestigial historical detailing, both were in a language that was forceful, regular, and determined in great measure by constructional logic. The Levantehaus was also Peters's first fully realized building—at least the first one in which he had a meaningful design role. Although Bensel's name was on it, Peters took great satisfaction from his part in its creation.

In the midst of all this, Peters had a crisis of conviction. For a time, he thought seriously about giving up architecture and becoming a full-time artist. In September, just before he began teaching in Essen, he wrote to Herta (then vacationing in Munich) that he was deeply frustrated with his work. He yearned, as he wrote, "to give to humanity something that would bring it to a higher plane. As long as I cannot find an expressive form, to say everything that is in my heart, I will remain unhappy."[64]

What emerges from their subsequent correspondence is a picture of an ambitious yet conflicted young man. One moment, Peters is cocksure, filled with a sense of his own destiny; the next, he is uncertain and self-effacing.

Some of Peters's work from this time shows evidence of a shift, in the form of a newfound interest in graphic art. Many of the drawings he produced were visual love notes to Herta. One is a frieze in the form of his nickname for her—Boegie—done up in the manner of Behrens's 1908 logo for the Allgemeine Elektricitäts-Gesellschaft, or AEG (fig. 14). Another is an ex libris plate depicting a nude female figure facing the rays of the sun, an allusion, perhaps, to her strict health regimen (fig. 15). Both convey a modern awareness in keeping with what was being stated in reformist German circles of that time.

These very personal renderings are a first hint at a quality that would become central to Peters's mature work, a preference for artistic expression and decorative play over the

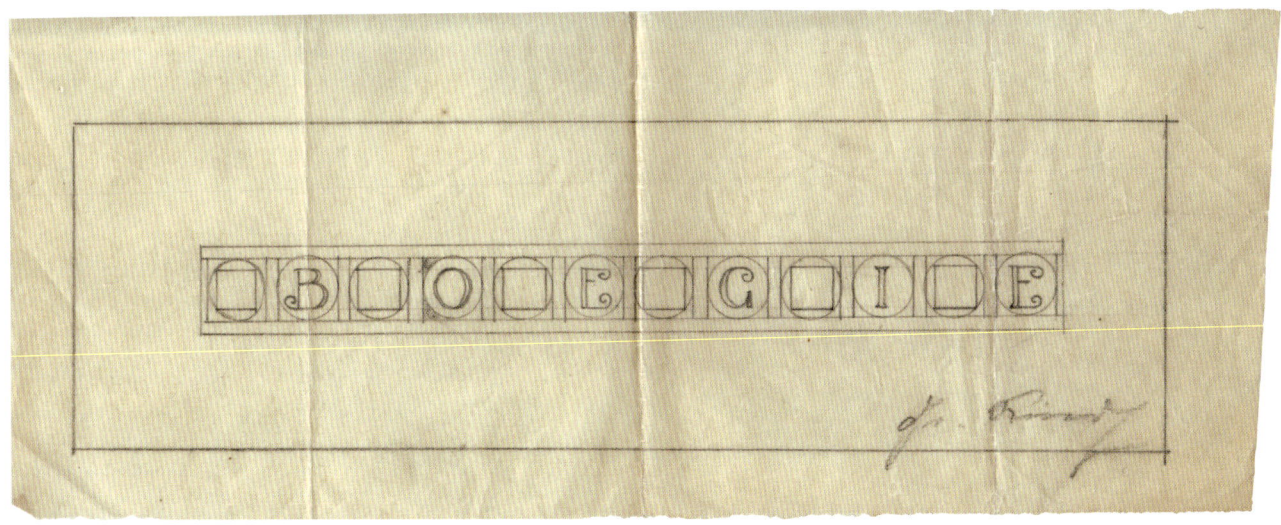

13. Franz Bach and Carl Gustav Bensel, Karstadt department store, Mönckebergstraße, Hamburg, 1912–13. Bildarchiv Foto Marburg.

12. Jock Peters with Carl Gustav Bensel and Franz Bach, competition design for the Levantehaus, Hamburg, 1913. Print on paper. Collection Jock de Swart.

14. Opposite bottom: Jock Peters, graphic frieze spelling out "Boegie," Herta's nickname, c. 1912. Pencil on paper. Collection Jock de Swart.

strictly architectonic. And it may be, as he demonstrated in his design for the ex libris, that he had already hit upon his real passion: shaping scenes or vignettes resting between modern reality and fantasy. Often, his drawings would have as their themes some intimation of escape, or a striving to flee the afflictions of modern life. It is telling, perhaps, that one of the etchings from this period is a scene of what can be described as modern-day alienation: an immense classical temple, dominating the diminutive human figures standing before it (fig. 16).

Peters may have meant this image as an allegory in another way—about the continued persistence of classicism, or, put differently, its great and enduring burden. For Peters, as for many young German modernists of the day, the question of what role history—and, more especially, the legacy of classical antiquity—might retain in contemporary practice was at the forefront of their concerns. It was easy enough to reject historicism, which appeared both outmoded and misguided. But the demise of the Jugendstil after 1905 (which, in the plainest terms, had been an attempt to dispense with historical forms altogether by embracing an aesthetic derived nearly or wholly from nature) had left the incipient modern movement at a crossroads. Almost all the younger progressive designers after the turn of the century had been educated in curricula that were still largely traditional. A few daring young designers rejected the past and existing models out of hand. Yet many, if not the majority, of up-and-coming German architects were then unresolved about the idea of shedding history fully. It appeared too drastic, too final, a move. If the revival styles had all seemingly lost their legitimacy, the language of a purified classicism—of the finest and most stringent aspect of the Western historical legacy—was more difficult to cast off. What nearly every aspiring German modernist of those years sought instead was to forge a synthesis between a modernist imperative and distilled classical form—in other words, a modernized classicism.[65] Peters fell firmly into this camp.

This idea of a modernized classicism was at the fore of another project Peters worked on for Bensel, a competition entry in 1913 for the HAPAG-Haus, for Albert Ballin's shipping concern (fig. 17). Bensel and perhaps Peters (for the authorship is far from clear) assembled a forceful composition of massive pilasters and muscular massing—all in a language not very different from Behrens's German embassy in St. Petersburg, Russia, completed the same year.

In June, he and Herta announced their engagement.[66] They were able to spend time together in June and early July, but by mid-August, he had left Düsseldorf again. This time it was to follow Bensel to Hamburg, where his boss had moved his practice. Peters spent most of the fall of 1913 and the spring of 1914 commuting back and forth between his teaching job in Essen and his work for Bensel in Hamburg.

Bensel's decision to relocate to Hamburg was bound up with his success with the Kontorhäuser. By this time, he had already built several of these huge structures, and he was hard at work on more. Flushed with his triumphs, and in response to encouragement from Vivié and Lichtwark to come back to Hamburg, Bensel moved north in the late summer of 1913. He opened a new office at Mönckebergstraße 9. Between that time and the end of 1914, he completed several additional buildings.[67]

Peters, who for a short time was commuting between Düsseldorf and Hamburg as he finished his studies, played a central part in the firm's successes (figs. 18, 19). Bensel now named him as his "Atelierchef"—the head of his studio—and a partner in the firm.[68]

Peters assisted Bensel with a competition design for a *Realgymnasium* (a sciences and mathematics high school) in Duisburg (fig. 20). Once more, he produced the final entry drawing; he was now making all the final presentation drawings for Bensel. It was another version of the heavy-walled Biedermeier language that had become the office signature, though it was less progressive—which is to say, less architectonically concise—than their commercial designs.

Peters also aided Bensel with the design of yet another project, the Bugenhagenhaus, for the H. & O. lumber concern. He prepared the preliminary drawing: a tight, mostly unadorned composition in brick, with traces of classical detailing (fig. 21). It was a premonition of what was to come in Hamburg, a new burly architecture of mass and brick.

Another unbuilt work of this period, a small house with a central octagonal rotunda, is one of Peters's few solo designs. He seems to have worked on it privately, outside his time in the office. Two variant drawings of it have come down to us, without any indication of a client or site. One is a classicized structure, with pilasters and a blank frieze (fig. 22). A second, probably later, version (dated November 1913) is rather plainer in form (fig. 23). It draws from the *Heimatstil* movement, an effort on the part of some conservative and nationalist architects who sought to combine traditional and German vernacular influences.

Peters and Herta finally married during his Christmas break from work, in late December 1913. Peters designed and printed the announcement in his own Jugendstil-inspired

15. Jock Peters, bookplate for Hertha (Herta) Boeger, c. 1912.
Etching on paper. Collection Jock de Swart.

16. Jock Peters, architectural sketch of a temple, c. 1912. Etching on paper. Collection Jock de Swart.

17. Jock Peters, competition design for the HAPAG-Haus, Hamburg, 1913. Pencil and colored pencil on paper. UCSB.

18. Jock Peters, c. 1913. Collection Jock de Swart.

19. Peters's business card, c. 1913. Collection Jock de Swart.

20. Carl Gustav Bensel and Jock Peters, competition design for a *Realgymnasium* in Duisburg, 1913. From "C. G. Bensel, Regierungsbaumeister a. D., Architekt, Hamburg," Sonderheft *Bau-Rundschau* (Hamburg: Konrad Hanf, 1914): 53.

21. Carl Gustav Bensel and Jock Peters, preliminary design for the Bugenhagenhaus, Hamburg, 1913. From "C. G. Bensel, Regierungsbaumeister a. D., Architekt, Hamburg," Sonderheft *Bau-Rundschau* (Hamburg: Konrad Hanf, 1914): 9.

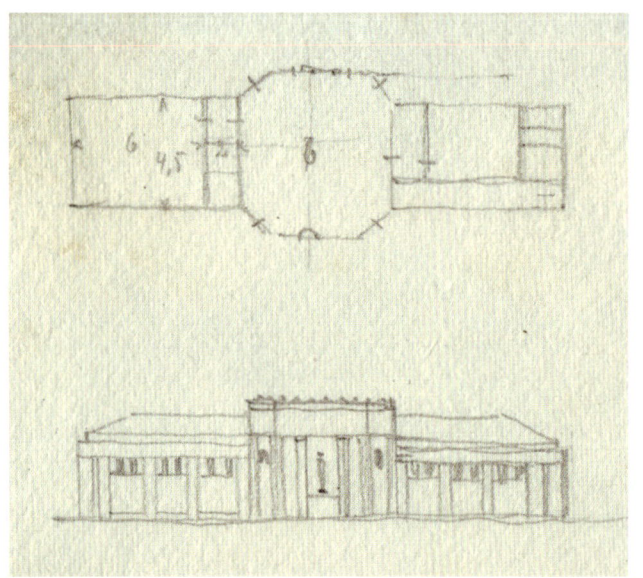

22. Jock Peters, design for a villa, c. 1913.
Pencil on paper. Collection Jock de Swart.

23. Jock Peters, design for a villa (variant version), 1913.
Pencil on paper. Collection Jock de Swart.

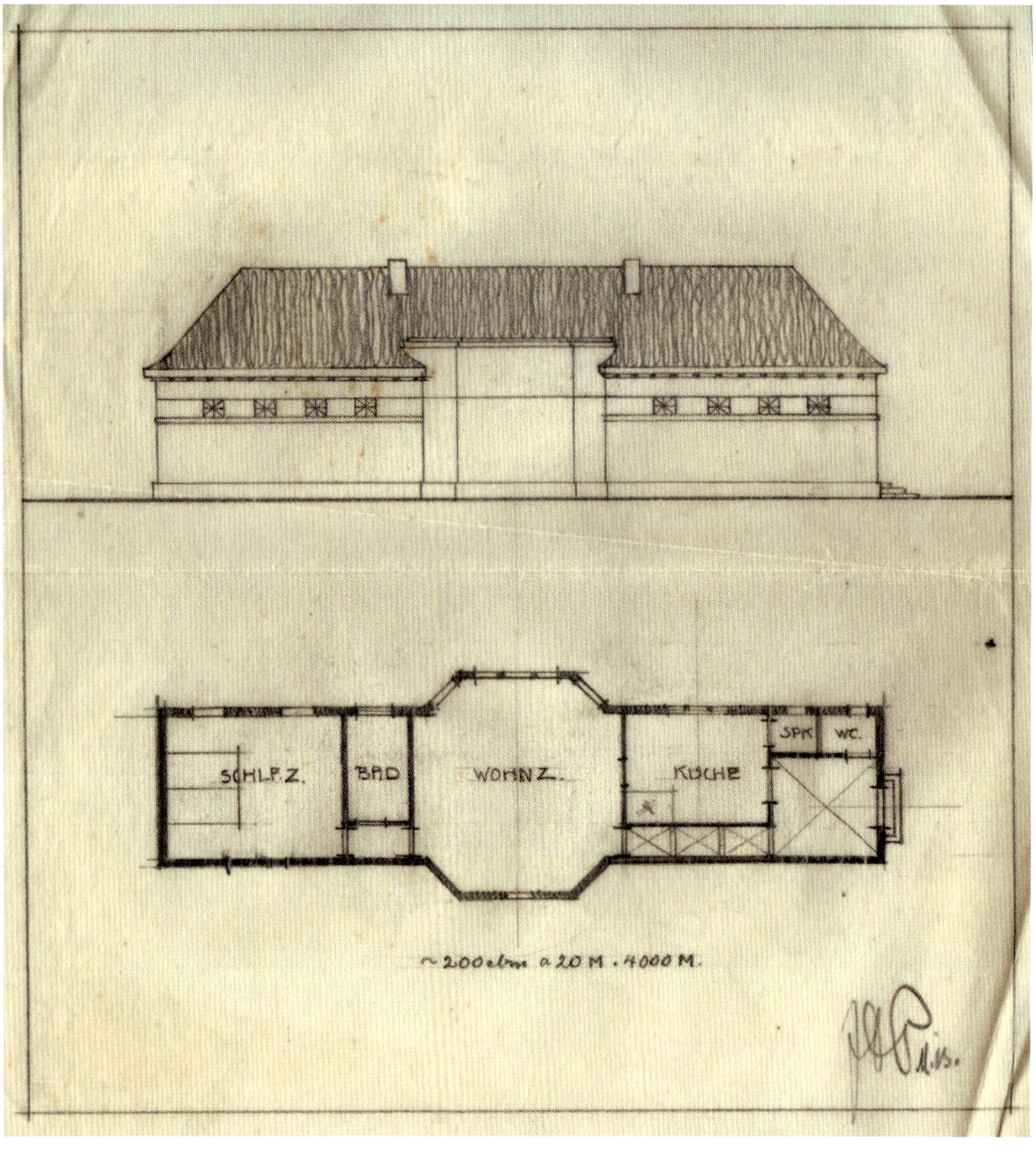

script (fig. 24). The official ceremony took place at the registry office in Düsseldorf. Shortly afterward, they settled in Hamburg, moving into a small house in Lokstedt, a district of tidy villas and gardens.[69]

By early 1914, Peters was involved in several new projects in Bensel's studio. One was the preparation of a development plan—in the basic guise of an English Garden City—for the Hamburg suburb of Wohldorf-Ohlstedt.[70] He and Bensel also worked on a proposal—ultimately unbuilt—for another massive commercial structure for the Mönckebergstraße.

The latter is a forceful composition, stripped down and regular—a statement of a new unbridled rationalism (fig. 25). It is a foreshadowing of things to come: a structure at huge scale, relying on its great mass and rhythmical arrangement to convey a sense of monumentality. A few similar works had been realized by then—though almost nothing quite at that scale, aside from a few American factories, department stores, and warehouses. In 1914, the design was at the outer edge of what constituted progressive architecture. In all likelihood, it remained unbuilt for that reason.

The more important project Peters worked on was a competition entry for a new Hamburg municipal power plant (Heizkraftwerk) in Tiefstack (fig. 26). Bensel's office again won first prize. Construction on the huge project began almost immediately, in 1914; it would carry on for three more years.[71]

With so much work now flooding into the studio, Bensel's attention was spread widely. Peters, as a consequence, had a hand in the design of the main power plant building and its associated structures. The complex's overall look was Bensel's, who, in turn, it seems, borrowed some elements from the heavy-limbed prewar factory aesthetic of Hans Poelzig. Peters, though, was responsible for several of the smaller structures, including the machinery building (fig. 27).

Peters also evidently came up with the initial version of the plant's dramatic giant twin stacks. He later made an etching of the stacks, which represents perhaps his most assertive work of the period before the war (fig. 28). He eventually produced several versions of the view, aware, it seems, of its visual force. The nature of the depiction was new for him: it was dark, foreboding, and starkly "industrial." Its dramatic presentation was a first indication of his interest in the new language of Expressionism.

It also revealed his growing attraction to dystopian imagery. While he was working on the Tiefstack drawings, Peters produced another etching, of a "Großstadt," a metropolis, with enormous, blocky buildings overwhelming the teeming masses in the streets (fig. 29). It is at once an inspiring and gloomy vision. What stands out even more, though, is its prescience: the buildings are reduced to featureless volumes, forcefully and predictively modern in their sparseness. Peters also extracts something else from the scene: a feeling of otherworldliness. It is a glimpse of his coming penchant for futurist fantasy.

In 1914, Bensel took part in one further competition, for an expansion of Alfred Lichtwark's Hamburg Kunsthalle. Lichtwark and Vivié had strongly encouraged Bensel to enter the competition, and, borrowing from a conceptual scheme made the previous year by Hugo Häring, Bensel produced a decidedly classicized structure with crisp detailing.[72]

Peters prepared at least one of the early designs for the project, which he later retained (fig. 30). It departs in significant ways from the final, submitted entry. It is, above all, a great deal simpler—without the side pavilions Bensel later added, which gave the proposed building a rather more conventional look.

What is notable in Peters's drawing is the confidence with which he handles the building's massing and its individual elements. The distance he had traversed as an architect since his first tentative school projects less than two years before is remarkable. The exhibition building's long, low profile is reminiscent of Ludwig Mies van der Rohe's design for the Kroller-Müller House of 1912–13; so, too, is Peters's depiction of the structure's oversized ashlar blocks. If less radical in its overall reductiveness than Mies's design, the drawing is no less compelling as an architectural image. Their submitted entry again won Bensel's office the first prize. It was never executed, in large part because Lichtwark died of stomach cancer at the beginning of 1914 and the final decision was first put on hold, then permanently shelved.[73] Had it been constructed as Peters proposed, it would certainly have been acknowledged at the time and afterward for its newness and vitality.

The Tiefstack and Kunsthalle projects brought an end to the first phase of Peters's career. His nearly two-and-a-half-year-long tenure in Bensel's office was his true architectural apprenticeship. The training he received and the experiences he gained in that time would serve him for the remainder of his days. Peters might well have continued working with Bensel: their collaboration and shared achievements had brought the two men close. But the outbreak of the war in late July 1914 would soon propel Peters onto an entirely different course.

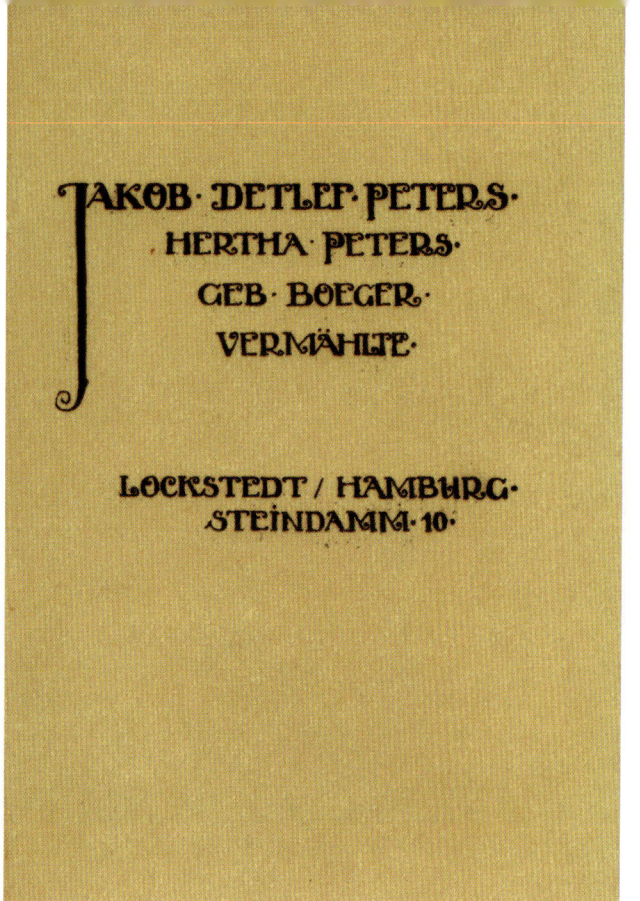

24. Jock Peters, announcement of his marriage to Herta Boeger, 1913. Collection Jock de Swart.

25. Carl Gustav Bensel and Jock Peters, design for the block of the Mönckebergstraße between Lange Mühren and Barkhof, Hamburg, 1914. From "C. G. Bensel, Regierungsbaumeister a. D., Architekt, Hamburg," Sonderheft *Bau-Rundschau* (Hamburg: Konrad Hanf, 1914): 2.

26. Carl Gustav Bensel and Jock Peters,
Tiefstack Electrical Power Plant, Hamburg, 1914–17.
Photographic print. UCSB.

27. Jock Peters, Machinery Building, Tiefstack Electrical Power
Plant, Hamburg, 1914–17. Sepia print. UCSB.

AN ARCHITECTURAL APPRENTICESHIP 41

28. Jock Peters, Boiler Building, Tiefstack Electrical Power Plant, Hamburg, 1914–17. Etching on paper. UCSB.

29. Jock Peters, *Großstadt* (Metropolis), c. 1914. Etching on paper. Collection Jock de Swart.

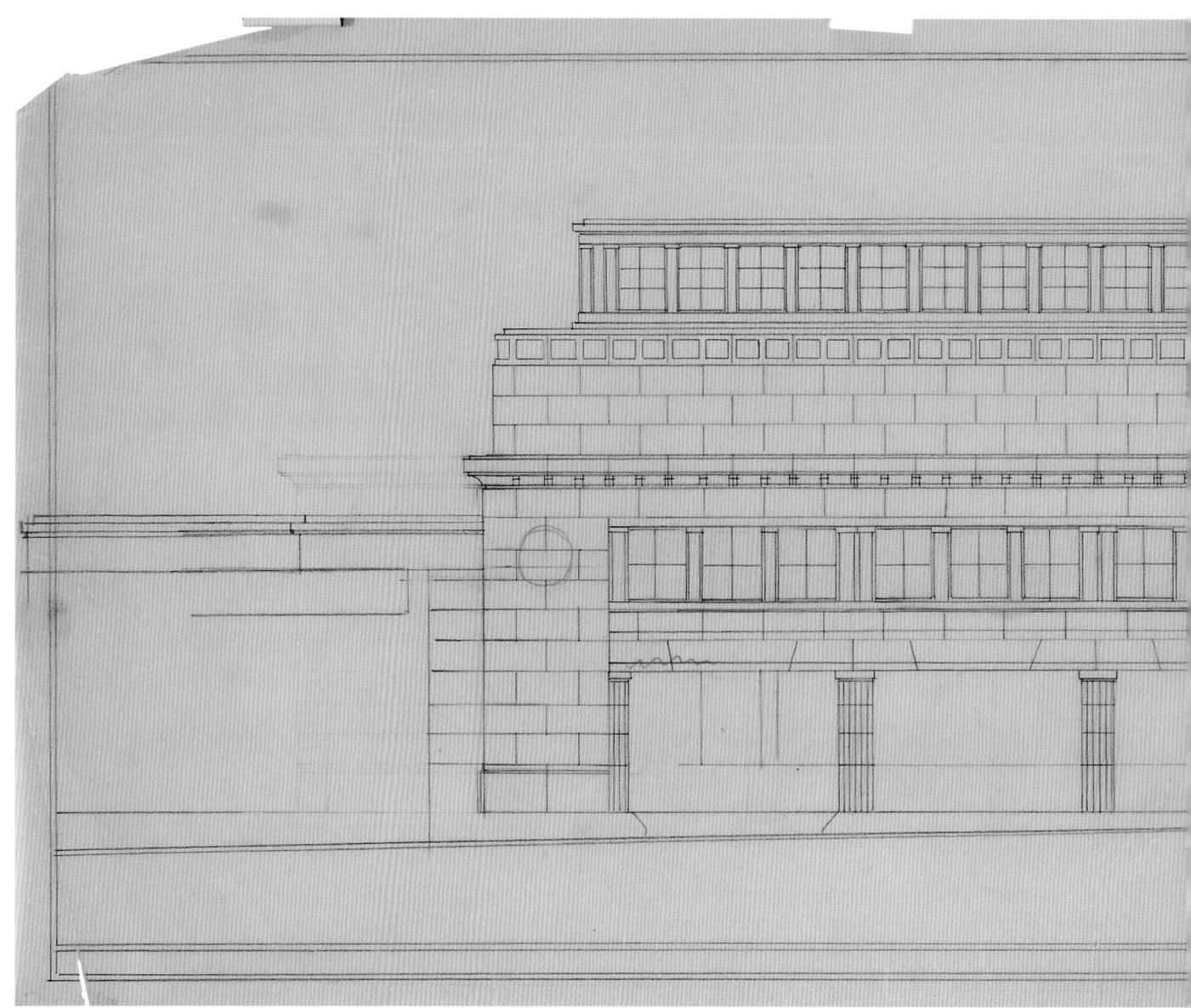

30. Jock Peters with Carl Gustav Bensel, competition design for the expansion of the Hamburg Kunsthalle, 1914.
Pencil and pen and ink on paper. UCSB.

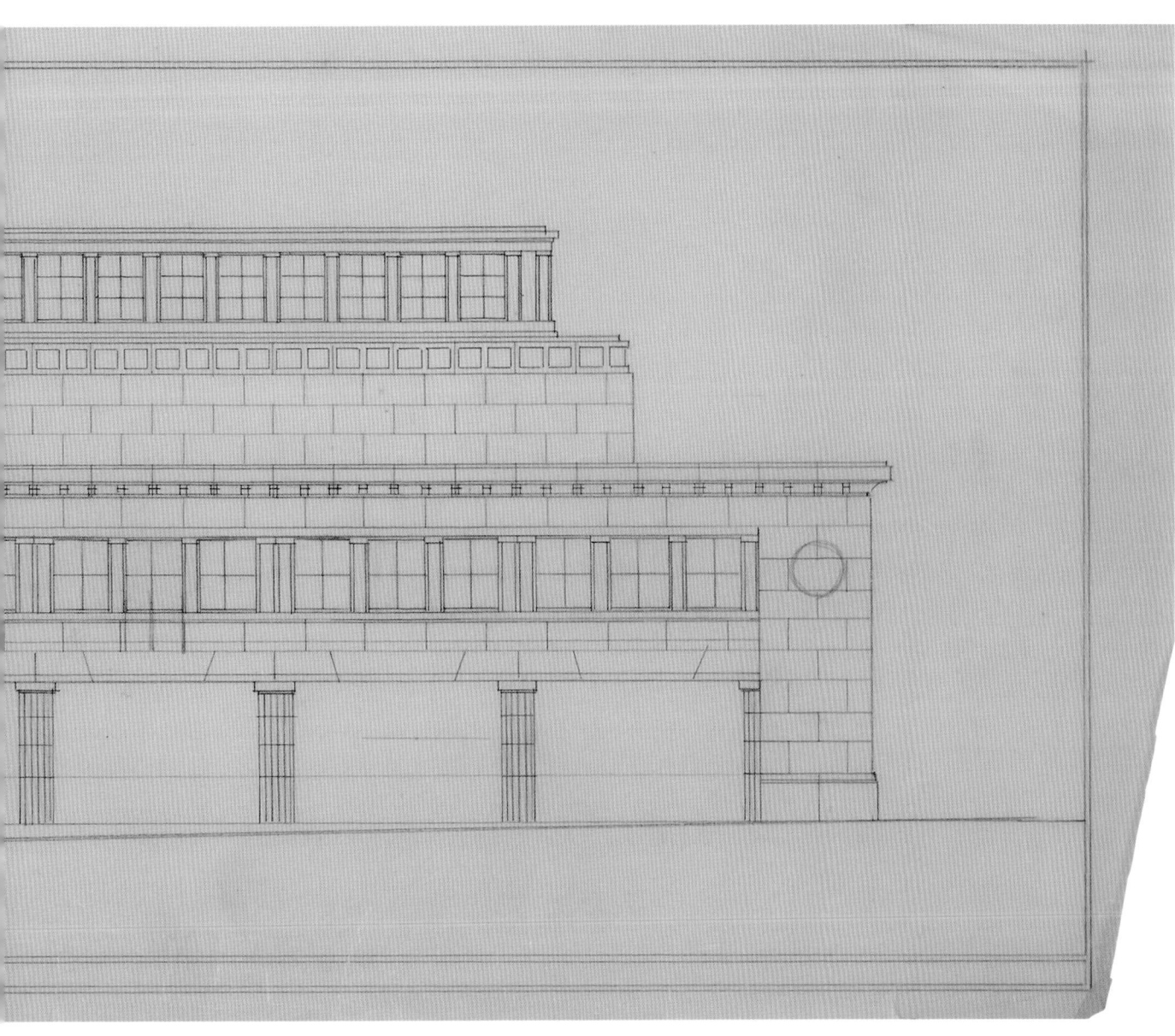

Chapter 3 |
OF LIGHT AND DARKNESS

As German soldiers streamed into Belgium in the late summer of 1914, Peters went down to the local army office and "volunteered for duty."[74] This act of patriotism was ever after a source of pride for him. It was not quite all that it seemed, however. Peters, like nearly every young German male not already in uniform, was a member of the reserves—in his case, the *Landsturm*, the provincial militia. Given his age, he would have been called up for service before long. In light of his stated willingness to fight, his time came sooner: he was told to report for active duty on September 24. He was promoted to *Gefreiter*—lance corporal—and assigned to a field artillery unit based in nearby Altona.[75]

Over the next several months, Peters underwent training to prepare him for service at the front. But with so many soldiers already in the field, and in view of the firm belief within the imperial government that Germany would quickly win the war, he was furloughed on February 9, 1915.[76] He went back to his old position in Bensel's office.

The previous December, Herta had given birth to their first child, a daughter they named Ursel.[77] After his discharge, Peters moved back in with them in the house in Lokstedt, commuting to work in the inner city each morning. In spite of the outbreak of the war, Bensel's office had remained active. No new commissions were coming in—most building activity not directly related to the war effort had been curtailed by the end of 1914—but construction on the Tiefstack power plant was in full swing, and countless details were yet to be worked out. Most of Bensel's other assistants had already left to join the war effort. That left only Bensel, Peters, and one other man to do the work.[78] (Breuhaus had stayed behind in Düsseldorf when Bensel moved to Hamburg.) Construction drawings were yet to be made, and the final details of the exteriors and spaces were still to be determined. The work was tedious, and Peters found it neither stimulating nor satisfying.

Some months before the outbreak of the war, he took up art again. He had stopped doing any drawing not related to his job; there was simply too much else to do. But as he would throughout his career in times of boredom or enforced idleness, he started sketching again. For the first time, he also began sculpting works in plaster. During his weeks of military training in Altona, he used his free time to make several pieces—all of them in some way about the experience of the war. The most ambitious was a small bust of a man (fig. 31).

31. Jock Peters, *Studie*, 1914. Plaster bust. Collection Jock de Swart.

Only a few photographs of the work, which Peters titled simply *Studie* (Study), survive; the piece itself has been lost. The face of the partial figure—only the front of the man's head and shoulders are depicted—is at once placid and anguished. What Peters was seemingly trying to portray was a trenchant sorrow, an apt theme for those early months of the war.

The look of his little bust was also perfectly in keeping with the newest art currents in Germany—more precisely, the advent of Expressionism. By 1915, Peters had joined a loosely formed group of like-minded Hamburg artists who were experimenting with the style.[79] They were well aware of what was going on in radical artistic circles in Germany, especially in Munich and Dresden: the striving to expose inner states of emotion, the mounting sense of unease with modern life, and the radical critique of Wilhelmine values.

Peters was drawn to the artists associated with Die Brücke, a group of Expressionist artists in Dresden that included Ernst Ludwig Kirchner and Erich Heckel.[80] His little sculpture, though, belongs more closely to another chapter of early German modernism. It brings to mind not the saturated color and jagged forms of the Dresden painters but the work of Ernst Barlach, who in the years before the war had exhibited with the Berlin Secession. Peters's bust exhibits the same rounded and swelling forms, even the oval and heavy-lidded eyes Barlach preferred.

Peters's most poignant and affecting work was a drawing he made in the middle of 1915 (fig. 32). It depicts a disembodied head, elongated and thinned, with an intense and unwavering gaze. It is possibly a self-portrait, for it bears more than a superficial resemblance to him. He may have also intended the drawing as a symbolic representation—an everyman, tormented, angry, and angst-ridden. Even though Peters was far from the fighting, as the conflict dragged on he became progressively more distressed by what he saw as its pointless cruelties.

He managed to escape the worst of it—at least for a time. By the end of September 1915, he had left Bensel's employ; the latter had been forced to close the office after being called up for service. Peters suddenly found himself out of work.[81] But he soon had a new job, working for Peter Behrens in Berlin.

Behrens had by this time emerged as the most renowned and admired architect in Germany (fig. 33). In the eight years since he had resigned from the directorship of the Düsseldorf Kunstgewerbeschule, he had become the unrivaled leader of the reform movement. His groundbreaking designs for electrical giant AEG—which encompassed everything from the company's stationery to its factory buildings—announced a novel vision of how products would be made and sold in the future. They represented a signal moment in the advance of industrial design, founded on an aesthetic of mass production and mass consumption. They were a statement, too, of a new simplicity. For even as Behrens had made the turn back to classicism around 1907, he had pushed toward a language of clarity and tectonic rigor that spoke directly to the rising interest in functionality.

Behrens's innovative designs drew to his atelier aspiring young architects from across Germany and abroad. In the years prior to Peters's arrival, Walter Gropius, Ludwig Mies van der Rohe, and Le Corbusier had all spent time in his office. By the end of 1915, Behrens had seen most of his assistants siphoned off for the war effort. There was still work, and hiring Peters, who was by this time knowledgeable and experienced, was a godsend for both men.[82]

Peters knew that the situation with Behrens would be temporary.[83] He and Herta kept the house in Lokstedt and rented a small apartment in Neubabelsberg near Potsdam, close to Behrens's home and office.

The office itself was in a large purpose-built studio in the garden of the Behrens family home. When Peters joined the practice, most of those working there were young men like him, who had been furloughed for one reason or another. He soon found common cause with one of them, Karl Schneider.

Born in Mainz in 1892, Schneider ascended early to the uppermost echelon of German modernism. After moving to Berlin in 1912, he found a position in the office of Walter Gropius and Adolf Meyer, just at the time that they were working on their Fagus Factory in Alfeld an der Leine. After Gropius closed his office in August 1914, Schneider eventually moved over to Behrens's office.[84]

Peters and Schneider formed a close friendship, united by ambition and their shared pursuit of the new architecture. For Peters, it was an important moment. From Schneider, he gained insight into the ideas and methods that Gropius and Meyer had been developing; from Behrens, he took in new lessons about what modernism could be.[85]

Behrens, though, was less radically modern than Gropius and Meyer, relying on more conventional ideas about materials and construction. He was also a more traditional German "atelier boss." Imposing and intellectually self-possessed, he assigned specific tasks to his assistants,

32. Jock Peters, self-portrait (?), 1915. Pencil on paper. Collection Jock de Swart.

with meticulous instructions about how to carry them out. Peters quickly found that he had far less freedom than he had enjoyed under Bensel—and few real opportunities to give input.

Behrens's office was then engaged with several large projects. On the boards were plans for a low-cost housing estate in Berlin-Lichtenberg and a competition design for the Haus der Freundschaft (House of Friendship), a meeting hall for the German-Turkish Union in Constantinople.[86] We know precisely which projects Peters was involved with, because Behrens detailed his activities in a letter of recommendation he wrote for him the following year (fig. 34). "While present [in my office]," he stated, "I assigned [Peters] to prepare preliminary and working drawings for a factory building in Hamburg and, in addition, a factory and administration building for the Nationale Automobil-Gesellschaft in Berlin-Oberschöneweide, which is currently under construction."[87]

The extent of Peters's role in either of these projects is unclear. The Hamburg factory project was typical of Behrens's work in those years: sturdy and solid, with an underlying but still perceptible classicism. The Nationale Automobil-Gesellschaft complex, on the other hand, shows a greater emphasis on clarity of form and line, a portent of the coming reliance on *Sachlichkeit*—austerity and "objectivity." Neither work displays any recognizable traces of Peters's hand. Given the force of Behrens's artistic personality, Peters's contribution to both projects was surely minor. In his first autobiography, Peters wrote that he had been Behrens's "1. Mitarbeiter"—his chief assistant.[88] That appears to have made little difference. The fact that he retained no drawings from this time is seeming confirmation that he did not consider any of the projects he worked on his own.

Peters did produce at least one independent project during this time. Shortly after he joined Behrens's atelier, he executed a rendering for a small festival hall and gymnasium on the shore of Alster Lake in Hamburg (fig. 35). It is an adept composition: a small, tightly composed cubic structure with truncated wings and a central block surmounted by a pyramidal roof. It resembles Behrens's aesthetic—or, perhaps, a melding of Peters's own ideas with those of Behrens.

But it was little enough to show for nearly a year's labor. Peters must have sensed that it was time for him to move

PROF. PETER BEHRENS
FERNSPRECHER: AMT NOWAWES 282 · NEUBABELSBERG BEI BERLIN

DEN 12.9.16.

Z e u g n i s

   Herrn Architekt Jakob Detlef P e t e r s bestätige ich hiermit, daß er von Ende September 1915 bis zum 30. August d. Js. auf meinem Atelier tätig war . - Herr Peters hat die ihm übertragenen Arbeiten mit Fleiß und gutem Verständnis ausgeführt . -

   Während seiner Anwesenheit beschäftigte ich ihn mit den Projektierungs- und Ausführungszeichnungen für ein Fabrikgebäude für Hamburg und ferner für das jetzt noch im Bau begriffene Fabrik- und Verwaltungsgebäude für die Nationale Automobil-Gesellschaft, Berlin-Oberschöneweide .

   Herr Peters verläßt mein Atelier, um einer Kriegsbeorderung, die er erhielt, Folge zu leisten .

Prof Behrens

34. Letter from Peter Behrens confirming Peters's employment in his office, September 1916. Collection Jock de Swart.

33. Peter Behrens, c. 1913. Photograph by Waldemar Titzenthaler. Private collection.

35. Jock Peters, project for a festival and gymnastics building, 1915. Pencil and charcoal on paper. UCSB.

36. Peters (on the left) with another German soldier in the foundry in Charleroi, Belgium, c. 1916. Collection Jock de Swart.

on. Some of those who had previously worked in Behrens's office, including Gropius and Le Corbusier, griped about their boss's overbearing character. Peters made no such complaints—at least none have survived. But though cordial, his relationship with Behrens never developed into the sort of deep friendship he had shared with Bensel. He seems to have taken away few explicit lessons from his time in Behrens's employ: there is little, if any, perceptible influence from Behrens in his subsequent works. Still, by the time he departed, he had spent a number of months at the very epicenter of German modernism.

The more than a year and a half Peters spent working for Bensel and Behrens in 1915 and 1916 was a rare gift for a young German man at that time. Peters knew all too well that it could not continue. In October 1915, not long after he started working for Behrens, he had received orders to report to his unit in Altona.[89] Once more, after only a few days, he was informed he was not needed, and he returned to Behrens's office in Berlin. But as the war dragged on, Germany began to commit its total resources. All reservists were being called up for duty, and in late July 1916, Peters received another letter ordering him to report for service.[90]

He was assigned to a reserve unit awaiting deployment to the front. After a few days, the men were sent to a base in the town of Lille, in northern France near the border with Belgium. Anticipating a long separation, Herta returned to Hamburg to sell all the furnishings from the Lokstedt house. She and baby Ursel then moved in with her mother in Düsseldorf.[91]

Though he was still distant from the fighting, Peters's first days in Lille were filled with anxiety. The army command, concerned about flagging morale, was sending commissions of inquiry to many units—even those far from the front—to ferret out soldiers who might be undermining confidence in the war effort, or even fomenting insurrection. Individual men in some cases were taken and subjected to intense, often hours-long interrogation. Peters confided in a letter to Herta that he thought it "all theater," but he still experienced some apprehensive moments while his unit was undergoing its "examination." He was also worried and depressed about a new order that soldiers would no longer automatically receive leave for Christmas to "prevent any increased demand on Germany's over-stretched food supply."[92]

He was also bored rigid. After the constant activity and stimulation of being in busy architects' offices, Peters found the sitting and waiting, the ceaseless drilling, and the frequent night guard duty unbearable. He wanted something "more interesting," he wrote Herta. After much anxious reflection, he went to his commanding lieutenant and volunteered to be an aide in the company office.[93]

On his first day, he discovered that his duties mostly involved routine clerical work—hardly more stimulating than what he had been doing. To his surprise and irritation, he found himself assigned that first evening to night duty, ordered to monitor the office and telephone.[94] The situation, as it would turn out—greatly to his relief—lasted only a single day and night. The next morning, as his unit prepared for its first rotation at the front, all soldiers underwent a final medical examination. Peters was determined to be medically "unfit" and was immediately reassigned to the rear echelon.[95]

He wrote about his reassignment in a letter to Herta, but he did not spell out the nature of his illness. Both already knew what it was: tuberculosis. In this letter is the first evidence of the disease that would redirect the course of his life and, ultimately, kill him. Peters must have been aware for some time that he was infected, though the knowledge that it had advanced to the degree to warrant his exclusion from front-line duty—at a time when Germany needed every man on the front—probably came as a shock.

It was, though, in a curious way, a stroke of luck. Because of his condition, Peters managed to avoid being sent to the trenches, which by that point in the war might well have killed him more swiftly than and almost as surely as the disease itself. After receiving the news—which, to judge from the tone in his letter to Herta, he took with resignation—he spent another week at the base in Lille, "guarding" the local populace.[96] Then, on September 18, 1916, he was permanently transferred to the Heereswerkstätte West, an army group utilizing Belgian factories and labor to manufacture weapons, munitions, and other materiel for the German war effort.[97]

The Heereswerkstätte West was a vast undertaking, a significant piece of Germany's total war strategy. Overseeing its command was a staff of army officers and a handful of civilians. Most of the men had been involved in manufacturing in Germany before the war and had some form of technical expertise. Peters, despite his lack of factory experience, was regarded as a perfect candidate for the work in light of his education as an engineer-architect (as all architects then were designated in Germany, because of their training in technical subjects). He was assigned to a foundry in the southern Belgian town of Charleroi, where large and small bronze and iron castings were being produced.

He was officially made a *Giesserei-Assistent* (foundry assistant) responsible for supervising a group of Belgian civilian laborers (fig. 36).[98] He was initially pleased with this new state of affairs, relieved to be far away from the trenches and excited to have the opportunity to learn a new trade. Because of his experience in Reimer's workshop, he soon picked up the techniques for fashioning molds. He was also put through a crash course in the science of smelting and casting metals.

In the factory section to which he was assigned, Peters was one of only a handful of Germans overseeing a large number of conscripted Belgian workers. He tried to maintain a good relationship with the men, in spite of the difficult circumstances. Over time, his responsibilities enlarged. At first, he was placed in charge of twenty-four workers; eventually, that number grew to some nine hundred.[99]

As conditions in the occupied areas of Belgium deteriorated, tensions between the workers and the Germans in command mounted. When Peters arrived at his office one morning in the latter part of 1916, he was confronted by an angry mob demanding more food. One man threw a metal fragment at Peters. It missed him and instead hit a vase of narcissuses on his desk, shattering it. Peters wrote a poem about the incident, which he sent to Herta. He describes how he grabbed the flowers in one hand and drew his pistol with the other. He went to the landing above the work floor and threw the flowers down on the men, "letting [them] rain down on their heads."[100] After a few moments of tense confrontation, the men withdrew one by one and went back to work.[101]

Nevertheless, working behind the front spared Peters from the worst of what the war brought. He had time to himself in the evenings and sometimes on Sundays, and he was not in immediate danger. In his later autobiography, he noted that he had been "briefly assigned to front-line duty."[102] He supplies no other detail, and there is no specific mention of this in his army records. It is possible Peters was sent to the front to confer with commanders about their needs for weapons or other articles. His time there, in any event, was brief.

While in Lille, in 1916, Peters had witnessed the explosion of a grenade and the death and maiming of several people. Afterward, sometime in 1917, he made an etching depicting the scene (fig. 37).

It is at once powerful and disturbing. Peters catches the force of the blast and the horrific impact on those caught up in it. Lines radiating out from the center of the image capture the energy of the detonation. The whole scene—its dark vision, its dramatic representation—is consistent with the visual language of prewar Expressionism. The way in which he renders the centrifugal lines also hints that by that time Peters was acquainted with works of the Italian Futurists.

The etching was once more Peters's way of coming to terms with the war. His inner feelings, though, are even more poignantly displayed in the many letters he sent to Herta. They reveal that he was often depressed, dismayed by what he saw as only wanton destruction and senseless murder.

Peters's early letters to Herta, written before their marriage in 1912 and 1913, give hints of his sensitive nature. His wartime letters are something else altogether. They disclose a genuine and deeply felt hatred Peters had developed for the army and German militarism. He found nothing redeeming in his wartime experiences, nothing that provoked in him feelings of patriotism or enthusiasm for the war effort. Not infrequently, he writes to Herta of his hopes and dreams for the future, but any positive feelings he expresses are tinged with acerbity. "You write a great deal of light and darkness," Herta replied to him in one of her letters, voicing her concern about his increasingly bleak moods.[103]

In a letter Peters wrote to his wife in December 1916, he declares, "Only with peace will we be able to return to consciousness of ourselves. Only with peace may we expect the sun, which will bring to life again all that we have put aside during this time. Then we will be able to enjoy again the work of our hands, to create freely, and act in accordance with morals and customs."[104] He adds, with palpable anger, "This association with people in the military straitjacket . . . makes one feel cast out from all culture."[105] In another letter, of just five lines, written a short time before, Peters tells his wife that only when she sees him at Christmas will she be able to gauge the level of his despair. He closes with a chilling declaration: "I cannot write anymore, because I want to scream!"[106]

In many of his letters from 1916 and 1917, Peters also expresses his hope to continue his career in architecture and, also, to make art. If for many the shock of the war had made art seem peripheral, for him it now became all the more essential. It became his emotional outlet, his best means of coping. As much as time and work permitted, he continued to make small artworks, including blocks for woodcuts, which he fashioned from scraps left on the shop floor. Sometimes he made drawings, often on the backs of used sheets of stationery from the foundry. Many of these he mailed off to his friends serving at the front.[107]

37. Jock Peters, *Grenade in Lille*, 1917. Etching on paper. Courtesy Ars Libri, Boston.

Peters also found spare moments to work on several architectural projects. Most were designs for war memorials.

Earlier, in 1915, he had worked on a competition design for a monument to the fallen for the main Hamburg cemetery in Ohlsdorf.[108] Peters apparently returned to the idea a year later, after he had started working at the factory. He prepared two versions, both in the form of a raised sarcophagus. In one, dated 1916, a continuous frieze of soldiers marching in single file is shown, reminiscent of ancient Egyptian or Babylonian bas-reliefs (fig. 38). Zigzagging lines extending along its upper edges give a foretaste of early postwar Expressionist architecture. His second version relies similarly on Expressionist detailing, but it is simpler, more condensed and direct (fig. 39).

More significant is his competition design for a memorial church (figs. 40, 41). Peters apparently worked on it during the second half of 1916, though the exact circumstances of its creation are unknown. Its blocky massing and colonnaded forecourt are suggestive of early Roman Christian basilicas, a vestige of his ongoing interest in a modernized classicism. Even more notable is the horizontal streamlining of the main body of the building, which Peters may well have taken over from Behrens's AEG Turbine Building.

The war monuments and church project, while very different, are more proficient in terms of their design and graphic presentation than any of Peters's previous efforts. They are also fresh and original statements: if, before the war, the young Peters had been a follower of trends, he was now showing a capacity to devise novel forms.

This newfound confidence is especially pronounced in another of his wartime projects. Around the time he was designing the memorial church, Peters began work on a series of projects for country houses. They would become for him a sustained investigation, his first true foray into a new and personal architecture.

The earliest version of his country house idea appears in the form of a small pencil drawing dated 1916 (fig. 42). It shows a remarkably innovative solution: Peters considers a low, flat-roofed, pavilion-like room—presumably an extension of the house—set upon a high base. Prominent are its framing surfaces, which he dissolves entirely on three of the four sides into glass panels affixed in very thin mullions. The effect, which he depicted in a second drawing showing the interior, is startling—its lightness very much unlike the works of other German architects of the time (fig. 43).

39. Jock Peters, project for a war memorial, c. 1916.
Alternate version. Pencil on paper. UCSB.

38. Jock Peters, project for a war memorial, 1916.
Pencil on paper. UCSB.

OF LIGHT AND DARKNESS 57

40. Jock Peters, project for a war memorial church, 1916. Forecourt.
Pencil on paper. UCSB.

41. Jock Peters, project for a war memorial church, 1916. Nave.
Pencil and colored pencil on paper. UCSB.

42. Jock Peters, project for a country house, c. 1916.
Window detail. Pencil on paper. UCSB.

43. Jock Peters, project for a country house, 1916. Window detail from the interior. Pen and ink and gouache on paper. UCSB.

Full curtain walls of glass were only then being realized in the United States. Gropius and Meyer had produced something of the sort in their two prewar factory complexes. Their glass walls, however, were set into self-supporting frames; they were not attached to (and carried by) the structural members—the columns and beams—as is the case in true curtain walls. Peters's version is similar, which is to say that it is not a curtain wall per se. His design instead announced a different solution: by means of a radical reduction of the framing elements in which the glass was held, he achieved the near dissolution of the supporting structure.[109] The early postwar crystalline fantasies of Bruno Taut would come close, but nothing comparable in German architecture would appear again until Mies van der Rohe produced his great skyscraper projects, with their sleek, diaphanous envelopes of glass, in 1921 and 1922.

From the outset, Peters intended to set his glass room into a complete country villa. His first full version of the villa, which he designated as Landhaus (or country house) I, was a sprawling one- and two-story L-shaped house perched on a hill. A perspective of the house, which he made in 1917, shows the degree to which Peters had absorbed not only the latest currents in European modernism, but also those in America, for the house has a distinctly Wrightian cast (fig. 44). Much of its formal language—its long, low profile, broad eaves, cantilevered roofs, and thickset brick construction—stems straight from Frank Lloyd Wright's vocabulary.

The similarities reveal that Peters was already intimately familiar with Wright's work. The most likely source of his knowledge was Wright's Wasmuth portfolio, his *Ausgeführte Bauten* (Executed buildings), that had been published in Berlin in 1911.[110] It is possible that Peters may have seen the portfolio before the war. But the fact that no Wrightian influences turn up in his previous designs suggests strongly that his acquaintance with Wright came later—most likely through Karl Schneider, when both he and Schneider were working in Behrens's office.

Schneider was well acquainted with the Wasmuth portfolio from his time with Gropius and Meyer, where, as architectural historian Winfried Nerdinger has written, it served as the "office bible."[111] Schneider had spent time poring over the plates, and it seems most likely that it was he who introduced Peters to it.[112] In any event, Peters had clearly seen and fully digested the portfolio by the time he was engaged with the country house project.

The first perspective view he prepared of the full house is still inelegant and unsure, with an oddly "tacked on" semi-circular glazed corner. A second drawing he made, depicting the house on its garden side, however, is less equivocal (fig. 45). Like his memorial church from the year before, it presents a clever union of styles and impulses. This time, he combined Wright's idiosyncratic mannerisms with the robust tectonic forms of Behrens, Hans Poelzig, and Bruno Paul.

What sets the design apart is Peters's stress on open and flowing volumes. Even with the knowledge that realizing such unrestrained spaces was limited at the time, Peters was confident new forms of space-making were in the offing. Though he does not explicitly allude to it in any of his letters of this period, his early Landhaus project points toward another impending architectural development: a pronounced accent on light and lightness. There is a luminous quality to his drawings: Peters was already envisioning a better, more radiant future—far removed from the darkness and despair of the war.

Peters's hopes for a better future were buoyed in April 1917 by the birth of his and Herta's second child, a boy they named Dierk. His day-to-day experiences, however, all too often brought him to despondency. He found the conditions in the foundry and the dismal reality of the war increasingly hard to bear. The mounting resentment of the Belgian workers weighed on him, as did the slaughter that was taking place not far away at the front. From time to time, he heard reports of the deaths of men from his former unit and of friends serving elsewhere. The worst blow came when he learned that his younger brother Fritz had been killed in action.

Toward the end of 1917, Peters became steadily more depressed. He lost weight and became progressively weaker as tuberculosis more and more affected his lungs. The damp and cold conditions at the factory and the poor quality of food then reaching the soldiers only made matters worse. In spite of it all, Peters continued to be a model soldier. An evaluation from his commander in September 1917 reported that his performance was satisfactory and his leadership "good"—genuine praise in an army that dispensed such judgments sparingly.[113]

Throughout 1917 and into early 1918, he was allowed few visits home; the work of making armaments was simply too crucial for the war effort. Peters complained bitterly to Herta, but there was little he could do. It was all the more frustrating for him because Düsseldorf was not far from Charleroi, though the journey could be agonizingly slow because the train system was severely overtaxed.

Over and over in his letters to his wife, Peters voiced his frustrations and resentments about his situation at the factory. In one letter from after February, he tells her of his dream of being back on the farm in Jarrenwisch and returning to his art:

44. Jock Peters, project for a country house (Landhaus I), 1916–17.
Print. UCSB.

45. Jock Peters, project for a country house (Landhaus I), 1917.
Exterior detail. Pencil on paper. UCSB.

I wish I could work with my father on the land and forget everything, the madness for which I have given my best years . . . This constant servitude, this obeying. The arrogance that increases with rank . . . I hate the whole thing down to my bones, and I want to withdraw into a hiding place and throw arrows out from my eyes so that no one will dare to touch me, and I can live for myself and for my art.[114]

In another anguished letter, from mid-March 1918, written on his twenty-ninth birthday, Peters complains that he had lost three years of his creative life to "militarism." He had been forced, he writes, to give his "best strength to destruction. We have sacrificed our life's springtime, our fortunes and possessions." He signed it "in the field gray" (the color of the German army uniform) "of 1918."[115]

Peters's situation finally saw a turnaround not long thereafter. He came to the attention of the head of the unit assigned to prepare grave markers and cemeteries along the entire western front, Captain Melchior von Hugo.

In personality and outlook, Hugo was very different from the other German officers Peters had encountered up to that point. Hugo had started his career in the service of the army of Saxony but resigned after a decade to pursue studies in art. He spent time at the Académie Julian in Paris and, later, in Munich, where he befriended the playwright Frank Wedekind. Hugo eventually moved to Stuttgart, and there he fashioned reliefs and other ornamental features for several of Theodor Fischer's buildings. He returned to the army when the war broke out, and in due course he was made responsible for planning the military cemeteries and fabricating all the grave markers in the whole of the western theater.

Hugo probably met Peters in the context of a commission for grave markers he had ordered from the foundry. He would have discovered that Peters had been a stonemason's apprentice and that he had considerable design experience. In late April 1918, Hugo had Peters transferred to his unit, headquartered nearby in Charleville.[116]

The chance to fashion funerary monuments—essentially, works of art—came for Peters as a momentous relief. Though the subject matter was grim, he found the task far more sustaining than what he had been doing up to that point: manufacturing instruments for killing. Hugo, as an artist himself, understood the needs and sensibilities of the young man he now came to increasingly rely on. He turned over to Peters the task of designing and making bronze and iron castings to adorn the many cemeteries.

Hugo also saw to it that Peters received a pass to travel to Hamburg on what he described as "urgent business." In reality, it was a chance for Peters to get away and see his parents and sisters after many months. Herta and the children traveled north for the reunion, and Peters saw baby Dierk for the first time (fig. 46).

Upon his return to Charleville, Peters resumed his work for Hugo. We have no evidence of what, precisely, he accomplished. In light of the deteriorating state of the German army, it is doubtful that much came of his efforts. If he was able to execute any grave markers of his own design, they probably mirrored his earlier projects for memorials: vaguely modern in style but imbued with traditional elements. In a letter of recommendation written after the war, Hugo praised Peters's "superior" abilities, his "work stamina," and his "organizational talents." He offers no specifics about Peters's work while under his command, other than to remark that although the younger man was a "modernist by conviction," he also appreciated the "fruits of earlier eras."[117]

Beyond the ever more dire situation of the Germans in 1918, what prevented Peters from doing more was that he was often ill and away recuperating. In mid-July, he contracted influenza—likely the dreaded Spanish flu that killed so many in those last days of the war. He spent two weeks in an army sanatorium. His illness led to a case of pleurisy, which was aggravated by his tuberculosis infection, and he was forced to pass a further three weeks at the German military hospital in Charleroi.[118] Finally, in late August, he was able to return to Charleville. He worked there for six more weeks, until Hugo had him transferred to the unit's head office in Berlin.[119] It was a small gesture, but the move probably saved Peters's life. He was so weakened by disease and poor nutrition that he could not have held out much longer.

Peters remained in Berlin only briefly. In mid-November, with the war at last over, he was released from service. Immediately afterward, he made his way to Hamburg to rebuild his life and career.

46. Peters on leave from the front, with Herta, Ursel, and baby Dierk, June 1918. Collection Jock de Swart.

Hamburg Chile-Haus

Chapter 4 |
EXPERIMENTS IN STYLE

In the aftermath of the German army's sudden collapse on the western front in early November 1918, the imperial government simply melted away. During Peters's last days in Berlin, he witnessed sporadic street fighting among the various militias connected with the political right or left. Soldiers and civilians, concealed behind barricades, fired Mausers and machine guns at each other, at times wildly. Furious mobs ransacked stores, and women and old men butchered dead horses for food on the boulevards.

When Peters arrived in Hamburg barely two weeks after the war's end, the situation there was nearly as frenzied and unsure.[120] Sailors and former soldiers, many recently returned from the front and still wearing their ragged uniforms, wandered the streets. The sense of a loss of order that would come to be the great black mark of the Weimar years was already beginning to insinuate its way into the national consciousness.

Peters, once more, was fortunate. In early December, even while the situation in Hamburg, as in Germany as a whole, remained confused and unstable, he found work in the office of architect Fritz Höger.[121]

Peters had known Höger before the war. The older architect had been involved in the rebuilding of Hamburg's inner city and the development of the Mönckebergstraße, and he had realized one of its essential landmarks, the Klöpperhaus, a massive edifice in the Neo-Renaissance style.[122]

In background and outlook, he and Peters shared much. Höger came from the far north, from Holstein, near the border with Dithmarschen; he had first been trained in the crafts, as a carpenter. Both men were committed to the mission of developing Hamburg into a modern city; both aspired to recast German modernism.

Nonetheless, Peters took the job reluctantly. Some months before the war's end, he had expressed his growing doubts about returning to architecture. "I will hold out," he wrote to Herta, "until the war is over . . . and then, dear Boegie, I don't know if I'll stay in my current profession. When the war is done, I can immediately find a good position in my present line of work [he is referring here to making metal castings] that would bring us financial health."[123]

Peters thought this plan would give him greater artistic freedom. He could readily earn a living making bronzes, he reasoned, and he could use his spare time to engage in artistic pursuits, without being tethered to the dictates of an architect's office.[124]

47. Postcard owned by Jock Peters of Fritz Höger's Chilehaus, Hamburg, 1922–24. Collection Jock de Swart.

In the closing days of the war, he reconsidered; he instead thought of opening his own architectural practice. But he was now forced by circumstance to take the expedient route, to find work in an established office. He had, he believed, precious little choice: he had a family to support, few prospects, and no means to fall back on. Ever after, he saw the decision as an unhappy compromise—an unavoidable choice, in his words, of having "to start over."[125]

Still, Peters knew that he was lucky. Many young architects returning from the war were out of work and would be for some time. He had only received the offer of employment from Höger because another prominent figure he knew in Hamburg, architect and urban planner Fritz Schumacher, who was a friend of Höger, had interceded on his behalf.[126] The union, in any case, was to both men's benefit: Peters needed the job, and Höger needed qualified assistants. Höger had just returned from the front, and he was trying to rebuild his practice. By the time Peters joined his staff, roughly a month after the war's conclusion, Höger was already at work on several projects.

The largest of these was the HAPAG-Haus, for Albert Ballin's shipping concern. Höger had begun work on the building in 1913, but its design and construction were halted during the war. Höger hoped to start the project anew, and on a very different basis. Before the war, he had built a reputation for his advocacy of heavy brick masonry construction, especially the use of "clinker" bricks (so called because during the firing process they are burned at higher temperatures and for longer periods and are, as a result, darker, harder, and often misshapen). He and his friend Schumacher had contended at the time that this rustic aesthetic should become the constructive language for modern Hamburg because of its associations with north German building traditions.[127]

Ballin, however, had other ideas. The HAPAG-Haus was an extension of an existing structure, designed in 1903 by an architect named Martin Haller, and Ballin insisted that it be of the same light sandstone and in the same style. Höger was forced to match a barely updated version of the Renaissance revival. When it was finally finished, in 1921, the completed work appeared at least two decades out of date.

Höger would go on to realize many other projects that bore the hallmarks of the sturdy brick aesthetic he championed, and Peters had the opportunity to assist on several of them. Peters was even briefly involved with the building that Höger is now best known for: the mammoth Chilehaus in the Kontorhausviertel, widely regarded as one of the triumphs of German Expressionist architecture.

Peters worked on the initial plans for the huge building, but he had already left Höger's office by the time construction ended in 1924. Ever after, Peters retained a postcard of it as a keepsake (fig. 47). With its angular lines, sweeping curvilinear façades, and dark brownish clinker-brick skin, the Chilehaus was Höger's most vigorous statement of what has been called "Hanseatic modernism," a brawny northern version of Expressionism.[128] Yet the building also represents an ending: by the time the scaffolding was removed, Expressionism in Germany was swiftly giving way to a new reticence in architecture and design. The completed Chilehaus rested at the divide.

Much lay before that moment, and Peters was involved with a great deal of it. His work of those years closely followed the progression of architectural ideas in early postwar Germany. Peters's personal development is readily discernible in the projects he prepared—many, as it would turn out, independently, outside of Höger's office. For, as time went on, Peters became disillusioned with Höger. He was happy for the position and income, but he often disagreed with Höger's approach. He also sorely missed the freedom of being able to make his own designs. Soon after joining the office, he was engaged in two parallel pursuits: working as a highly competent employee for Höger during business hours, while moonlighting in the evenings and sometimes on the weekends with his own work. He was astonishingly active in those first several years after the war, absorbed with various competitions as well as making more than a few fantasy projects—and most of these designs had nothing at all to do with his regular day job.

One of these early "supplementary" designs was for Peters's own dining room and study. He and Herta moved the family back into their old house in Hamburg as soon as he returned from Berlin, and he hurriedly went to work to furnish their new interiors, collaborating with an unknown but highly skilled cabinetmaker.

The dining room, captured in a photograph taken not long after its completion, bears the marks of the two main impulses in Peters's early postwar work (fig. 48). The heavy turned legs of the dining table show his penchant—taken over, it seems, from Höger—for over-scaled, burly forms. The bookcase along the wall, on the other hand, exhibits, in its slender, pointed inlays, the characteristic motifs of a more refined Expressionism. (Visible in the image is Peters's *Studie*, his plaster bust of 1914, resting on the bookcase.)

48. Jock Peters, dining room of the Peters house, c. 1919–20. UCSB.

49. Jock Peters, project for the renovation of the pavilion on Alster Lake, Hamburg, 1919. Pencil on paper. UCSB.

This more ornamental variant of Expressionism is on display in another of Peters's projects, an entertainment pavilion on Alster Lake in the heart of the city (fig. 49). The design is related to the festival hall Peters had made in 1915, around the time he was first working for Behrens. He appears to have returned to it during the first half of 1919, spending a considerable amount of time on its redesign.

The central portion of the new structure is tentlike, a fitting bit of imagery for what was supposed to be a communal *Lusthaus*, or garden pavilion. Flanking it on either side are rectilinear blocks, with glazing and decorative panels. In formal terms, the arrangement—absent the "tent" roof—exhibits some similarities with Gropius and Meyer's model factory at the 1914 Werkbund exhibition in Cologne. Peters's application of finely modeled Expressionist motifs, however, rendered the building at once festal and forceful, severe and light—an appropriate design idiom for those years.

Peters was also engaged with another civic project, a massive tower in the inner city, at Ferdinandstor, across from the Hamburg Kunsthalle. It was intended both as a war memorial and as an art exhibition space (fig. 50).

What is immediately obvious is Peters's interest in generating a soaring monumentality. The drawing itself is enormous, nearly a meter and a half tall. The upper tower rests on a broad, solid base, which was meant to house the exhibition spaces. Once more, it is possible that Peters was looking at a prewar precedent: Joseph Maria Olbrich's Wedding Tower in Darmstadt, completed in 1908. But Peters's design was more hard-edged, more strident, a statement very much in the mood of the time. Had it been erected, Peters's tower would doubtless now be viewed as one of the key statements of the early postwar era of German architecture. It remained unrealized, as did the Alster Lake pavilion. The political stability and the financial means to complete such civic projects were still some years off in the future.

Another of Peters's projects is a competition design for a secondary school in Hamburg, at the corner of Breitenfelderstraße and Curschmannstraße (fig. 51). This time he was working within the scope of his duties in Höger's atelier, and the design won the first prize. The sole surviving drawing is in his hand. It shows a ponderous building with a bulky

50. Jock Peters, project for a war memorial and exhibition tower, 1918. Pencil on paper. UCSB.

51. Jock Peters, competition entry for the Lyceum at the corner of Breitenfelderstraße and Curschmannstraße, Hamburg, 1919. Pencil and pen and ink on paper. UCSB.

corner tower block. Continuous vertical stone mullions elevate the work; as a whole, though, it is unresolved and fussy. The main body of the structure is broken up with needless horizontal banding, which undermines its better features. It was never realized, but later Höger erected his own design on the site.

Peters also worked on a competition project for an electrical power plant in Rendsburg, a small town on the Elbe River in central Schleswig-Holstein, that also won a first prize. It, too, remained on the drawing board. Peters made several other designs for competitions, though it is not known whether he did so on his own or as one of Höger's assistants. Nothing is indicated on any of the documents that remain to us.

Among these is a design for a city hall for the small town of Gadebusch, near Lübeck.[129] Only a single drawing of the building, shown in perspective, has survived. Dominating the front is a large Dutch or Friesian parapet, a standard architectural form of the region. The robust look of the building suggests the influence of Berlage and Cuypers; its overall cast, though, is more closely wedded to the Netherlandish vernacular. It, too, came to naught.

Peters seemed barely to notice or to care. He was increasingly preoccupied with his experimental designs for country houses.

All of these designs were extensions or modifications of his Landhaus project from the war years. Over the course of the roughly two years after his return from the army, he produced at least three more versions of the house. These projects chart, even more conspicuously than his other designs of those years, his developing architectural ideas.

At the end of 1918, after he had begun working for Höger, Peters prepared what he called his Landhaus II. On at least two drawings, he added the legend "House for Dr. Paulsen," who was likely the prospective client for all the Landhaus projects.[130] Like his variant Landhaus I of 1917, it is again Wrightian in appearance—this time, even more insistently so (fig. 52). The L-shaped structure is low-slung and firmly grounded. In comparison with his first wartime version of the Landhaus project, Peters greatly condensed its massing, and he took pains to work out a full interior and landscaping plan (fig. 53). There is a pronounced cantilever at one end, in form and effect much like Wright's Robie House in Chicago. Underneath is a projecting, full-length window, glazed on three sides, which doubtless was another of Peters's efforts to bring light into the interior.

Despite its derivative quality—it could nearly be a work by Wright—the Landhaus II was Peters's most complete and coherent architectural statement up to that point. That he presented it in the form of a woodcut, with radiating lines and a stylized sun—in a manner not so dissimilar from the stars and aura of Lyonel Feininger's slightly later "Cathedral" woodcut for the cover of the 1919 Bauhaus manifesto—discloses his interest in allying Wright's form language with that of German Expressionism.[131] Spatially, though, the design was a departure from German domestic architecture of the time—at least until Mies van der Rohe commenced his volumetric experiments a few years later. The rooms are large and the spatial progression nearly continuous.

A short time after this, Peters—predictably, one could say, and consistent with his usual restlessness in matters of style—investigated the idea of wrapping a cloak of a more or less unalloyed Expressionism over the same basic design. This version of his project has almost the identical form and plan. Yet its detailing is converted to a more homegrown—north German—modernism (fig. 54). Peters even adjusted the manner of his rendering to make it all harmonious.

This cluster of independent projects reveals once more Peters's ability to move from style to style with an effortlessness that is almost uncanny. It suggests the consolidation and affirmation of an approach that at first came through necessity, as Peters learned his trade as an architect. In contrast with his more formally educated peers, he learned on the job, and part of what he learned was how to adopt a new visual language with each move to a new employer. This facility, a feature even of his apprenticeship with Reimer, became central to Peters's identity as a designer, and to his understanding of modernism.

Throughout the early postwar years—and ever after—Peters tried out new and diverse options, seeking always to find the one that matched his own mood and the times. He was hardly the only modernist of the period to do so. What would shape Peters's career, however, was his demonstrated willingness to try out diverse forms of expression, different styles and idioms, without ever quite settling on one. He never came to articulate the idea in his writings, but he seems to have believed that the spirit of modernism extended well beyond any single stylistic expression. There is a tacit acknowledgement in his work that modernism was and should ever be "polyglot." For the remainder of his working life, he would promote a form of modernist eclecticism, freely exploiting whatever he deemed useful and appropriate.

As Peters was cycling through the many modernist currents of the early postwar era, he did skip a few. He was not interested in Russian Constructivism or De Stijl. Perhaps they were too foreign for him—or too rational and

52. Jock Peters, project for a house for Dr. Paulsen, (Landhaus II), 1918. Woodcut on paper. Collection Jock de Swart.

53. Jock Peters, project for a house for Dr. Paulsen, (Landhaus II, variant design), 1918. Plan. Pencil and pen and ink on paper. UCSB.

54. Jock Peters, project for a house for Dr. Paulsen, (Landhaus II, variant design), 1918. Perspective. Print on paper. UCSB.

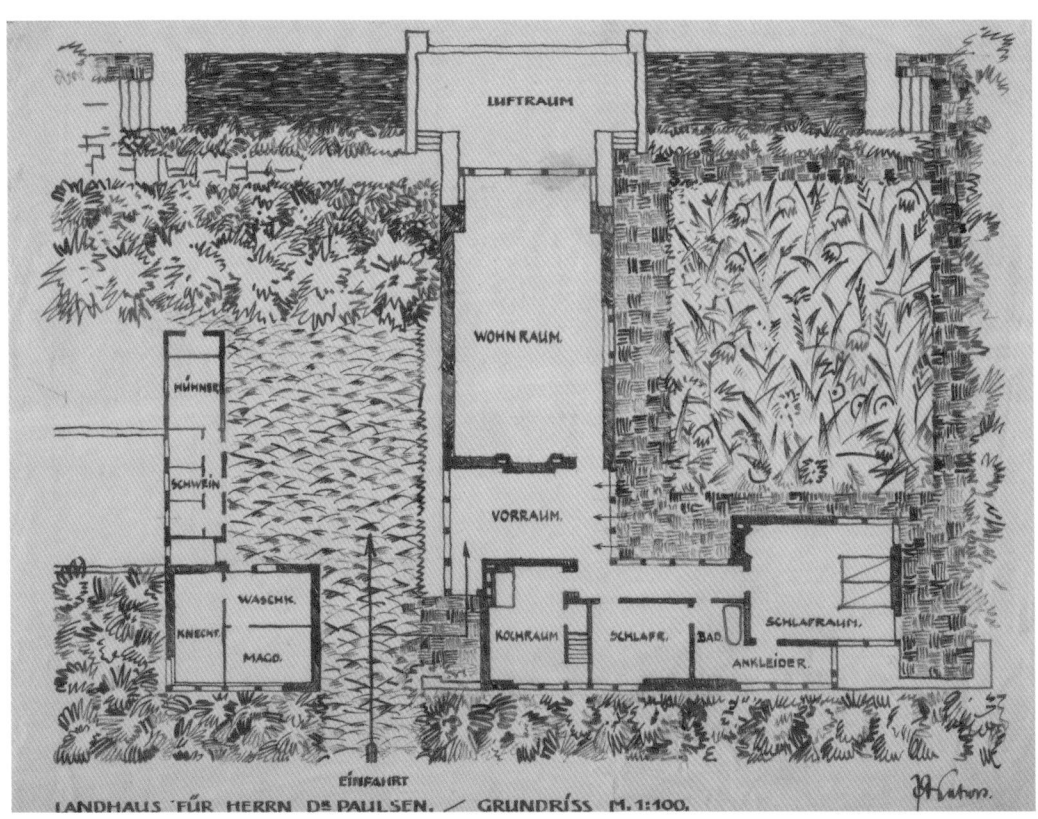

EXPERIMENTS IN STYLE 75

controlled. He did, however, find inspiration—as was true for many others at the time—in the sweeping contours of Erich Mendelsohn's dramatic new streamlined aesthetic.

Mendelsohn had first publicly announced his radical vision of curving, flowing forms in 1919, at an exhibition of his drawings at the Paul Cassirer Gallery in Berlin. Peters's exposure to the new style likely came slightly later, after Mendelsohn published some of his renderings. Whatever the case, by 1920 Peters was experimenting with Mendelsohn's visual language, albeit in an idiosyncratic way. He took what was for Mendelsohn essentially a gesture of urban and technological realism and set it into a world of imagination rooted in the countryside. In one remarkable instance, in 1921, he sketched a thatched-roof, two-story cottage, the roof softening and blurring into the walls (fig. 55). Truly extraordinary—and wonderfully peculiar—are the two versions he prepared for an even more cottagey structure for an unspecified site in Holstein, a domicile ostensibly for an industrial-age Hansel and Gretel (figs. 56, 57).

But Peters remained ever restless, always investigating some new idea or direction. In the early 1920s, he returned again to his Landhaus project—which seems to have held some steady and special power for him—and converted it to a dynamic Mendelsohnian streamlined image (fig. 58). And he was not content to stop there: he also considered an idea for a closely related formal dynamism, a country villa that was seemingly part machine, part motion study (fig. 59).

There are clues to what Peters was thinking about in his writings of this period. For nearly two years, from late 1919 to early 1921, he wrote for, and helped to edit, *Bau-Rundschau*, the local Hamburg architecture journal. The majority of his pieces were reviews of others' works or announcements of competitions or their results. A few of his writings, however, expose the ideas that informed his own designs or reveal his reactions to the buildings and trends he was witnessing at the time.

Bau-Rundschau was owned and edited by Konrad Hanf, the leading publisher of Hamburg Expressionist literature and art. Hanf was also the treasurer of the local chapter of the German Werkbund and a vocal supporter of its program. Peters, who joined the organization around this time, may have known him from the local Werkbund group or, perhaps, through Höger or Schumacher.

Peters's first piece for the journal was an impassioned assault on the neo-Biedermeier (and neoclassicism more generally), and a plea for a new architecture. "Iron and concrete," he writes, are not "ersatz building materials," meant merely to replace traditional ones; "they are materials that demand their own form, just as new transportation methods and living conditions are needed."[132] He titled the piece "Architektonischer Götzendienst," or Architectonic Idolatry.

This statement of a new emphasis on materiality and modern conditions was a repudiation, in a sense, of everything he had believed and achieved before the war. Peters explained his new understanding, writing, "Our way of living is fundamentally different from [that of] those living around 1800. We travel in express trains, automobiles, and ocean liners, and we have invented a new language for our transportation and factory complexes. . . . Our language, our literature is not borne by classical pathos; it is freer, abbreviated, and concerned with the internal substance of things."[133]

Nothing here is in any way surprising for a young German modernist of those years. The belief that the world had changed and that those changes necessitated a different, more "functional" aesthetic was shared widely among those who sought reform. A few of Peters's writings for the journal, though, touch on issues or solutions that were more personal. At a time when many German architects were already beating the drum for collective architecture and standardization, especially when it came to worker or mass housing, Peters, in a piece from March 1920 titled "Build Space, Not Cells!" argues for a more humane approach: "To design living spaces for people requires a close interaction [the word he uses here is the Latin *fluidum*] with the inhabitant himself. And where this personal relationship is impractical, as in the case of a housing estate for a large number of people, it is important that the architect be deeply focused on the inner life of those who will live there."[134] Peters goes on to describe what he sees as the transformative power of large rooms—how devising open, free-flowing spaces would enhance and improve the lives of those who lived within.

The next issue of the journal featured a profile of Peters, written by another young Hamburg architect, Hugo Koch. Koch saw in Peters's work the same emphasis on the human and the spiritual that Peters had written about: "Pure functionalism is not enough for him. As a true builder, he regards that which is merely practical as a starting point . . . he seeks to master life in its fullness in architectural garb."[135] Accompanying the article was a short text from Peters and a group of his drawings featuring the wartime Landhaus projects.

By the early summer, Peters had become the journal's managing editor and one of its principal authors. His published texts over the following year focused on the problems facing architects in the wake of the war, especially the shortages of materials and the need to develop a new form of expression. He is never dogmatic in his views. His essays

55. Jock Peters, project for a country house, 1921.
Pencil on paper. UCSB.

56. Jock Peters, project for a farmhouse in Holstein, 1920. Pen and ink and watercolor on paper. UCSB.

57. Jock Peters, project for a farmhouse in Holstein, 1920. Pencil on paper. UCSB.

58–59. Jock Peters, project for a country house, c. 1920. Pen and ink on paper. Collection Jock de Swart.

EXPERIMENTS IN STYLE 79

are often complimentary of more conservative approaches, especially when he thought the buildings or landscapes were well done.

Writing for *Bau-Rundschau* greatly raised Peters's visibility. By 1921, he had become well-known in Hamburg's architectural circles. He was also increasingly active in the local art scene, especially the newly formed Hamburg Sezession.

The Hamburg group was a latecomer to the roster of these early modernist organizations; most of them, including those in Berlin, Munich, and Vienna, had formed some two and a half decades before. The Hamburg Sezession was also neither as radical as its predecessors, nor as important as a wellspring of ideas. Most of its members subscribed to some variant of late Impressionism or a gentler version of Expressionism, without quite fully embracing either one.

Peters was active in the organization for a time, and he exhibited drawings in the Sezession's first and second group shows. (In the first one, he showed his memorial tower at the Ferdinandstor.)[136] He enjoyed the camaraderie, the sense of belonging, which he had missed during the years he spent in Belgium.

Yet, however much Peters found joy and solace in the Hamburg Sezession, his engagement with the group proved to be only a fleeting interlude. Far more important for him and his career at this time was his reconnection to his old acquaintance from his stint in Behrens's office—Karl Schneider.

After leaving Behrens in 1916, Schneider spent the remaining war years in the army, building railroads in the Balkans. After the war (and a brief spell in a Romanian prisoner-of-war camp), Schneider returned to Hamburg, where he found employment in the office of local architect Heinrich Straumer. Peters and Schneider rekindled their friendship, and Peters encouraged Höger to hire Schneider. Soon, though, the two young architects were discussing the possibility of leaving the office and setting up their own practice.

At first, the economy still appeared too fragile; but in the spring of 1921, together with another young architect named Karl Witte, they made their move. On the first of May, they opened an office at Spaldingstraße 160, not far from the main Hamburg train station.[137]

Their new partnership turned out to be more of a loose association than a standard architectural practice. Each man pursued his own projects independently. Peters and Schneider, however, did complete at least two joint works, both in 1922: a renovation and addition for the home of the artist Lore Feldberg-Eber in Hamburg-Blankenese, and a freestanding suburban dwelling, the Haus Schluck, in Volksdorf. Neither reflected Peters's ideas for a new architecture of space, light, and movement. The first was still mostly traditional; the second, an ornate brick structure complete with a steeply pitched roof, was indebted to Dutch forms and to Höger's "Hanseatic modernism."[138]

Peters, in any event, was already occupied with another undertaking. In the late winter of 1920, he received an appointment from the city of Altona to teach at the Handwerker- und Kunstgewerbeschule, the Handicrafts and Applied Arts School.[139]

Established in 1901 as a secondary school for "manual training" and graphic design, the institution was part of a larger network of such institutions throughout Prussia devoted to raising the quality of the crafts and providing future employees for small manufacturing and design firms.[140] The curriculum in those early days was broad: around 1907, the school even briefly offered a course in watchmaking. Later, the plan of studies was refocused on wood- and metalworking, textiles, and drawing, and those were still the emphases when Peters started teaching there in the fall of 1920.[141]

Most of the school's students were, and long had been, part-time. In 1904, only 61 of 239 were full-time students, since most held regular day jobs.[142] The enrollment grew to more than 300 in the years just prior to the outbreak of the war, but it fell off steeply after most of the younger males began being called up for military service. By the end of 1917, there were only women, girls, and a few invalid males left. In the immediate aftermath of the war and the ensuing economic turmoil, the school languished.

When Peters was hired, the institution was thus in crisis and close to shutting down. He quickly sought to remedy the situation, reforming the curriculum and actively recruiting students. When the post of director of the school suddenly came open in the early fall of the same year, the local Altona city authorities (who funded and oversaw the school), impressed with Peters's efforts, decided to appoint him to that role.[143] Among those who wrote enthusiastic letters in support were Behrens and Schumacher.[144]

Peters took up the challenge with his customary energy, revamping the course offerings and hiring additional faculty. Being at the school also provided him an outlet for his interests in making furniture and connecting him with craftspeople across the area. From the outset, he was intent upon remaking the school according to the principles of the German Werkbund.[145] By this time, he had come to believe fervently in the Werkbund's stated mission of allying the crafts with architecture, and his position at a crafts school gave him even more reason to support its aims (fig. 60).

60. Jock Peters's membership card from the German Werkbund, 1922–23. Collection Jock de Swart.

Peters faced daunting challenges, however. Funding for the school was meager, and its facilities were far from ideal. Before he began working there, the school had been moved to an old palace, the Donner Schloss, a rambling neo-Gothic pile built in the mid-1850s. Peters, without approval or even the faintest chance of securing financing, began to explore the idea of building a complex to replace it.

He sat down and drew several versions. In one drawing, the main body of his visionary new campus is shown with a two-story classroom and office wing, and an attached one-story structure for studios and offices (fig. 61). Dominating the complex is a massive tower, streamlined, with a cascading wall of glass. It is a seeming homage to Mendelsohn's Einstein Tower, finished two years before. On another sheet of drawings, Peters tried out several variants, some in the form of officelike blocks (fig. 62). He eventually settled on one with a low profile and pylon (shown in the rendering on the lower right).

Within the principal classroom and office wing of this scheme, he planned a large courtyard—in effect, an academic cloister. In contrast to the streamlined language of the exterior, he introduced a sturdy and vigorous "tectonic" Expressionism, fashioned with multi-angled piers and lintels (fig. 63).

He was evidently not satisfied with the look, because he considered other alternatives. A second version he prepared of the same general layout is similar in its broad outlines (fig. 64). Yet, as was so typical of Peters, he gave it a wholly different stylistic dress. This time it was a forceful and more integral version of Expressionism, less reliant on ornament than on massing and form. It was also, in contrast to many of his other derivative postwar designs, strikingly original. Why he did not develop it further is, like so much else about his work in this time, lost to us. In the end, nothing came of his proposal. He put it away; though, as it would turn out, he would not entirely forget it.

During the course of 1922, Peters worked on several other visionary projects, all made in collaboration with Danish architect Knud Lönberg-Holm.

Lönberg-Holm was younger than Peters by some six years. They met through a mutual friend, Werner Jakstein, who was the head of the Altona *Baupflegeamt*, the municipal office charged with overseeing local historic preservation efforts.[146] Jakstein was well connected in Denmark—he had many Danish friends and a Danish wife—and he hosted Lönberg-Holm in Altona during his stay there.

Lönberg-Holm was already a practiced architect and designer. He had spent time in Berlin after the war, closely watching the advance of German architecture and developing a strong predilection for modernist forms and ideas. He became deeply disaffected after returning to Copenhagen, where a conservative neoclassicism still reigned, and he went to Hamburg seeking allies and stimulus. After he arrived in Altona, he and Peters quickly hit it off. Soon, they were collaborating on several competitions, working out of Lönberg-Holm's studio.[147]

One of their joint projects was a competition design for a large building complex, a cultural center, possibly for the city of Stuttgart (fig. 65). It is very different from Peters's other works of 1922, massive and forceful, suggesting that Lönberg-Holm had probably taken the lead in its design.

For their second project, an office building in the East Prussian city of Königsberg, each architect prepared his own

61. Jock Peters, project for an art education center, 1921. Print. UCSB.

62. Jock Peters, project for an art education center, 1921. Pen and ink on paper. UCSB.

63. Jock Peters, project for an art education center, 1921. Interior courtyard. Print. UCSB.

64. Jock Peters, project for an art education center, 1921. Alternative design. Pencil on paper. UCSB.

EXPERIMENTS IN STYLE

Grundriß Erdgeschoß. M. 1:600

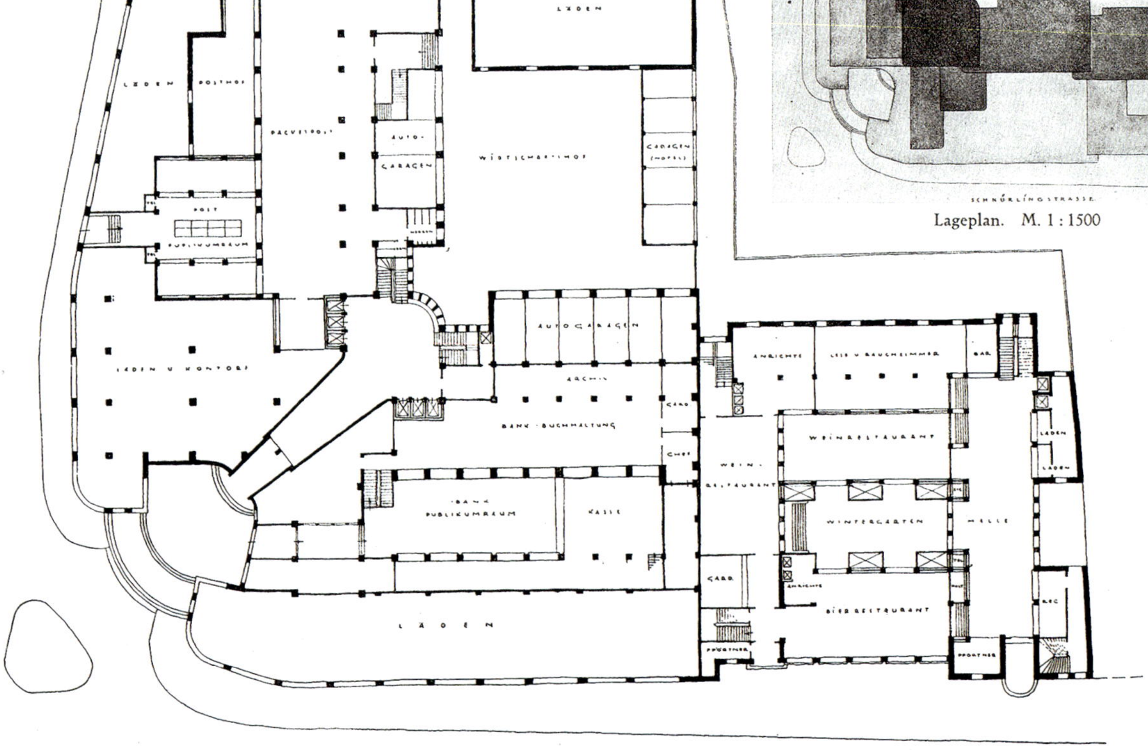

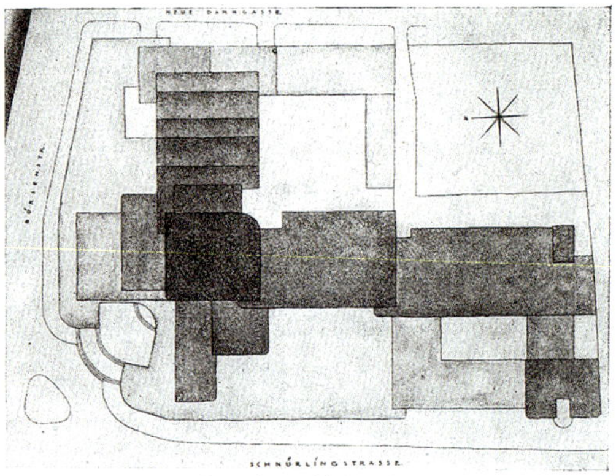

Lageplan. M. 1:1500

Wettbewerb für ein Büro- und Geschäftshaus in Königsberg i. Pr.
Kennwort: »Proportion«. Verfasser: Architekten J. D. Peters, Altona und K. Lønberg Holm

68. Knud Lönberg-Holm and Jock Peters, entry (not submitted) for the *Chicago Tribune* tower competition. Clay massing model. Private collection.

67. Jock Peters, model for the *Chicago Tribune* tower competition, c. 1921. Collection Jock de Swart.

65. Knud Lönberg-Holm and Jock Peters, competition project for a building in Stuttgart, 1922. Private collection.

66. Knud Lönberg-Holm and Jock Peters, competition project for a commercial building (Börsenhof) in Königsberg, 1922. From *Wasmuths Monatshefte für Baukunst* 7, Heft 9/10 (1922–23): 291.

EXPERIMENTS IN STYLE 85

design. Lönberg-Holm's was a squat composition, again with powerful, block-like massing; Peters's design—characteristically—was a more romantic and expressive composition, based on a free-form conception.[148] Peters thought that Lönberg-Holm's version was the better of the two and helped him work out the final design, which they submitted together (fig. 66). Although it did not win a prize, it was singled out by the jurors.[149]

The most important of their collaborations, however, was their project for the famed *Chicago Tribune* competition in 1922. According to Steven Clarke, a young student at Yale who interviewed Lönberg-Holm in 1966, the men "tried the same dual approach" they had for their Königsberg project.[150] Peters came up with an extraordinary concept: a streamlined tower with broad, cantilevered awnings (fig. 67). It was—once more—Mendelsohnian, though arranged in a manner that was insistently novel. Lönberg-Holm, for his part, proposed a more ordered and blocky tower. Peters agreed to help Lönberg-Holm with a preliminary massing model based on the latter's design, but, as Clarke writes, "the rift between their concepts was so marked that Peters felt he could not help him develop the clay model" (fig. 68). Peters withdrew, and Lönberg-Holm continued to rework and refine the design on his own. Lönberg-Holm missed the final November 1 deadline for the competition and did not submit it.[151] His drawings for the tower project were subsequently published in numerous European journals and books, and the design made Lönberg-Holm's reputation. Peters's early involvement in the project was completely ignored.[152]

By the time Peters came to work on the Tribune Tower, he was at the end of an exceedingly good stretch. He had started to see success with his reforms at the school in Altona, and he was gratified when the Prussian Ministry for Trade and Commerce notified him that he had officially been awarded the title of "Professor" in September 1922.[153] He also was experiencing his best health in years.

When Peters returned from Berlin in 1918, he had appeared gaunt and worn out. During his bout with influenza, one of his lungs had collapsed, and it became mostly useless. The damage was permanent, but he managed to put on some weight after his homecoming to Hamburg. He took frequent walks with his dachshund to build up his stamina (fig. 69). The Donner Schloss was situated in a large park, along the banks of the Elbe. Whenever he could, he took the opportunity to leave his office and stroll through the adjacent green spaces.

He and Herta had three more children, all girls: Annemarie, born in 1920; Eva, born in 1921; and Herta, born in 1922.

Toward the middle of 1922, his health began to decline again. The late winter and spring of that year had been exceptionally cold and damp, and the episode of German hyperinflation, which reached its dismal heights that fall, made it difficult to afford healthy food—or, on occasion, any food at all. In 1921, Peters had earned more than sixty-two thousand marks, a respectable, middle-class salary; a year later that same amount was worthless due to the mounting inflation.[154] He had grown careworn, worried about how to provide for his family and in doubt about how to keep the school afloat. He began losing weight, and while he was out walking he sometimes had to stop and catch his breath.

He was also becoming ever more pessimistic about Germany's future. The country was sharply divided between the political left and right and deeply burdened by the punishing terms of the Treaty of Versailles. The national mood was somber and depressed. Peters wanted a way out.

In late summer, he received a letter from his brother George in America. George was now in Pasadena, California, making his living as a draftsman and builder. He invited Peters to come for a visit—and suggested his brother might consider moving to Southern California permanently. There was more than enough work for an architect, George reported.

Peters pondered the offer, though not for long. Within days, he had decided to go. A quick trip to an astrologer, who made a set of charts of his projected future, seems to have allayed any lingering apprehensions he had.[155]

On August 25, 1922, he wrote to the Altona municipal authorities requesting a three-month leave from the school for "health reasons." He also cited his desire to "conduct a study of American trade schools and their facilities."[156] With dollars George wired to him, Peters purchased a third-class ticket for passage to New York.[157] He made a quick trip to his doctor, who, in an effort to speed his patient's way through Ellis Island, wrote a letter certifying Peters as healthy, when he most decidedly was not.

On November 15, 1922, he departed for America, leaving Herta and the children behind.

69. Jock Peters with his dachshund, 1922. Collection Jock de Swart.

16

Prof. Jakob Raloef Peters

HAMBURG–AMERIKA LINIE, HAMBURG,
JOINT SERVICE WITH
UNITED AMERICAN LINES, INC., NEW YORK.

S.S. Reliance sailing at 15. Nov. 1922 from HAMBURG

CABIN SECOND CLASS   MANIFEST SHEET H   NUMBER ON SHEET 25

NAME Prof. Peters

COMING FROM A NON-INFECTED DISTRICT.

THIS CARD TO BE PRESENTED UPON ARRIVAL TO THE IMMIGRATION AUTHORITIES.

Chapter 5 | AMERIKA

After bidding farewell to Herta, their children, and friends, Peters boarded a train bound for the port of Cuxhaven, at the mouth of the Elbe River (fig. 70). There he embarked on the S. S. *Reliance*, an American-flagged steamer. The ship made brief stopovers in Cherbourg and Southampton before sailing on to New York. Ten days later, it docked at Ellis Island. Peters set foot on American soil for the first time on November 25, 1922 (fig. 71).[158] George had arranged all the papers in advance, signing the required affidavit agreeing to be his brother's financial guarantor.[159]

After a frenetic half day of sightseeing in Manhattan, Peters caught an express train to Los Angeles, traveling via Chicago. The last leg of the long journey took him across the mountains and high deserts of the West. He wrote to Herta aboard the train as it approached Salt Lake City, describing the landscape as evening set in: "the salmon-red grass of the steppes . . . the clouds burning red and the brightest gold . . . the violet sky." The whole scene, he thought, was pro-phetic. He closed the letter: "I expect everything from California and hope I will not be disappointed."[160]

When he arrived in Los Angeles, George met him at the station. They had last seen each other before the war, in 1913, when George had sailed for the United States. George had first worked for a builder in Dysart, Iowa, before moving out to Southern California; soon, he took up work as a draftsman for Pasadena contractor Clarence P. Day.[161] Time had altered them both. Peters wrote to Herta that when he disembarked from the train he recognized George immediately, despite his brother being, in his words, "burned brown." It took some time, however, for George to find Peters in the crowd, so changed was he from his illness and the privations he had endured during and after the war.[162]

Peters moved into George's room at the Young Men's Christian Association in downtown Pasadena. Immediately, they began to formulate a plan. Peters's request for leave from the school in Altona had stated that he would return after his "three-month study trip." In his first letter to Herta, he informed her that he had no intention of ever returning to Hamburg. Before departing Germany, he had considered the idea of settling permanently in the United States; now, after seeing Southern California, Peters was certain.[163]

---

70. Jock Peters, passport photograph, c. 1922. Collection Jock de Swart.

71. Jock Peters's landing card from the S. S. *Reliance*, November 1922. Collection Jock de Swart.

But Peters miscalculated how to handle his departure from the school in Altona. He failed to resign his position before his leave ran out; because of the lag in the mail, his letter notifying the authorities of his intentions arrived in mid-February, after the three months had elapsed.[164] What followed was a string of exchanges between Peters and the Altona officials concerning the salary Peters was still owed and whether he should receive a promised retroactive pay raise. The city bureaucrats in Altona, irked by Peters's actions and believing that he had simply abandoned his duties, instituted disciplinary proceedings. The charges—which were serious, because Peters was technically a civil servant—were eventually dropped, but the raise in his back pay was denied.[165]

Peters was resolved nevertheless to make a new start. The brothers, as he wrote to Herta, had already worked out a detailed strategy of how to support the family once she and the children could join them:

> George and I want to rent a house and furnish it so that you can come as soon as possible. The house will cost about $25 to $30 per month. George now earns $45 a week. At first, I will probably earn $150–$200 a month. Since George knows the construction business well, we intend to build a little house and either keep it or sell it again. We might build one house after another with Sunday labor and then sell them. We also want to get a car as soon as possible so that we can live in a nice area and drive to work.[166]

Peters added some consoling words in an effort to allay Herta's fears, who at all times was worried that her ailing husband might literally work himself to death:

> I want to lead a quiet, insular life with you here and shall try to avoid ambition and fame. That is why I would not like to work in the city; it is even more restless than ours. George will see to it that I do not overwork because he likes to work in order to live, but not to live in order to work.[167]

Peters's expressed wish to live a less demanding life was no doubt sincere. He was convinced that he had at last found a way forward that would be less taxing and stressful than his last year in Altona. The benign climate and inviting landscape of Southern California, he was sure, made it the ideal place to put down roots.

He had fallen instantly in love with the Pasadena suburbs. The houses, he described to Herta,

> lie bedded in lawns, under palms. . . . You cannot believe what pleasure I get just from walking through the residential streets. The streets are wide and paved, then [there is] a broad stripe of lawn with palms and many flowers under them. Then comes a wide sidewalk and beyond it a cultivated lawn right up to the house. The houses are not separated by plantings or fences, and the neighbors do not indicate any boundaries between them. It seems as if everyone respects others as a matter of course.[168]

He began searching for work straightaway. In spite of his earlier declaration that he could "probably earn $150–$200 a month," he found the reality far different. Few architects in Southern California were making that kind of money, and the fact that he was an immigrant—and a German one, at that (at a time, in the wake of the recent war, when being German was a decided liability)—limited his prospects. That he knew barely any English was equally of no help. "I ran through Los Angeles with my drawings under my arm," he reported to Herta. "I saw an announcement that architects were being sought to work in a film company. George and I went there, in vain, not because of my work, they said, but because of my poor English."[169] Peters met with the same response at a number of architecture firms. After several more days of diligently pounding the pavement, his search at last yielded a job, a position with a "German architect." He was now, he wrote his wife, greatly relieved, and "glad to be among people who speak my language."[170]

The German architect was Otto H. Neher. Neher had immigrated to the United States in 1902. He had first worked in St. Louis. After a few years there, he moved out to Los Angeles, where he entered a partnership with prominent local architect Charles F. Whittlesey, who had once been a draftsman for Louis Sullivan. The two eventually went their separate ways, and Neher teamed up for a time with another local architect, Chauncey F. Skilling.[171] By the time Peters came to work for him, Neher had his own thriving practice, with an office in downtown Los Angeles. Peters told Herta that there was a Viennese-born architect in the office, who, he noted, had once "studied with Josef Hoffmann." One of the reasons Peters had been hired was that this unnamed "Viennese" had admired his "modern works."[172]

For the first time in years, Peters was genuinely excited about his prospects, as he wrote to Herta on December 6, eleven days after his arrival in "Amerika":

> The city is a good field for architecture. I expect to learn much in this office since there are only the three of us,

and we do all the work. At the moment, we are working on a big skyscraper; I am designing the façade; Neher is doing the floor plans. Both the partners and the client favorably received my work. I have no fear that I will make progress here. Maybe in a few weeks I will try the movies because one earns good money there.[173]

Peters confessed, though, that having to take another job in someone else's office was dispiriting: "In the first days of 1918 I started as a draftsman with Höger, and it is the same again here." Yet, he tried to hold on to his optimism: "If I get along as well here as I did in the five years there, things will go well for us. Let us hope so."[174] He also reassured Herta that his health was good: "You may be worried about my physical condition. Do not be, my dear, I have more to eat here than you have."[175] The last statement was doubtless true, in light of the ever-worsening crisis in Germany. Rationing had begun in earnest, and Herta was finding it ever more challenging to find food for herself and the children.

Peters wrote to Herta that on Sunday, his only day off, he and George took long hikes in the hills northwest of Pasadena scouting for a lot on which to build their family house. He complained in another letter that his pay from Neher was low—a mere fifteen dollars the first week, a fraction of what he thought he could earn—and that he was thinking about leaving to work with George as a carpenter.[176] In the end, he stayed on. He was reluctant to give up the steady income, however small. He and George continued to do all they could to earn money on the side to pay for the family's passage from Germany and to set up a household for them once they arrived.

The tone of Peters's daily letters home, despite his occasional grousing, remained mostly buoyant. A little more than a week later, he informed Herta that Neher had raised his weekly salary five dollars and promised another five-dollar raise in a few weeks.[177] On Christmas Eve, he wrote to Herta, encouraging her to keep her spirits up: "In this land and in the coming years you will be compensated for all the sorrowful times since 1914." He also sought to reassure himself:

I shall try to forget for the present that there is more culture over there. I have had many disappointments, but after a while one finds other things; little by little, one does not compare so much. Here it will be possible to live simply and contentedly, and to give form to inward things. One does not vegetate here. People who are spiritually rich do not need the whole ballast of art and ideas in order to feel human and happy.[178]

Peters was hardly the only recent arrival from Europe to find Los Angeles culturally wanting. Even so, he continued to view much of what he found around him with wonderment. He was now also writing to Ursel, the only one of the five children old enough to read and write. He sent her printed and illustrated letters—in one instance, with a drawing of a giant agave. He included a depiction of her and her mother standing next to the plant for scale so that she could begin to imagine her future home. Before departing Hamburg, he had made Ursel a visionary rendering of his journey to a shining Los Angeles perched on a mountaintop (fig. 72). He reassured his daughter that the reality was even more marvelous.

The situation in Germany continued to deteriorate. Herta's letters to her husband from this period are filled with ever more dire news about the spiraling inflation, and she shares her mounting worry that the Ruhr crisis (which had been brought on in late 1922, when French and Belgian troops occupied the Ruhr region after Germany was unable to make reparation payments) might lead to war. He replies angrily, "Evidently a right-wing putsch is to be expected; then things will really go downhill!! And when those men are at the oars, I will certainly never go back."[179]

Beyond his resolve to escape the unsteady political and economic situation in Germany, Peters had found another reason to stay in California. He was convinced that living in Pasadena was having a salutary effect on his health. In early January, he wrote to Herta that the "change of air" in Los Angeles was bothering him: "the old places [in his lungs] make themselves felt." He was sure, however, this was part of a "healing process," and he proudly informed her that he was gaining weight: "You can't see my neck bones, and no collar fits me anymore."[180]

Despite the euphoria Peters felt at times, he found it hard to adjust "to expectations" at the office. He was especially troubled by what he kept hearing from Neher and the clients —namely, that he should work faster and design architecture that would be cheaper to build:

At times, I find myself so resentful of the criticisms . . . that I just want to throw all my stuff away. But I bite my tongue and stifle my instincts. You can't believe how far behind people are here in aesthetic terms. . . . Decorating with the worst imaginable fakery is an art here. Over there, we thought about artistic things in ways that were ten times more American than any American does here.[181]

72. Jock Peters, drawing for his daughter Ursel, 1922. Pencil and watercolor on paper. Collection Jock de Swart.

Peters consoled himself with the thought that "Wright and his *Meister* [Sullivan] had persevered. I have the feeling that I, too, will triumph, and I have no thoughts of compromising. . . . I feel I have the strength to take up the fight."[182]

Peters used every spare moment looking for ways to earn extra money so that the family might make the voyage to America as soon as possible. At the start of 1923, when he was not working in the office, he was moonlighting in the evenings, designing houses. In a letter to Herta from early January, penned while he was riding the streetcar home after work, Peters announced that he was now earning good money. "There is a ready market for well-planned small houses; I am doing plans for ten houses for a building firm. They pay $70–75 per house." He also disclosed that he was still thinking about going into business with his brother: "George and I feel the firm of Peters and Peters is imminent. I hope things develop that way for I cannot endure this office work much longer, nor do I want to ride into the city each day."[183]

At that moment, less than two months after Peters had arrived in America, the idea of establishing a firm of their own was unrealistic: the brothers had neither the necessary capital nor the requisite connections. The house designs Peters was able to sell to builders would continue for some time to bring in much-needed income. The next step for them remained elusive.

Peters's broader mission of promoting modernism in America faced formidable challenges. Despite his reassuring words to Herta about living a less harried life, he knew that the struggle would be a long one. In early 1923, the groundwork for modern architecture and design in Los Angeles had barely been put down. The Arts and Crafts movement had already mostly come and gone, and those who had made the first brush with the new forms—including the Greene brothers (Charles Sumner Greene and Henry Mather Greene) in Pasadena and Irving Gill in San Diego—were fading from view. Bungalows continued to be built in the outer districts, especially to the east and south of downtown Los Angeles, but the movement was dying out. In its place was a new emphasis on historic revivalism, especially the Spanish Colonial Revival.

Only a few modernists were then working in the city. Vienna-born and -trained R. M. Schindler, who had moved west at the behest of his then employer, Frank Lloyd Wright, to oversee the construction of the theater complex for Aline Barnsdall on Olive Hill, had just finished his prescient house on Kings Road in West Hollywood. But he was still finding it difficult to secure his own commissions, mostly making do with small jobs.

Another early modernist, Lloyd Wright, Frank Lloyd Wright's son, who had come west to assist with the landscape design of the 1915 Panama-California Exposition, was then in the process of completing the Bollman House, the first of several visionary houses he would build in the Los Feliz and Hollywood districts of the city. He, too, was just starting out, experiencing the same problems as Schindler—finding willing clients.

German-born designer and architect Kem Weber had arrived in the city in 1921 and was working as the chief designer for Barker Brothers department store, the largest furniture retailer on the West Coast. But the company, while it employed the most forward-thinking management and sales strategies, was decidedly conservative when it came to aesthetic matters. Weber's efforts to persuade the firm's higher-ups to embrace modernism met with stiff resistance, and he was limited to designing with traditional forms.

Most of the other early Southern California modernists, including Richard Neutra and J. R. Davidson, were yet to arrive.

The scene was no more promising when it came to modern furniture. In those days, there were essentially no outlets for progressive furniture design in Los Angeles, and few interested customers. Even if the Peters brothers had some clear sense of a modernist program—which they did not—launching a practice of their own and promoting a progressive design agenda would have been daunting.

In spite of his ambitions, Peters stayed on with Neher, and every evening after returning to the brothers' room at the YMCA, he worked on house plans for various builders. Peters did take two firm steps forward in this period, both crucial to his future success. For one, he began to learn English; by the middle of 1923, he was fairly proficient in his new language. Just as important, he adopted a new first name: Jock. He had used it sometimes with Herta and friends back in Hamburg, though never professionally; English nicknames had been popular in arty circles in Germany before the war. When he first arrived in Los Angeles, his given name proved to be a liability: it sounded too German at a time when anti-German sentiment was still widespread. He could hardly disguise his accent, which remained instantly noticeable, but the more English-sounding variant of his name, "Jock," had a sturdy ring to it, and it came across as quintessentially American. Within weeks of his arrival, he had become, unalterably, Jock Peters.

Through the end of January 1923, Peters worked at a frenzied pace, doing all he could to earn money. He churned out house plan after house plan, mostly without

investing any real interest in the projects. By early February, he had set aside enough to purchase steamer tickets for the whole family. He and Herta began making the final arrangements for the voyage, now scheduled for late March. At the last minute, she proposed bringing along the family maid. Peters explained to her that that would be impossible; it was simply more money than he could come up with.[184] A few days later, she and the five children, along with one of his younger male cousins, sailed from Bremen aboard the S. S. President Fillmore.[185]

The family arrived in Los Angeles in early April to a joyous reunion. In preparation, Peters and George had rented a small, two-bedroom, Craftsman-style bungalow in Eagle Rock, just west of Pasadena.[186] They initially slept on mattresses on the floor. Herta had sold all of the family's furniture before departing Germany, including the pieces Peters had designed just after the war. Gradually, Peters and George built most of what they needed, including various chairs, tables, and bedframes.[187]

Though rudimentary, the pieces offer a foretaste of his coming aesthetic. A family photograph of the house's living room shows two of the objects the brothers designed and constructed: a combined bookcase and end table, and a larger étagère (fig. 73). (The third piece visible to the left in the image is a simple wooden packing crate with a cloth covering it). The form and execution of both pieces are modest, elevated only slightly from a "do-it-yourself" aesthetic. Conspicuous, though, are soft traces of Asian influences—Japanese in the base of the étagère (perhaps transmitted through the Arts and Crafts designs of the Greene brothers and others, which Peters would have seen in Pasadena), and Chinese in the end table (examples of which he may well have observed in local decorating and antique shops).

By the second half of 1923, Peters was already beginning to develop a more nuanced and personal response to what he was seeing around him. At some point after the arrival of Herta and the children—probably early that summer—Peters began freelancing for other architects.[188] And, when time permitted, he also continued to make and sell his house designs—in most cases, it seems, directly to builders. Almost all of these have been lost. They were likely in no sense different from the standard small houses being constructed across the region at the time—either some version of the nearly ubiquitous California bungalow or adaptations of historical revival styles.

A few of his house projects, the more experimental ones, from this period do survive, likely because he was unable to sell them. One is a Mission-style bungalow (fig. 74). It bears the inscription "Peters and Peters," suggesting that he and George might have tried to sell it in a "design-build" arrangement.

74. Jock Peters, project for a Mission Revival–style house, c. 1923. Perspective. Pencil and watercolor on paper. UCSB.

73. Jock Peters (designer), George and Jock Peters (makers), small bookcase with end table and étagère for the Peters House in Eagle Rock, c. 1923. UCSB.

75. Jock Peters, project for a Mission Revival–style house, c. 1923. Alternative version, elevation.
Pencil on paper. Collection Jock de Swart.

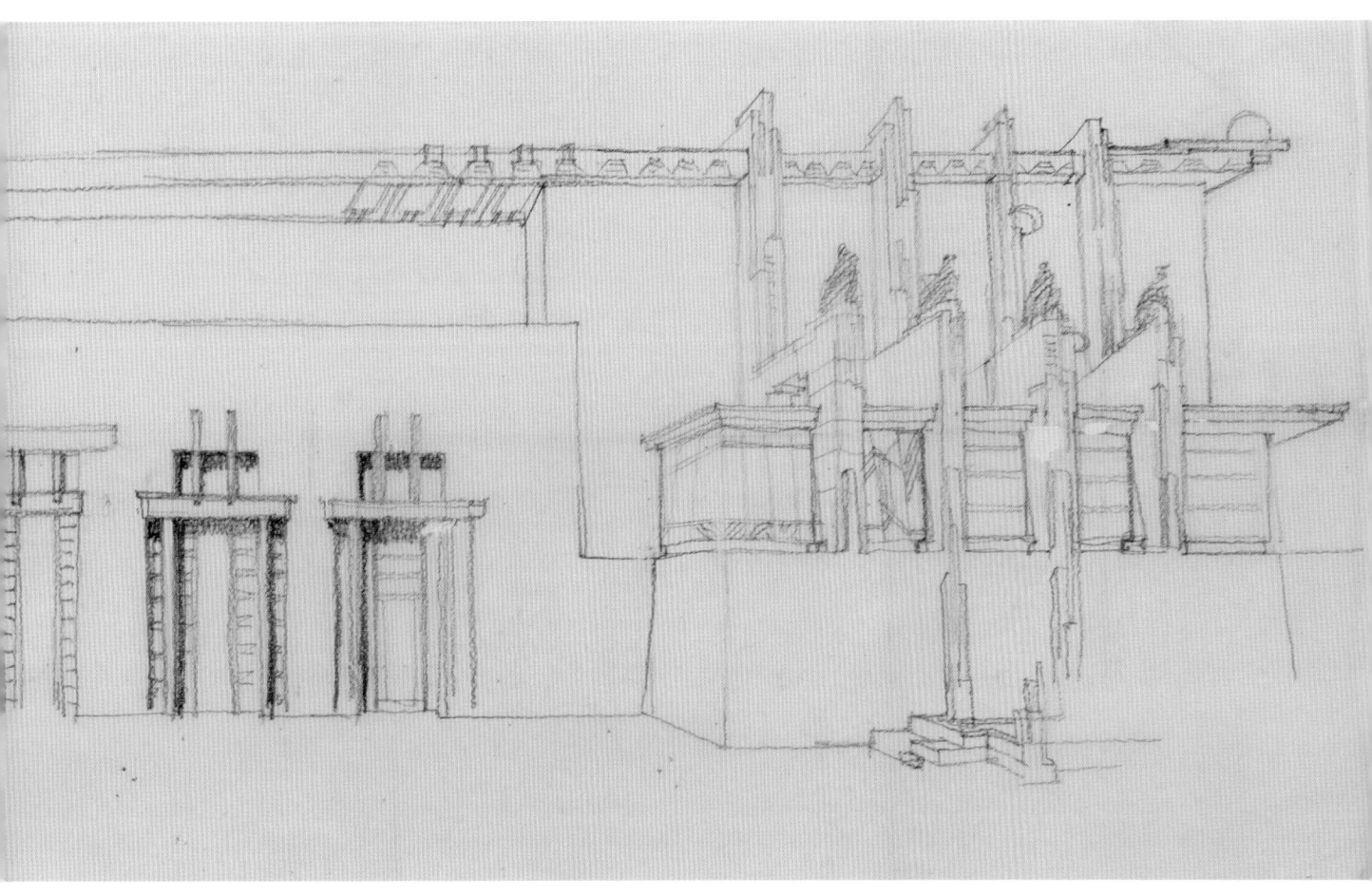
76. Jock Peters, project for a house in the style of Frank Lloyd Wright and Lloyd Wright, c. 1923. Elevation. Pencil on paper. UCSB.

Several of its features stand out. The sheet, for one, is finely rendered—far more so than any of Peters's other surviving projects from this time—perhaps because he believed that the quality of the drawing would enhance the design's marketability. The rendering also displays a technique that was new for him: the house is shown in perspective, with partly flattened vegetation and subtle watercolor highlighting, in the mode of Japanese woodcuts and Frank Lloyd Wright's drawings.

The design of the house itself was unusual for Peters (though common for Los Angeles at the time). Its large set-in porch, extended pergolas, and clean lines amounted to a historicist mélange, with a few modernist gestures. The squared lantern, set on a corner pergola near the door, is unadulterated Greene and Greene. Some of the detailing, such as the stair-stepped transom over the main door, points toward another current influence in Southern California design, an exoticism drawn from New World precedents in the form of the contemporary Mayan and Aztec revivals.

Peters also prepared a variant design of the house that was at once more conventional and more modern (fig. 75).[189] Its overall look is consistent with the Mission Revival. Yet the detailing is greatly pared down: the composition relies instead on elemental, blocky massing. Its one distinctive feature, the tall, four-columned pergola that frames the front façade, seems to have come directly from Peters's imagination. The general form of the house suggests, though, that he may well have been looking at another Southern California precedent: the work of Irving Gill. It is conceivable that Peters had seen Gill's Dodge House in Los Angeles or published photos of some of the many buildings Gill had built in San Diego.

Another of Peters's surviving house projects, a low, elongated villa, with highly wrought ornamental features, looks decidedly Wrightian—though in this case he was borrowing, it seems, from both the father and son (fig. 76).

Lloyd Wright was by that time putting the finishing touches on the Taggart House in Los Feliz; Peters's design, with its boldly contrasting horizontal and vertical forms, appears to draw from it. Peters likely had also visited the elder Wright's Hollyhock House on Hollywood Boulevard (where local lectures on art and various exhibitions were frequently held). This design was perhaps intended as a fusion of the two.

It is also something else. At first glance, Peters's own aesthetic is nearly imperceptible. On fuller inspection, it becomes evident that the resulting conception is surprisingly original. Everything is recognizably "borrowed," yet remade. The design is *of* the Wrights, but it is not exactly theirs. This is especially apparent in Peters's extended and thinned roof pergola and his dramatic, fully three-dimensional ornamental supports and pylons.

Notable, too, is the extent to which his design is not solely architectonic. It looks almost scenographic. There is a strangely flat quality to it all, like a painted set for a play about modern life.

Another of Peters's unrealized works from this period is documented in an early sketchbook. The tiny pencil rendering again shows a design that is as much image as building: several stacked cylinders set upon a rise (fig. 77).

The curious structure was a project for the festival hall at the Loheland Settlement, an experimental school for girls near Fulda, in central Germany. Established in 1919, Loheland grew to have dozens of buildings spread over an expansive wooded site. The two visionary women behind the school, Louise Langgaard and Hedwig von Rohden, had commissioned Peters in 1922 to provide designs for two buildings, a dormitory for ten girls and a larger community center; the latter was intended to house a dining hall, a theater, and more living spaces.[190] Peters had worked on both designs in the early fall of 1922, not long before he left for the United States. Neither building was realized, but in February 1924, in response to a request from Langgaard and Rohden, he sent two additional designs, both variations for a festival hall on the same site as the unbuilt community center. His two schemes for the larger building played on the notion of a round structure positioned upon a hill, their sweeping forms an expression, in part, of progressive ideas going back to Rudolf Steiner's first Goetheanum projects. What Peters showed in his small sketchbook drawing was, however, in key respects an original statement. The design is integrated and consistent in a way that is impressive for the time. Even without being fully developed, it is a remarkable experiment in modern form-making.

Peters hoped that at least some of these independent projects might pay off, and he could finally leave Neher's employ and open his own office. Without clients or capital, however, this was simply out of the question. Peters instead did what he had been considering almost from the moment he had first set foot in California: he went to work as a set designer in the Hollywood film industry.

77. Jock Peters, project for a festival hall for the Loheland Settlement, near Fulda, Germany, n.d. [1924]. Perspective. Pencil on paper. Collection Jock de Swart.

Chapter 6 |
FAMOUS PLAYERS-LASKY

The details of how and when Jock Peters came to work in the Hollywood movie industry are now lost to us. His earliest set designs are dated 1923, suggesting that he may well have started making them while he was still employed in Neher's office. Peters would go on to be involved in the production of film set designs for the next four years, until the spring of 1927. Sadly, little of what he created survives. The great majority of the drawings that he produced for sets remained with the motion picture companies and are now gone, discarded after they ceased to be any use; and many of the movies themselves are lost, casualties of neglect and unstable cellulose nitrate film. Of the roughly three dozen drawings that survive in Peters's papers, many are missing labels, and most are undated, making it difficult to identify the films for which they were made or to establish a reliable chronology. But Peters's stints in the film industry at this time and later (during his second stint in the business in the 1930s) would form a central chapter in his life's work. The set designs he devised spoke in powerful ways about modernism, its visual force, and its possibilities for shaping contemporary and future life.

From a letter Peters wrote in May 1923, we know that he initially freelanced for one or more of the movie studios.[191] Two pen-and-watercolor drawings, both dated 1923, likely represent set designs he made while still working for Neher (figs. 78, 79). One is a view of a soaring, majestic interior; the other is an entry gate. According to their legends, they depict a palace. No film title is indicated, but they appear to have been made for a science fiction movie.

Their stylistic language is an amalgam of Peters's postwar experiments, bringing together an ardent Expressionism and Mendelsohnian streamlining. They are skillfully handled, yet nothing about them reflects American reality as it was portrayed in Hollywood films at the time; they could have readily appeared in any German silent film of the era. They reveal that Peters—unsurprisingly—was still immersed in the artistic world of postwar Germany.

Peters's lingering attachment to German trends of the day is evident in another of his early set designs. It depicts a prison scene, with a solitary figure chained to a wall (fig. 80). Here, he makes direct reference to Gothic imagery, so abundant in the early German silent films. Two other drawings he made the following year also display his continued affinity for German Expressionism. One portrays a large room, with a gesturing figure seated in the center; a tall, open French

78. Jock Peters, set for an unknown film, 1923. "Palace entrance," perspective. Pen and ink and watercolor on paper. UCSB.

door to one side admits light and a sharp wind (fig. 81). Here, Peters employs a chiaroscuro effect, which accentuates the room's detailing of chevrons, triangles, and other angular forms. A corresponding drawing of a futuristic chamber with Christian symbols is titled "Last Judgement [sic]"—likely a description of the scene rather than the name of the movie (fig. 82).

The fact that Peters retained these drawings suggests that they were never used. Which company or companies might have engaged him to produce his first set designs is unknown. But by the late summer or early fall of 1924, when he made the latter two drawings, he was employed by one of the leading Hollywood studios, Famous Players-Lasky.

The Famous Players-Lasky Corporation was formed in 1916 from the merger of Hungarian-born Adolph Zukor's Famous Players Film Company and pioneer producer Jesse L. Lasky's Feature Play Company. Established as a joint motion picture production and distribution company, it screened its films through Zukor's Publix Theaters chain. One of the original "big six" studios, it would become Paramount Pictures in 1927.

Soon after its founding, Famous Players-Lasky became a leader in the emerging star system. Zukor signed some of the biggest names in Hollywood: Mary Pickford, Douglas Fairbanks, Rudolph Valentino, and Gloria Swanson.[192] Of greater consequence for Peters, though, was that the head of the studio's art division was another German-born designer, Hans Dreier.

Dreier is now credited with shaping the distinctive look of the Famous Players-Lasky and later Paramount films. His sets were luxurious and glamorous but also determinedly modern—"modern," it should be said, in the German sense. The early films the company made under Dreier's leadership were sated with a German Expressionist moodiness; at the end of the 1920s, under the Paramount name, that changed into a sumptuous, though still dark, Art Deco. Later, in the mid-1930s, Dreier would embrace the forceful lines of Bauhaus functionalism. But always there was the Dreier stamp, a persistent elegance and richness.

Like Peters, Dreier came from north Germany. Born in Bremen in 1885, he studied architecture in Munich with Theodor Fischer.[193] In 1919, he joined UFA, the Universum Film-Aktien Gesellschaft, the preeminent Berlin motion picture studio of the era, as an assistant art director. He was at UFA for almost four years, during the heyday of German film. Dreier left for Hollywood in 1923, recruited by director Ernst Lubitsch, who had himself a short time before been lured from Berlin to work for Famous Players-Lasky.[194]

From the start, Dreier established a creative and supportive atmosphere in the art department at Famous Players. In contrast to Irish-born Cedric Gibbons, the legendary art director at Metro-Goldwyn-Mayer, who was feared—and just as often loathed—for his imperious and controlling manner, Dreier gave his production designers the freedom to express their own artistic visions. He personally took charge of the films directed by Lubitsch and Josef von Sternberg, but he recruited talented designers for the studio's many other productions and left them alone to do their work.[195]

It was Dreier who hired Peters. He started as a freelancer, working directly with Dreier. In an October 1924 letter to her mother in Germany, Herta notes in passing, "Jock is blissfully working on a picture for [Ernst] Lubitsch for eight weeks, for which he will receive a lot of money."[196] Likely in early 1925, Dreier hired Peters full-time.

Peters's German-inspired modern aesthetic fit perfectly with what Dreier was trying to establish at the studio. The two men worked together closely; at times, they collaborated on projects, including the aforementioned Lubitsch film. And it was Dreier who assigned Peters to what at the time must have been regarded as one of the art department's choice jobs: designing the sets for a new science fiction feature film, *The City of the Future*.

Famous Players-Lasky staked a great deal on the project, hoping it would be a blockbuster. Peters worked on the designs through the end of 1924 and the early months of 1925. The project was to be his first true masterwork.

Nothing is known of the script or who might have been considered to direct or star in the film. Almost all the records concerning the production have been lost. Peters's involvement is documented solely in a notebook and the few renderings he retained.

Of the three bigger drawings, two are perspective views of a cityscape set in a not too distant future. Both are labeled in pencil "City of the Future," with the name of a specific scene. One, a "general view," shows a great megalopolis, with immense, bulky skyscrapers and superhighways (fig. 83). The other is of a massive arched bridge and elevator tower—a detail of the same grouping, depicted under construction (fig. 84). A third drawing, much smaller, shows Peters working out the specific shapes of individual structures (fig. 85). The buildings echo the American skyscrapers of the early postwar period, but they are more massive and monumental.[197]

A surviving notebook Peters filled with notes and sketches for the project reveals that he expended a considerable amount of thought and effort in crafting the look of his futuristic city. In one jotting in the notebook, he writes

79. Jock Peters, set for an unknown film, 1923. "Palace entrance," perspective. Pen and ink and watercolor on paper. UCSB.

80. Jock Peters, set for an unknown film, 1923. "Prison scene," elevation. Pen and ink and watercolor on paper. UCSB.

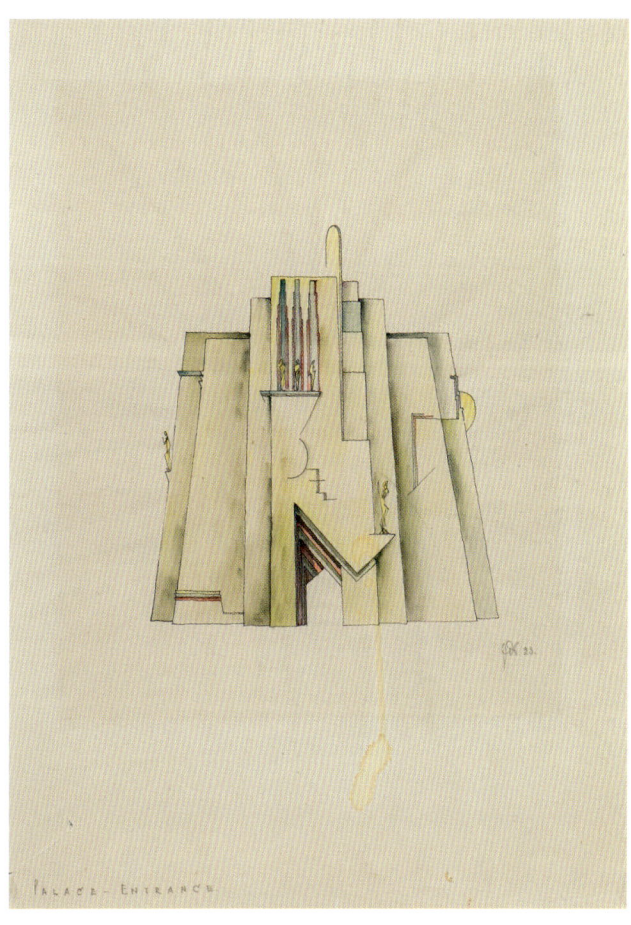

81. Jock Peters, set for an unknown film, 1924. Interior perspective. Pencil on board. UCSB.

82. Jock Peters, set for an unknown film, c. 1924. "Last Judgement" (handwritten and misspelt on back), perspective. Pencil and colored pencil on board. UCSB.

83. Jock Peters, set for *The City of the Future*.
Famous Players-Lasky (not produced), 1924.
Colored chalk on paper. UCSB.

84. Jock Peters, set for *The City of the Future*.
Famous Players-Lasky (not produced), 1924.
"Elevator station." Colored chalk on paper. UCSB.

85. Jock Peters, various skyscraper designs for *The City of the Future*.
Famous Players-Lasky (not produced), 1924.
Perspectives, elevation, and plan. Pencil on paper. UCSB.

that his inspiration for the terraced skyscrapers was the Hanging Gardens of Babylon, a decidedly nonmodern source.[198] Yet throughout, Peters depicts the buildings in a way that would suggest that they were truly functional—as if he were building an actual city. He ruminates in the notebook about how the traffic might best flow, how the apartments might receive the maximum light and sun, and what materials might be used to construct his city. On this last matter, he writes, "In point of fact, only ferro-concrete and glass come into question. . . . The concrete should be cloaked in glass."[199]

For every scene, every vignette, Peters investigated the ways in which specific features might be applied. In one sketch from his notebook, he shows how the different levels of his constructed urban landscape would be used: living areas on the upper level of the skyscrapers, and, below, descending in order, offices and shops, roadways, spaces for loading and unloading, and utilities (fig. 86). In other sketches, Peters considered how the transportation network might be arranged and how the roads could connect to the structures (figs. 87, 88). On other pages of his notebook, he pondered the form of a department store of the future; on another, he fashioned a tall, streamlined tower; and on yet another, he considered a bridge structure that could carry cars on multiple levels (figs. 89–91).

Peters's fantastical designs paralleled related proposals of the 1910s and 1920s for a futuristic cityscape, including Harvey Wiley Corbett's "City of the Future" of 1910 and Moses King's almost contemporary depiction of a yet-to-come New York.[200] The strongest similarities are to the "City of 1950," published in *Popular Science Monthly* in August 1925—almost a year after Peters started working on *The City of the Future* project (fig. 92).[201]

What sets Peters's urbanistic vision apart from these other schemes is its greater openness: his city idea dispenses with the standard grid and has much broader avenues. Peters's buildings also show a consistency of stylistic language; Corbett's and King's views depend on existing skyscraper designs, in disparate styles and from earlier periods. There is also an unavoidable sense of restlessness and unease embedded in their scenes, while Peters's version is neither dystopian nor an interim solution. It is an earnest and thoughtful attempt to devise a new city form that would be practicable and appealing—more akin to the futuristic urban visions of Antonio Sant'Elia or Richard Neutra.

The sets for *The City of the Future* were to be the crowning achievement of Peters's first years in California—or so he hoped. But the project was abandoned while it was still in development. The higher-ups at the studio had caught wind of the coming release of Fritz Lang's film *Metropolis* (begun by UFA in Berlin at the same time but only released, after a number of delays due to its complex filming, in 1927).

The suspension of what for Peters had very clearly been a labor of love came as a blow. He was bitterly disappointed.[202] He remained busy, but never again would he invest quite the same energy or passion in any of the films he was assigned. Mostly, he worked quickly, solving whatever problems came up, with few second thoughts. How many projects Dreier turned over to him during the course of the next few years is difficult even to guess. The number must have been relatively large. Although the studio released a mere seven films in 1924, it completed more than fifty in 1925, and another forty followed in 1926. Peters must have been involved with the planning for a considerable number of them, though which specific films he designed is now impossible to say. In those days, assistant art directors always went uncredited.

Only one completed film from this period can be attributed to him with certainty, and it was not for Famous Players-Lasky but for the Fox Film Company.

The film was *What Price Glory*, a 1926 war drama and comedy directed by Raoul Walsh and starring Victor McLaglen, Edmund Lowe, and Dolores del Río. Set mostly on the battlefields of France during World War I, it is the story of a flirtatious daughter of a local innkeeper, played by del Río, who becomes the target of the two men's ardor—both sergeants serving in the American army.[203]

How Peters came to work on a Fox Film production is unknown. It is possible Famous Players-Lasky lent out his services, not an uncommon practice at the time. All that is certain is that Peters delivered a set of vignettes that were used in the filming.

What stands out in his *What Price Glory* boards is their dreamlike effect. In one drawing, Peters depicts a war-torn French village (fig. 93). In another, a battle scene, soldiers take shelter in a partially collapsed building in the same village (fig. 94). The drawings exhibit a strange vividness—almost a form of hyperrealism. This quality of a magnified realism, new for Peters, is also evident in one of his surviving preliminary sketches, a dramatic interior view rendered in pencil in a muted chiaroscuro (fig. 95). In spite of their inherent battlefield "grittiness," all of the drawings he made evoke a sense of retreat into make-believe and artistic imagination.

The drawings for *What Price Glory* also bear for the first time Peters's personal signet. In the early 1920s, he usually

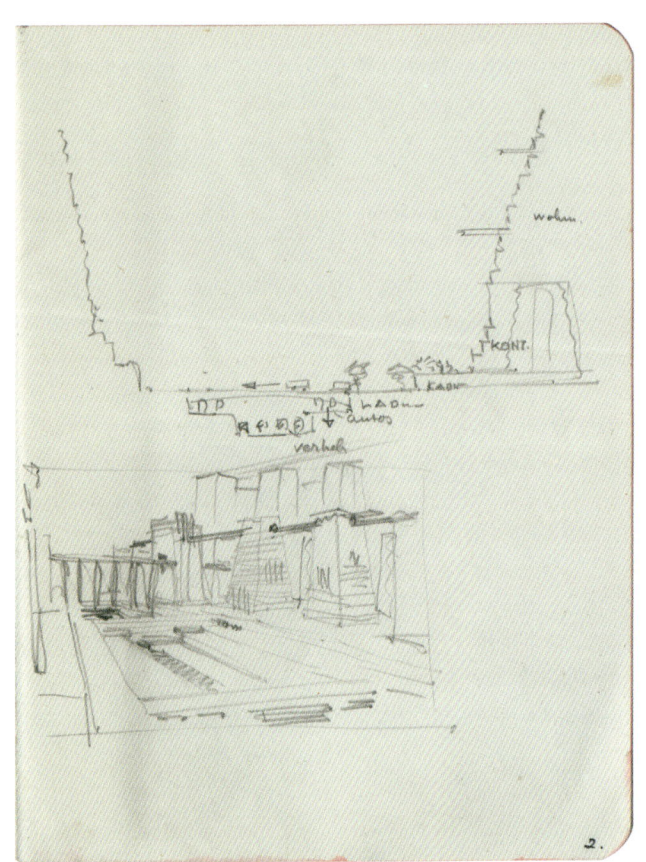

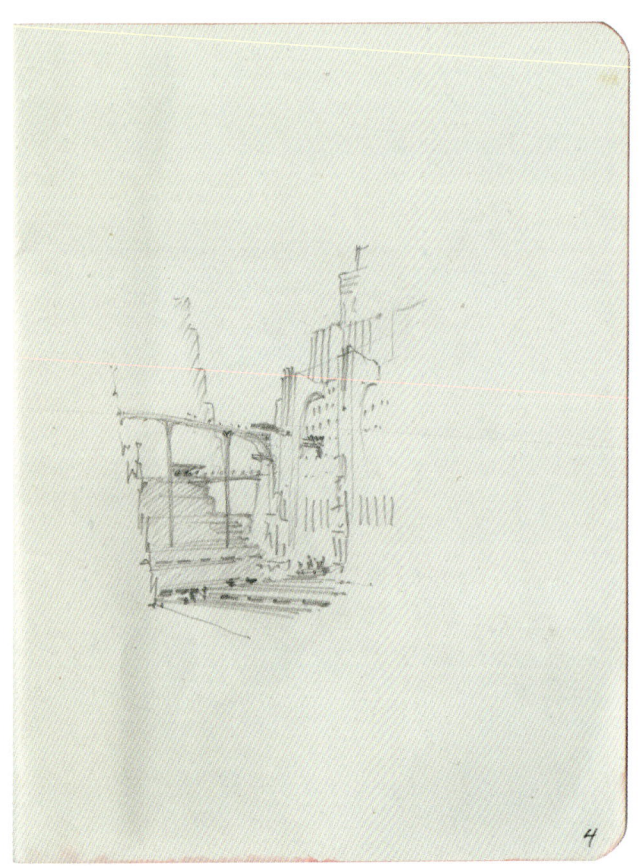

90. Jock Peters, notebook sketch for *The City of the Future*. Famous Players-Lasky (not produced), 1924. Streamlined tower. Pencil on paper. UCSB.

91. Jock Peters, notebook sketch for *The City of the Future*. Famous Players-Lasky (not produced), 1924. Bridge and tower. Pencil on paper. UCSB.

92. "City of 1950." From *Popular Science Monthly*, August 1925.

86. Jock Peters, notebook sketches for *The City of the Future*. Famous Players-Lasky (not produced), 1924. Section and perspective of a typical building and surroundings. Pencil on paper. UCSB.

87–88. Jock Peters, notebook sketches for *The City of the Future*. Famous Players-Lasky (not produced), 1924. Overview with buildings and transportation forms. Pencil on paper. UCSB.

89. Jock Peters, notebook sketch for *The City of the Future*. Famous Players-Lasky (not produced), 1924. Department store. Pencil on paper. UCSB.

93. Jock Peters, set for *What Price Glory*. Fox Film Company (director: Raoul Walsh; released 23 November 1926). Village scene. Pencil, pen and ink, and watercolor on paper. UCSB.

94. Jock Peters, set for *What Price Glory*. Fox Film Company (director: Raoul Walsh; released 23 November 1926). Combat scene. Pencil, pen and ink, and watercolor on paper. UCSB.

95. Jock Peters, set for *What Price Glory*. Fox Film Company (director: Raoul Walsh; released 23 November 1926). Interior scene. Pencil on paper. UCSB.

signed his drawings "JD Peters," or simply with his initials, "JDP." Later, Peters experimented with different combinations of the three letters (fig. 96). By 1925, he had come up with an intricate logo, fusing his initials with an ancient Egyptian ankh, the symbol of life. He had a small brass figurine cast in the guise of an Egyptian pharaoh, with the signet formed into its base. Occasionally, he used it as a stamp. Eventually, he had a standard rubber version made, with which he sometimes "signed" his drawings (fig. 97). The mark of eternal life became his trademark.

In 1926, and possibly continuing into early 1927, Peters worked on a project titled *Mars* for Famous Players-Lasky. Little is known about the film, since it seems not to have gone beyond the initial planning stages. The title suggests that it may have been based on the 1912 serialized story *A Princess of Mars*, written by Edgar Rice Burroughs.[204]

The sense of a flight from reality, so palpably portrayed in many of Peters's drawings is also manifest in the designs he made for *Mars*. One of the most dramatic of these drawings is of the elevator station on Mars (fig. 98). It is presented in a relentless perspective: everything seems alive, everything is moving. Even the indications of what lies beyond—the edges and spaces—are disclosed in pale tracings. We are able thus to see inside the building and, simultaneously, to view it from without. Peters's form-language here is exceptional: a few elements of Mendelsohnian streamlining endure, but they are subsumed within an intricate and original play of geometries, both linear and curvilinear. (It is worth noting that the tiny female figure at the rear is wearing a suit that brings to mind the theatrical costumes for Oskar Schlemmer's productions at the Bauhaus.)

Peters's presentation board for the power station on Mars is equally striking (fig. 99). It is even more restive than the elevator station, with lines and shapes jutting forth and interpenetrating with full force. It is, literally, an electrifying prospect—vigorous, radiant, alive. There are angles and wires extending in every direction, overwhelming the tiny figure at its center, who forms a counterpart to the workers who man the great engine in *Metropolis* (which had still not been released at that time), part human, part slave to the machine.

Also for the *Mars* project, Peters made a rendering of the story's Martian princess seated in an immense hall (fig. 100). It is a grand Art Deco hallucination—glowing, mystical, fantastical. Some of its architectonic forms are prophetic, soon to arrive as elements of actual buildings in Southern California. The pylon at the center right, for example, would find its counterparts on the front of Wurdeman & Becket's Pan–Pacific Auditorium in Los Angeles, finished in 1935.

Other elements in the drawings are prescient in a different way. Another board he prepared depicts a mechanical robot, complete with an antenna, fixed metal hair, and a nonthreatening grin—a precursor to the many anthropomorphized robots of today's Hollywood (fig. 101).

One more of Peters's surviving drawings, dated 1927, shows what appears to be a courtroom, with strangely disembodied heads attached to the walls (fig. 102). It is at once fantastical and recognizable, a scene that is again predictive of what was to come in the movies. Peters's handwritten legend indicates that it is for a "stage setting." Whether it was intended for *Mars*, another film, or a theatrical play is unknown. He may simply have added the caption later, since he often repurposed his drawings.[205]

Peters's drawings for the *Mars* project are startlingly original and visually spectacular, replete with what seems to have been a compelling need on his part to foster a mood of movement and energy.

That same energy propelled Peters's departure from Famous Players-Lasky. He enjoyed his collaborations with Dreier, and the two men parted on good terms. But Peters had grown steadily more tired of having to fulfill the dictates of a large and often dysfunctional company, of having to please capricious studio bosses and directors. The California newspaper reporter who wrote about his early life laconically summed up Peters's feelings: "The work was hard and his abilities leashed. He waited for an opportunity to free himself from the bondage of his employers."[206]

The sentiment, if not the exact words, were certainly Peters's. In the early spring of 1927, he resigned.

96. Jock Peters, sketch for his logo, c. 1926. Pencil on paper. Collection Jock de Swart.

97. Jock Peters, "Ankh" logo, c. 1927. Detail. Rubber stamp and ink, and pencil on paper. Collection Jock de Swart.

98. Jock Peters, set for *Mars*. Famous Players-Lasky (not produced), c. 1926. Elevator station. Pencil, pen and ink, and watercolor on paper. UCSB.

99. Jock Peters, set for *Mars*. Famous Players-Lasky (not produced), 1926. Radio station. Pencil, pen and ink, and watercolor on paper. UCSB.

100. Jock Peters, set for *Mars*. Famous Players-Lasky (not produced), 1926. Palace scene. Pencil, pen and ink, and watercolor on paper. UCSB.

102. Jock Peters, unidentified motion picture set (possibly for *Mars*, 1927). "Stage setting." Pencil, pen and ink, and watercolor on paper. UCSB.

101. Jock Peters, mechanical robot for *Mars*.
Famous Players-Lasky (not produced), c. 1926.
Pencil, pen and ink, and watercolor on paper. UCSB.

Chapter 7 |
PETERS BROTHERS

Jock Peters had been quietly planning his exit from Famous Players-Lasky for some months—even before he commenced work on the *Mars* project. He had grown happily accustomed to drawing a regular paycheck, and he was concerned about the possible financial insecurity that leaving the studio would bring.[207] But he was now more determined than ever to chart his own course. The prospects looked bright. The nation, and Southern California even more so, were in the midst of an unmatched economic boom. For some months, Peters had been designing a few furniture pieces and other works on the side; he was sure that he could do better on his own.[208] What tipped the balance was the news he received in the spring of 1927 that he had won one of the two top prizes in a competition sponsored by the S. Karpen & Brothers Company of Chicago to fashion "new designs for furniture suitable for the modern home."[209]

S. Karpen & Brothers was one of the nation's largest manufacturers of furniture. It was also one of the first American furniture companies committed to producing modern designs. The firm worked with the Art Alliance of America, a coalition of applied artists and a force in the cause of modern art and design, to sponsor the competition. The judges were some of the country's leading design authorities: William Henry Fox, director of the Brooklyn Museum; Helen Koues, editor of *Good Housekeeping*; prominent New York architect Harvey Wiley Corbett; and Charles R. Richards, a noted authority on industrial design who had organized a US traveling exhibition of French design after the 1925 Paris Exposition des Arts Décoratifs et Industriels Modernes.[210] Many of the top American designers took part in the competition, including Paul T. Frankl and Kem Weber, who garnered the eighth and eleventh prizes, respectively.[211] Peters, who was still unknown outside the tight orbit of Hollywood art directors, took his chances and submitted pencil drawings of a small suite of furnishings and lamps.

One of the pieces, a low-slung bookcase, resembled the one he and George had built early on for his family's house in Eagle Rock.[212] It was a simple and unprepossessing design, modern but not *too* modern, an approachable form of the new aesthetic. What attracted the judges and the higher-ups at Karpen, however, was the relaxed quality of Peters's designs. Walter Rendell Storey, the design critic for the *New York Times*, put it best when he singled out their

103. Jock Peters, business card for
Peters Brothers Modern American Furniture, 1927.
Collection Jock de Swart.

"offer of comfort." Peters, Storey wrote, "strikes a responsive chord in the hearts of many a householder who has discovered that period furniture does not always suit the lounging habits of twentieth-century Americans."[213] Storey also highlighted one other feature of the designs—their up-to-date practicality: "On the top shelf in a small cupboard is a place for a radio set."[214]

Peters, emboldened by his success in the high-profile national competition (and the hefty $1,250 first prize, nearly $20,000 today), decided that the time at last was right for him to leave the studio. He and George formally established their firm, Peters Brothers Modern American Furniture, in the spring of 1927, listing Jock's home address as their office (figs. 103–105). In the basement of his nearby house on Buena Vista Terrace, George began fabricating prototypes for each model Peters had designed.[215] To generate marketing materials, the brothers staged the designs in various ensembles in Jock's house and had them professionally photographed.

One grouping featured a leather chair, an open-shelved bookcase, and a lamp (fig. 106). A second group had a related chair design, a different shelving unit with doors, and a lamp-and-table combo (fig. 107). Their look was singular, unlike anything then being made in Southern California—or anywhere else, for that matter.

The standout was the low lounge chair. It had a wood frame, elaborated arms and back, and a hanging leather seat (fig. 108). It was a herald of what was soon to come in Southern California: furnishings that were light and thus readily moveable. Peters's design was the perfect expression of the new West Coast lifestyle of leisure and informality. The chair design was also a reaction against an earlier belief (going back to the heyday of Art Nouveau) that modernist furnishings should be a statement of aesthetic ambitions divorced from practical considerations. Peters's design concept—as Storey had observed—was an essay on how to live in a relaxed and easy way after the day's toils.

The bookcase in the first ensemble offered a statement in a different way: it expressed Peters's belief that the new design could be lively and fun—without abandoning traditional forms entirely (figs. 109, 110). Most of his designs relied on this simultaneous evocation of the new and the familiar. One of his end-table-and-lamp combos brought together elements of East Asian form with the contemporary "modernistic" idiom, merging them in a nearly seamless way (fig. 111); and for a few of the pieces, Peters borrowed from late Expressionism—especially its more decorative features.

By the time Peters left Famous Players-Lasky, Expressionism was swiftly fading from the scene in Germany. Sep-

104. Advertisement for Peters Brothers with a drawing by Victor Mall. Collection Jock de Swart.

105. Business card for Peters Brothers, c. 1927. Collection Jock de Swart.

arated by a full continent and an ocean from Europe, he was slow to respond to the shift in design sensibilities. This is evident in another ensemble he and George made and installed for an unknown client. It features an Expressionist-inspired fireplace screen, similar to those made by Bruno Paul in Germany in the early 1920s (fig. 112).

But Peters was not limited to German models. For another commission—again for an unnamed client, presumably in 1927—he inserted detailing from French and American Art Deco (the latter most visibly in the zigzag lines), mixing this language with more characteristic Expressionist motifs (fig. 113). The ceiling lamp, one of the first examples of what would grow to a large number of lighting pieces he would design, is similarly blended, relying once more on forms that had been popularized by Bruno Paul, while the twin corner bookshelves, positioned on either side of the settee, borrow from another important influence of the period: Paul T. Frankl's Skyscraper furniture.

How successful Peters Brothers Modern American Furniture was as a business enterprise is difficult to gauge. At least a few of their pieces—represented today only by a handful of drawings and photographs—were evidently made and sold. The standouts include an elaborate coffee table and several other pieces commissioned by Hollywood businessman Harry Blaine (figs. 114, 115). The brothers also executed a dining room for a client named Hofmann in Beverly Hills and an interior in a mock English Arts and Crafts style for the Watson and Son tailor shop on Hollywood Boulevard (fig. 116).[216]

In 1927, Peters did come up with at least one architectural design of note, a house project for *Hi-Hat Magazine*. A glossy monthly, sometimes bimonthly, culture and lifestyle publication for the Hollywood community, *Hi-Hat* appeared briefly in the late 1920s. Its editors aspired to the suave sophistication and broad intellectualism of the recently launched *The New Yorker*. The magazine fell a good deal short of those Olympian heights, but it did play an important part in nurturing and promoting the Los Angeles modernist scene. Many of the city's artists and designers, and even a few of its better local writers, appeared in its pages. Peters, in a bid to earn publicity—in a magazine that nearly everyone who mattered subscribed to and read—also submitted several other designs, including his perspective view of the radio station on Mars.[217]

His house project appeared in the December 1927–January 1928 issue. It was a considerable leap ahead from what Peters had been making just a year or two before for Famous Players-Lasky.[218]

The drawing is remarkable (fig. 117). Through visual reduction and a trick of perspective, Peters conveyed a powerful sense of space and movement. The house, sited atop a steeply sloping lot, appears fully volumetric: the main body of the structure is arrayed around a massive central fireplace and chimney, with a double-height living room set into its right front corner. Framing the entrance is a sculptural porch—presumably of reinforced concrete—while, on the rear, balconies and terraces seemingly cascade outward, echoing the terraces on the front.

The house's openness is an unmistakable response to the benign climate of Southern California. Even more striking is its dynamism. Peters's use of a full array of forms, positioned in different directions, and his manipulation of scale in the rendering—achieved mostly through the oversized potted succulent in the foreground and the receding flights of stairs—generate an uncommon sense of energy. The repeated and continuous lines on the façades, in the form of full-bodied stringcourses, give the composition a feeling of restlessness—one that departs noticeably from the work of his California peers. Even the contemporary houses of R. M. Schindler, the only other Los Angeles designer then employing closely related compositional strategies, show a less animated handling of surface and volumes.

There is no indication—on the drawing or in the accompanying magazine feature—that Peters had a prospective client for the house. It was evidently a "fantasy" design.

The same is likely true for the two interiors he published in *Hi-Hat*. One was a reception room, the other a living space and library. The former, dated 1927, is less forward-looking, repeating what were already becoming standard "modernistic" forms and finishes (fig. 118). But the drawing of the living space and library of 1926 (which, notably, is shown hanging on the wall in one of the ensembles Peters and George had arranged and photographed; see fig. 107) has some of the qualities of the house project: a strong underlying sense of geometry stemming from Peters's insistent use of "modules," executed in a manner vaguely reminiscent of Gerrit Rietveld and the other postwar Dutch modernists (fig. 119).

The publication of Peters's drawings in *Hi-Hat* marked his coming out in the small Los Angeles design community. By then, he had become acquainted with most, if not all, of the other local modernists, including Kem Weber, R. M. Schindler, Richard Neutra, J. R. Davidson, Lloyd Wright, and German-born artists Jacob Asanger and Eugene Maier-Krieg.

Peters had first met Weber shortly after he arrived, in 1923.[219] Weber was living in a large Arts and Crafts bungalow just east of downtown Los Angeles, not far from the Peters house in Eagle Rock.

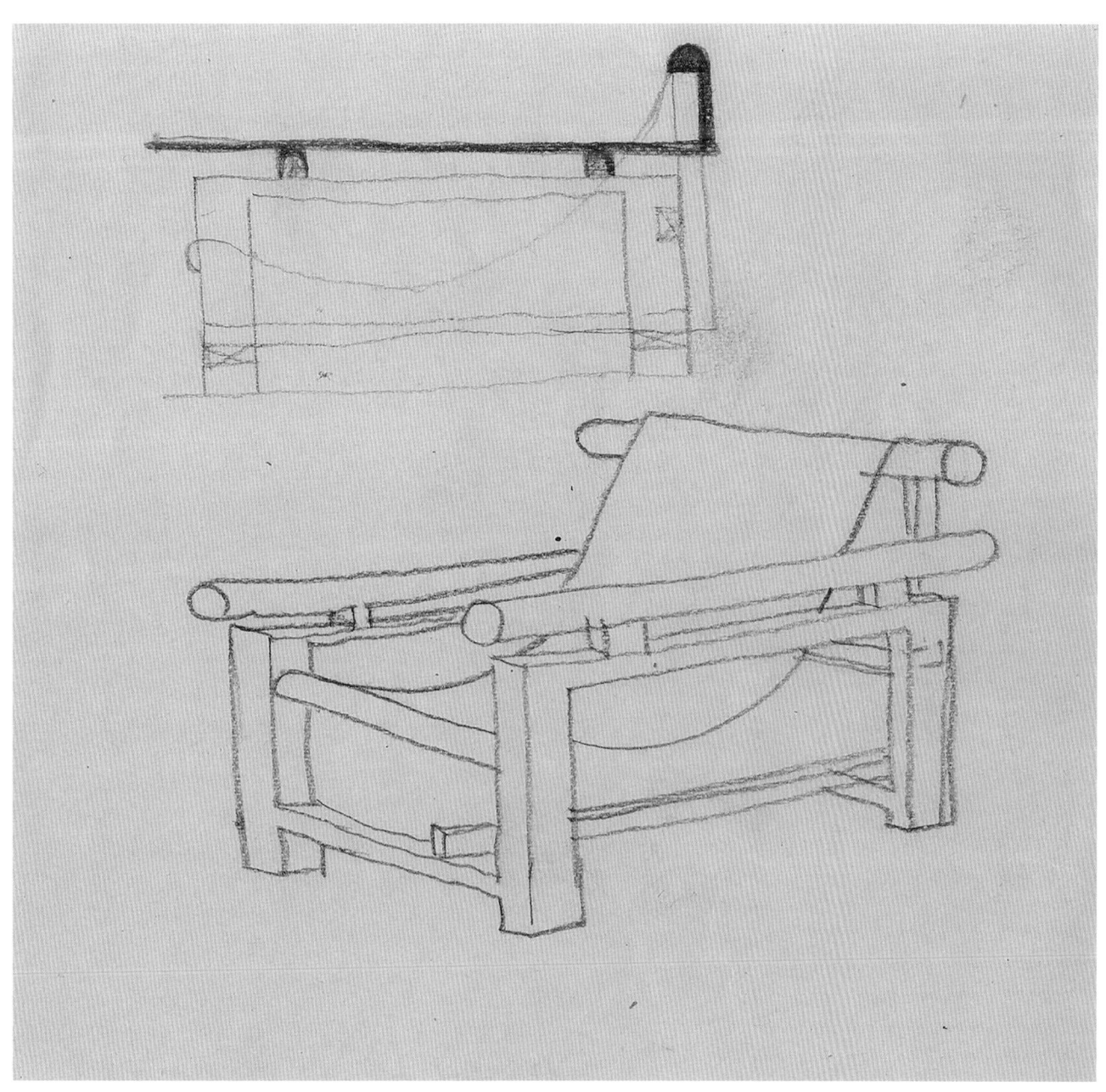

108. Jock Peters, sketch for a lounge chair, 1927.
Perspective and side elevation. Pencil on paper.
Collection Jock de Swart.

106. Jock Peters, lamp, bookcase, and chair
for Peters Brothers Modern American Furniture, 1927.
Collection Jock de Swart.

107. Jock Peters, chair, shelf with doors, and lamp-and-table combo
for Peters Brothers Modern American Furniture, 1927.
Collection Jock de Swart.

109. George Peters with one of the Peters Brothers bookcases he built, c. 1927. Collection Jock de Swart.

110. Jock Peters, bookcase made by George Peters, c. 1927. Collection Jock de Swart.

112. Jock Peters, installation of Peters Brothers furniture, including a bench, fireplace screen, combination lamp and table, and end table, c. 1927. Collection Jock de Swart.

111. Jock Peters, sketch for a table and lamp, 1927. Perspective. Pencil on paper, Collection Jock de Swart.

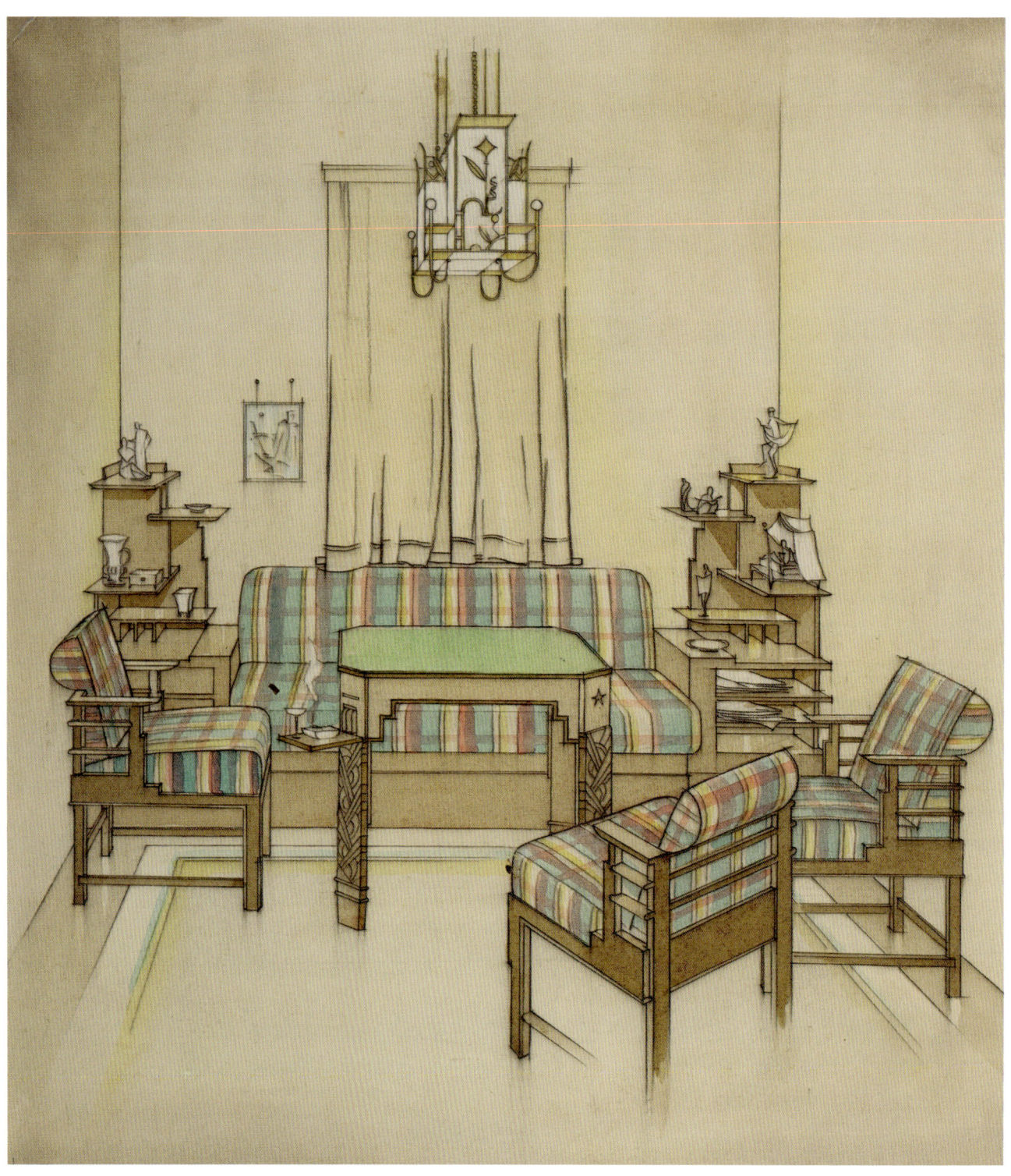

113. Jock Peters, design for a seating group, table, and bookcases, c. 1927. Pencil and watercolor on board. UCSB.

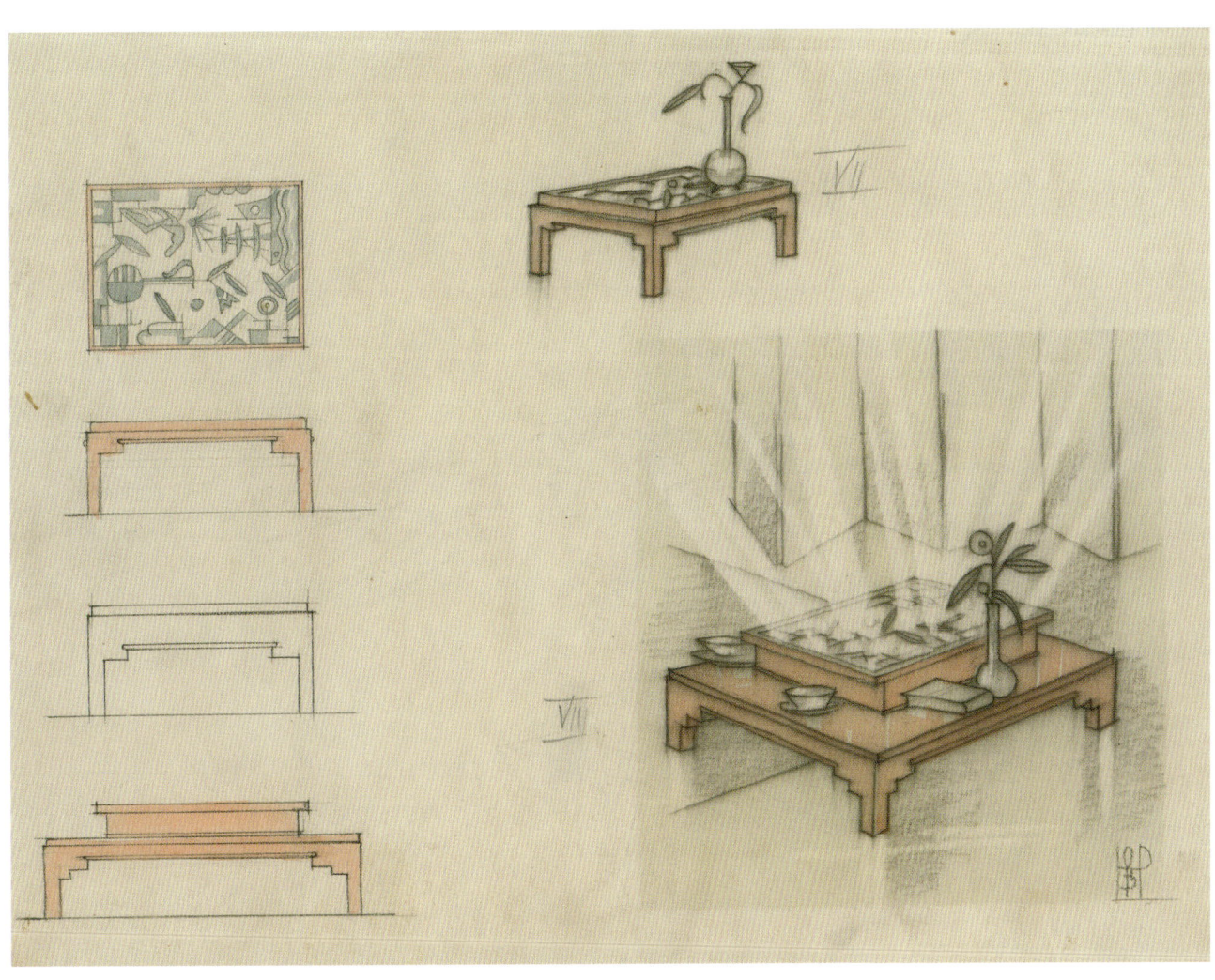

114. Jock Peters, design for a coffee table for Harry Blaine, c. 1927.
Pencil and watercolor on paper. UCSB.

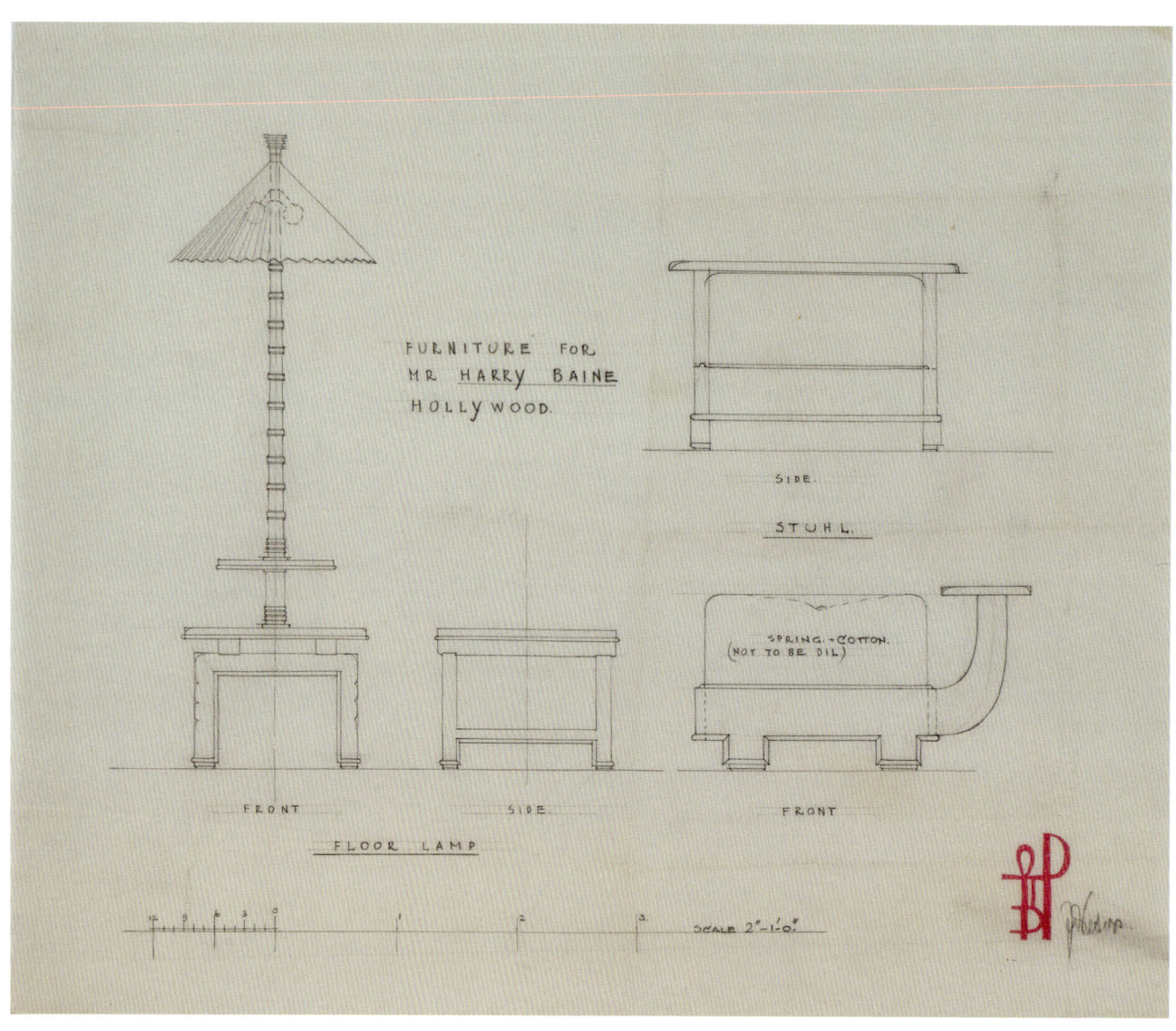

115. Jock Peters, designs for an end-table-and-lamp combo for Harry Blaine, c. 1927. Pencil and rubber stamp on paper. UCSB.

116. Jock Peters, Watson and Son tailor shop, Los Angeles, c. 1927. UCSB.

118. Jock Peters, design for a reception room, 1927. From *Hi-Hat Magazine*, February 1928 (Midwinter Sports issue), 34. UCSB.

117. Jock Peters, design for a house for *Hi-Hat Magazine*, 1927. Pencil and colored pencil on board. UCSB.

119. Jock Peters, design for a sitting room and library, 1926. From *Hi-Hat Magazine*, 15 December 1927, 28. UCSB.

They and their families—Weber and his wife also had several small children—were soon meeting up regularly. The two families formed part of a larger community of German-speaking émigrés, most of whom resided in and around Pasadena. Herta and Jock held Sunday-afternoon coffee and cake get-togethers at their house, inviting the Webers and many of the German, Austrian, and Swiss-born professors and researchers (and their families) from the nearby California Institute of Technology. By 1927, through Weber, Peters had also developed at least a passing acquaintance with the other progressive architects, designers, and artists.[220]

Professionally, though, Peters preferred to go it alone. He wanted to make his business with George a success, without outside help or interference. But at the end of 1927, the two brothers were bringing in just enough money to scrape by. George continued to augment his income by taking on work as a draftsman and contractor; Peters was compelled to seek other opportunities. When Weber asked him to help with the design of the new Barker Brothers store in Hollywood, he jumped at the offer.[221]

The two men enjoyed the chance to work together. Peters was especially pleased to collaborate with Weber on the new store's interiors, which included some of the most innovative spaces in Southern California from that time. For a few weeks, he also assisted Weber with furniture designs for Barker's production lines. Soon afterward, Peters decided to end the working relationship: he had no desire to be someone else's employee, however congenial the working conditions.[222] He left to pursue other possibilities.

One was an ongoing project that he had begun working on even before he resigned from Famous Players-Lasky. In 1926, William Lingenbrink, a local German-born developer, had hired Peters to design a new retail and housing complex on a barren stretch of the Pacific Coast north of Malibu, between Oxnard and Port Hueneme.[223]

The plot of land, which Lingenbrink named Silver Strand Beach, had nearly a mile of broad, white-sand beaches. The real cachet of this remote spot, however, sprang from the filming of the desert scenes of Rudolph Valentino's immensely popular 1921 movie *The Sheik* in the dunes nearby. (*Blood and Sand*, the follow-on Valentino vehicle, was also filmed there, in 1922.) Soon afterward, the portion of California Highway 1 that passed nearby was paved, and Valentino fans streamed into the area, strolling along the beaches, hoping thereby to come closer to their idol.

Lingenbrink sought to capitalize on the interest. In a sales brochure, he announced that the site was the only strip of similar coastline north of Santa Monica "dedicated to the public," and he claimed that most of the lots had already been hurriedly sold. (In the 1920s, Southern California developers were quick to announce property sales even when only very small deposits had been put down.[224]) Work on the eighty-acre development began in the early fall of 1925. Construction crews graded the dunes and paved a grid of streets as well as a main thoroughfare, Ocean Boulevard, fronting the Pacific.[225]

Lingenbrink first called in Peters to design the sidewalk that would front the shops facing the water along Ocean Boulevard—part of his strategy to lure potential buyers for the land. The ebullient concrete walkway, which Peters infused with colorful sunbursts and geometric patterning, was poured and stained along the still-undeveloped commercial strip (fig. 120).

But sales of the lots, despite the bullish reports, were weak, and Lingenbrink asked Peters to design several storefronts in an attempt to draw attention. The only drawing to survive—one of Peters's distinctive pencil renderings reproduced in the sales brochure—brought together much of what was then current in American architecture, including zigzag patterning and an intricate interplay of verticals and horizontals (fig. 121). The form of the doors and display windows, like the building as a whole, was conventional, but the detailing was up-to-the-minute—very near the edge of West Coast modernism in 1927.

Lingenbrink, who was equal parts hard-nosed developer and modernist Svengali (among the local modernists he would commission was Schindler), operated an art gallery in addition to his real estate ventures. He fancied himself an expert on the new design, self-publishing a folio book of photographs of shop façades in Los Angeles, a number of which he himself had commissioned.[226]

Much to Peters's relief, especially financial, Lingenbrink constructed at least two of his store designs—possibly three—at Silver Strand Beach. (They have since been altered beyond recognition.) The commission from Lingenbrink would turn out to be Peters's first substantial foray into modern store design, the practice and direction that would at last bring him renown.

Over the course of the second half of 1927, Peters worked on several other projects. He designed a grand house for a Mrs. C. O. Blachley in Hollywood. It was never built, and little now survives of the effort, aside from a few

120. Jock Peters, sidewalk design for Silver Strand Beach, California. From a Silver Strand Beach Company sales brochure, c. 1927. UCSB.

121. Jock Peters, design for a store façade for Silver Strand Beach, California, c. 1927. From a Silver Strand Beach Company sales brochure. UCSB.

122. Jock Peters, winning competition entry for a rug design for Mohawk Carpet Mills, 1928. Photographic print. UCSB.

First Prize Rug Design for Mohawk Carpet Mills   by   Jock D. Peters.   1928.

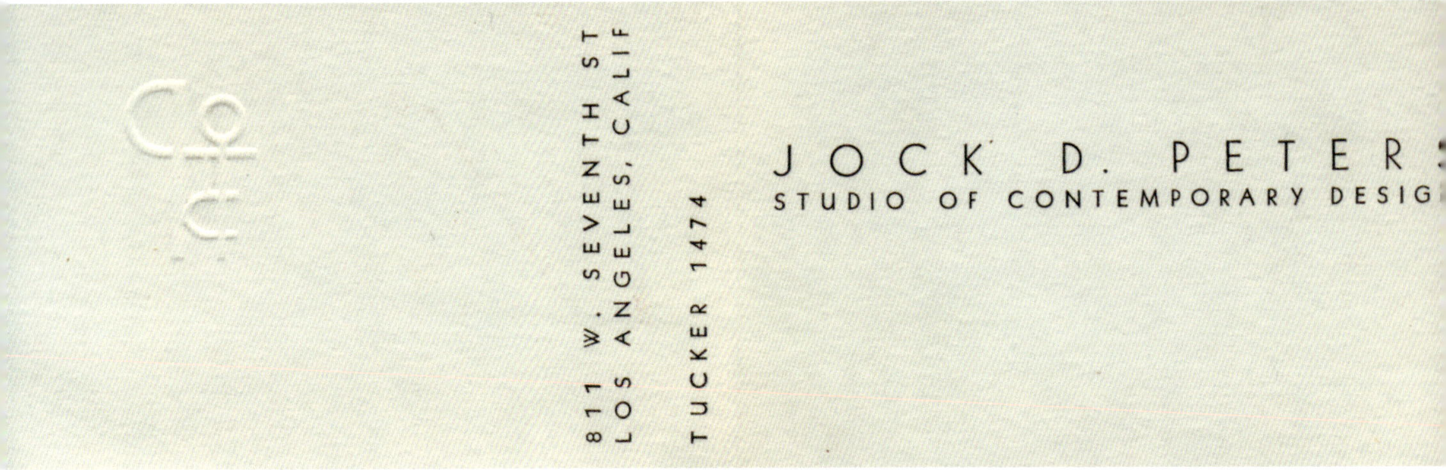

811 W. SEVENTH ST
LOS ANGELES, CALIF

TUCKER 1474

JOCK D. PETERS
STUDIO OF CONTEMPORARY DESIGN

123. Jock Peters, Studio of Contemporary Design business card, c. 1928. Collection Jock de Swart.

124. Jock Peters, Studio of Contemporary Design office in the Fine Arts Building, c. 1928. Collection Jock de Swart.

125. Jock Peters, design for a label for Ju' Nice Avocado Skin Food, c. 1928. Pencil on paper. Collection Jock de Swart.

rudimentary sketches. Most of his other jobs were modest—a living room here, a foyer or a brick fireplace there—all for unnamed clients.

Throughout this time, Peters continued to take part in national design competitions. And one of them, for a rug for Mohawk Carpet Mills, in New York State, brought a change in his fortunes.

Mohawk Carpet Mills had mounted the competition in conjunction with the Art Alliance of America. Peters again won one of two first prizes, which came with a check for one thousand dollars—enough to keep him afloat for several months.[227] His design, a stylistic amalgam of forms arising out of French Art Deco and late German Expressionism, was—at least in the American context—boldly new (fig. 122). It presented figural elements—stylized animals, vegetation, and, even, a sailing ship—which Peters married with straight-edged and curvilinear patterning. New York critic N. C. Sanford, writing in *Good Furniture*, described the design as "a maze of detail, with a curious Egyptian feeling." One can distinguish, she wrote, "in conventionalized form the lotus, the asp, the gazelles, and the strange birds that are so often seen in Egyptian sculpture." But Sanford added that though the design was "extremely ingenious . . . by its very great employment of variety one is sure to require wise and careful color treatment if it is to be made to 'stay upon the floor' as all good rugs should do."[228]

How Egyptian the rug design truly is can be debated. (It comes closer in many ways to the Nordic neoclassicism of the day.) Sanford, however, was no doubt correct in her belief that it would pose challenges in an actual room with other furnishings. The market bore out her judgment: few, if any, examples were ever made or sold.

The widely publicized prize nonetheless brought Peters a good deal of notice and several commissions for textiles and wallpaper. Despite the new work coming in, he decided to dissolve the partnership with George, who was, in any event, still preoccupied with his contracting business. It was a decision he would ever after regret.

In the late summer of 1928, he finally opened an office under his own name. He called it "Jock D. Peters—Studio of Contemporary Design" (fig. 123). He rented space in the recently completed Fine Arts Building, on Seventh Street in downtown Los Angeles, which housed the offices of many other architects and art firms. Shortly after moving in, Peters designed and installed the office interior (fig. 124).

His first job came from the C. R. Blackburn Company in Hollywood, for the packaging of a skin lotion made from

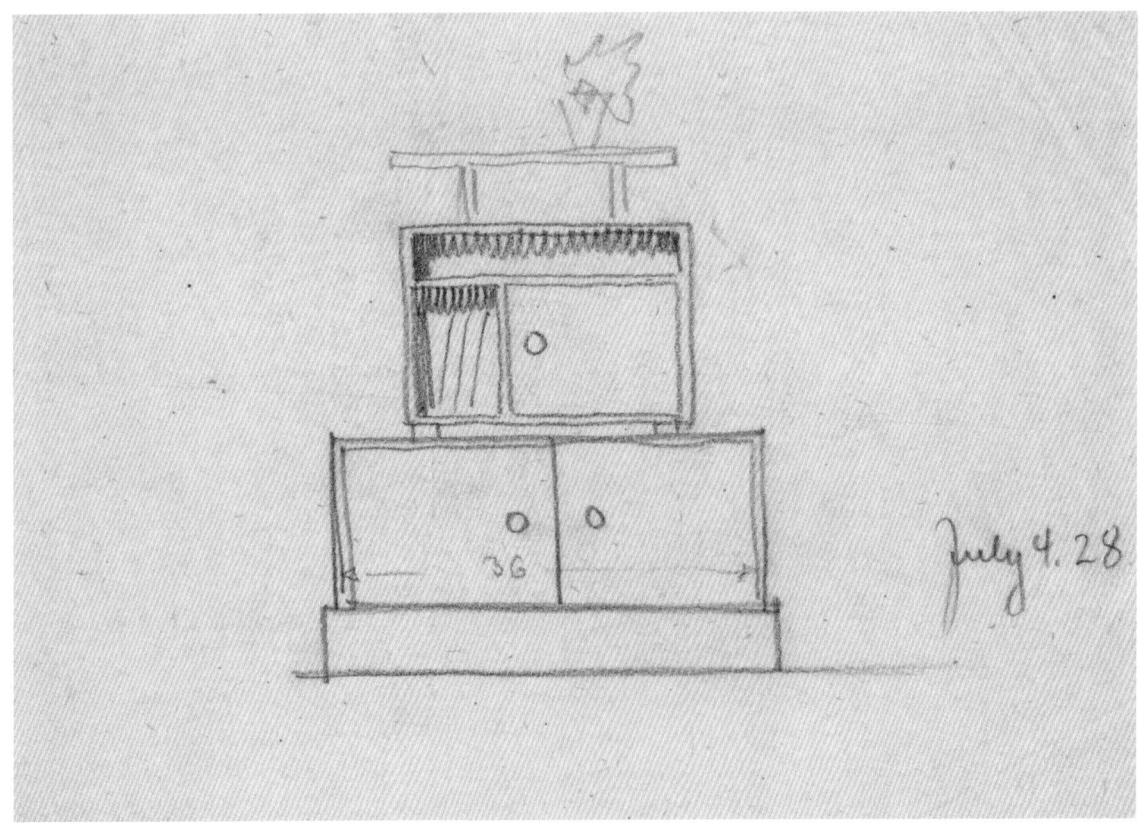

avocado oil. The design Peters devised was based on angular geometries in the spirit of the day (fig. 125). He also busied himself with various "spec" designs for furniture, which he hoped either to manufacture or sell to a major producer of furnishings.

One was a planar chair. It had a flat seat that widened toward the front, a high, stiff back, and elongated rectangular supports for the arms (fig. 126). It was an echo of previous modernist seating designs, including those of Rietveld, "constructed" in the manner of the Dutch and Russian avant-gardists but altered so that it was at least marginally more body-fitting and therefore more comfortable.

Peters also produced a related design for a small case piece. It was, in essence, a modified cabinet-on-stand (fig. 127). What occurred to him immediately after he finished was that it was inherently modular; it could thus be reordered in manifold ways. Straightaway, he began to devise a variety of configurations.

These came at first in the form of a set of related case pieces, then as larger assembled units (figs. 128, 129). Peters soon discovered that he could make a limited group of standard units and then, because they had correlated dimensions and proportions, stack or connect them into larger wholes for specific purposes. The name he came up with for the system, "Universal Assembling Furniture," perfectly captured his concept.

Peters produced drawings for a full set of pieces, including occasional tables, chests, bookcases, and sideboards. With the inclusion of a mirror, he found that he could also fashion dressing tables and vanities (fig. 130). In two days, in a lather of energy, barely stopping to rest or eat, he churned out twenty-three sheets of drawings. Among the designs were several seating modules, including sofas and corner couches, complete with footstools (fig. 131). He sent the entire set of drawings, dated July 5, 1928, off to the Copyright Office of the Library of Congress in Washington, DC.

It was a bold and surprising move, given the state of the law at the time. Copyright laws in the United States in that period did not normally convey rights for decorative arts designs. (This was the principal reason why the early American and foreign modernists so often saw their furniture and decorative arts ideas pilfered.) It was only with the passage of the Vestal Bill in Congress, in July 1930, that the situation changed.

The bill was named for its sponsoring legislator, Indiana congressman Albert Henry Vestal, who chaired the House Committee on Patents. It allowed for the copyright registration of "industrial 'patterns,' 'shapes,' and 'forms,' original in their application to a given material, artistic or ornamental in effect, and devoid of mechanical utility"—in other words, on the basis of their treatment or appearance alone.[229]

In 1928, however, there were no such protections. Peters, either through some knowledge of the existing laws or, perhaps more likely, on the advice of an attorney, applied for his patent citing not the pieces' aesthetic attributes but their "technical character." He was thus able to copyright a system involving the assembling of smaller standardized components into complete pieces of furniture—but *only* the system. In due course, he received a reply from the Copyright Office granting him exclusive rights for his system for "the first term of 28 years."[230]

It was a brilliant and largely original idea. A few other designers were developing related concepts around that time—in Southern California, particularly Schindler, who was experimenting with an analogous system, his idea for "Unit Furniture."[231] Peters's concept, though, was better adapted for commercial application. It was more practical and "less challenging" stylistically. But as would prove all too often the case for him, he was unable to capitalize on his breakthrough: Peters lacked the financial wherewithal to manufacture the pieces himself, and he had no luck finding a suitable partner.[232] In the end, the concept and drawings remain—nothing else. There is no evidence that he fabricated even a single prototype.

Peters's failure to find commercial success with the Universal Assembling Furniture idea had much to do with the times. In America, in 1928, there was only a tiny market for modern mass-produced furniture. Even modern designs that retained some connection with classical forms and motifs, such as the mitigated French-inspired Art Deco furniture lines then being made by some of the large manufacturers in Grand Rapids, Michigan, and elsewhere, found only a limited number of buyers. The broad public taste still ran to period revival styles or what remained of the Arts and Crafts. The major manufacturers accurately gauged the popular mood: they continued to make what were essentially replicas of older pieces. Their modernist lines were mostly experimental—intended only for limited release.

126. Jock Peters, design for a chair, c. 1927. Pencil on paper. Collection Jock de Swart.

127. Jock Peters, preliminary design for a cabinet in the Universal Assembling Furniture series, 1928. Pencil on paper. Collection Jock de Swart.

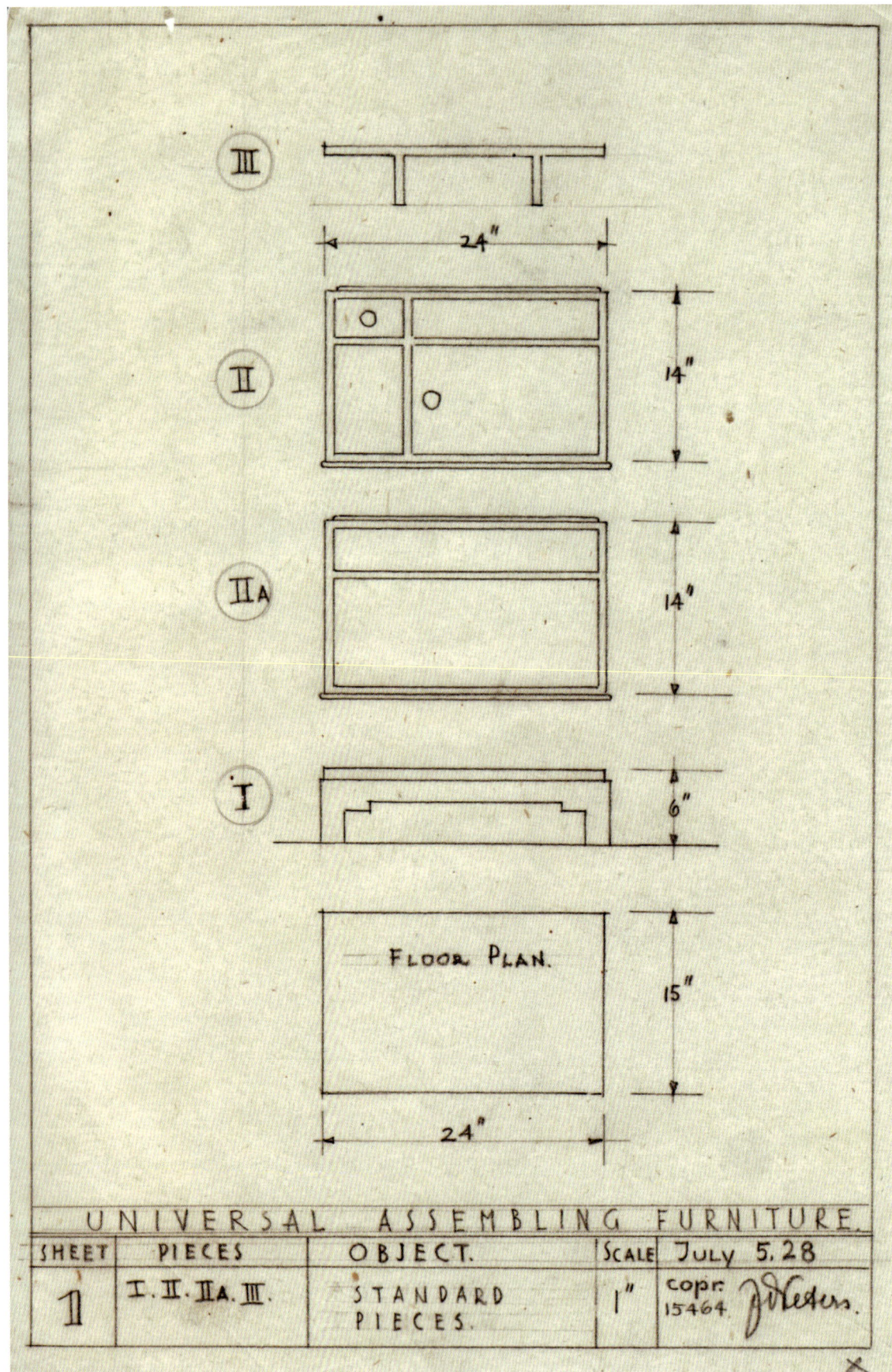

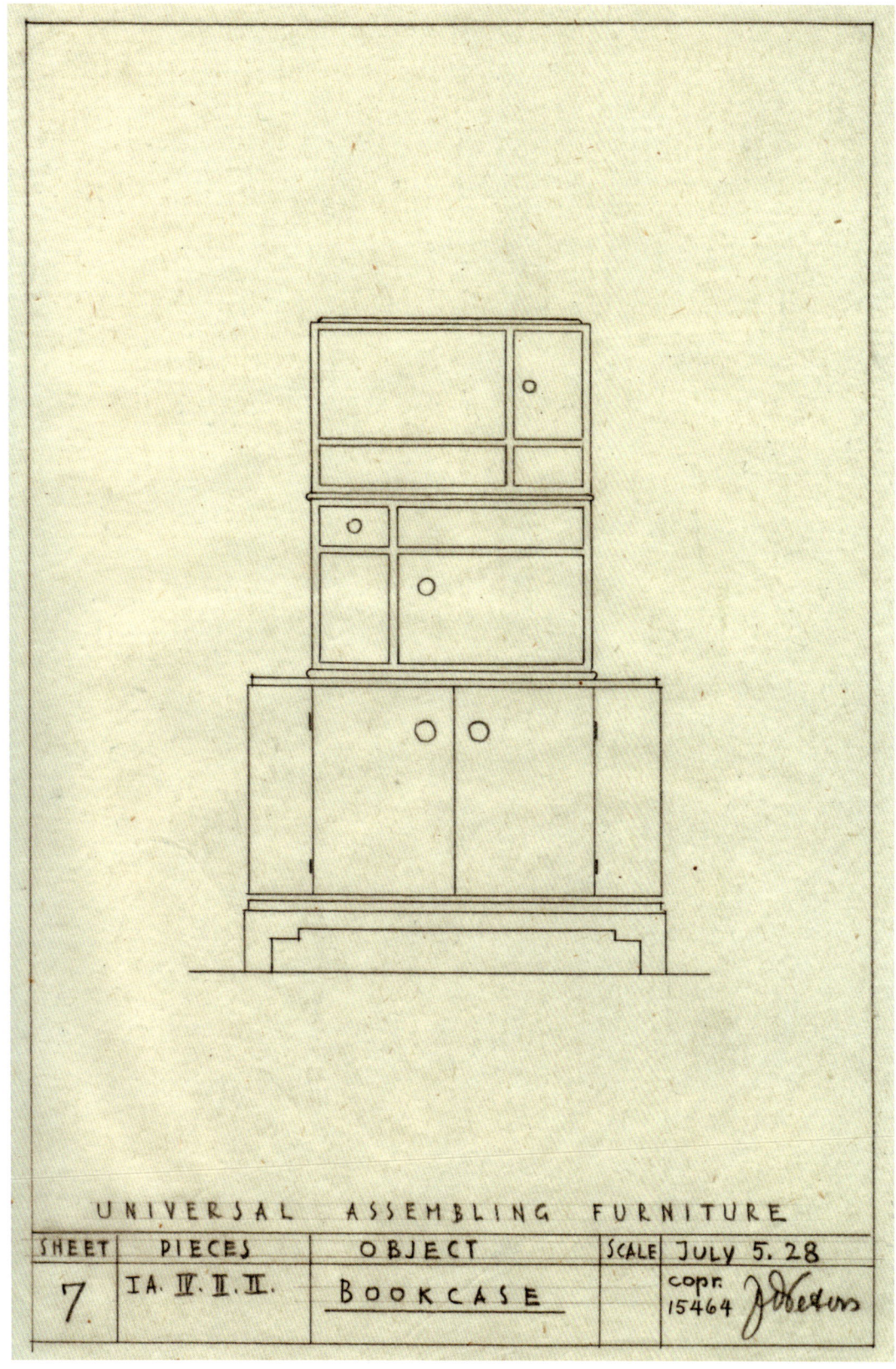

128. Jock Peters, Universal Assembling Furniture, 1928. Standard pieces. Pencil on paper. Collection Jock de Swart.

129. Jock Peters, Universal Assembling Furniture, 1928. Bookcase. Pencil on paper. Collection Jock de Swart.

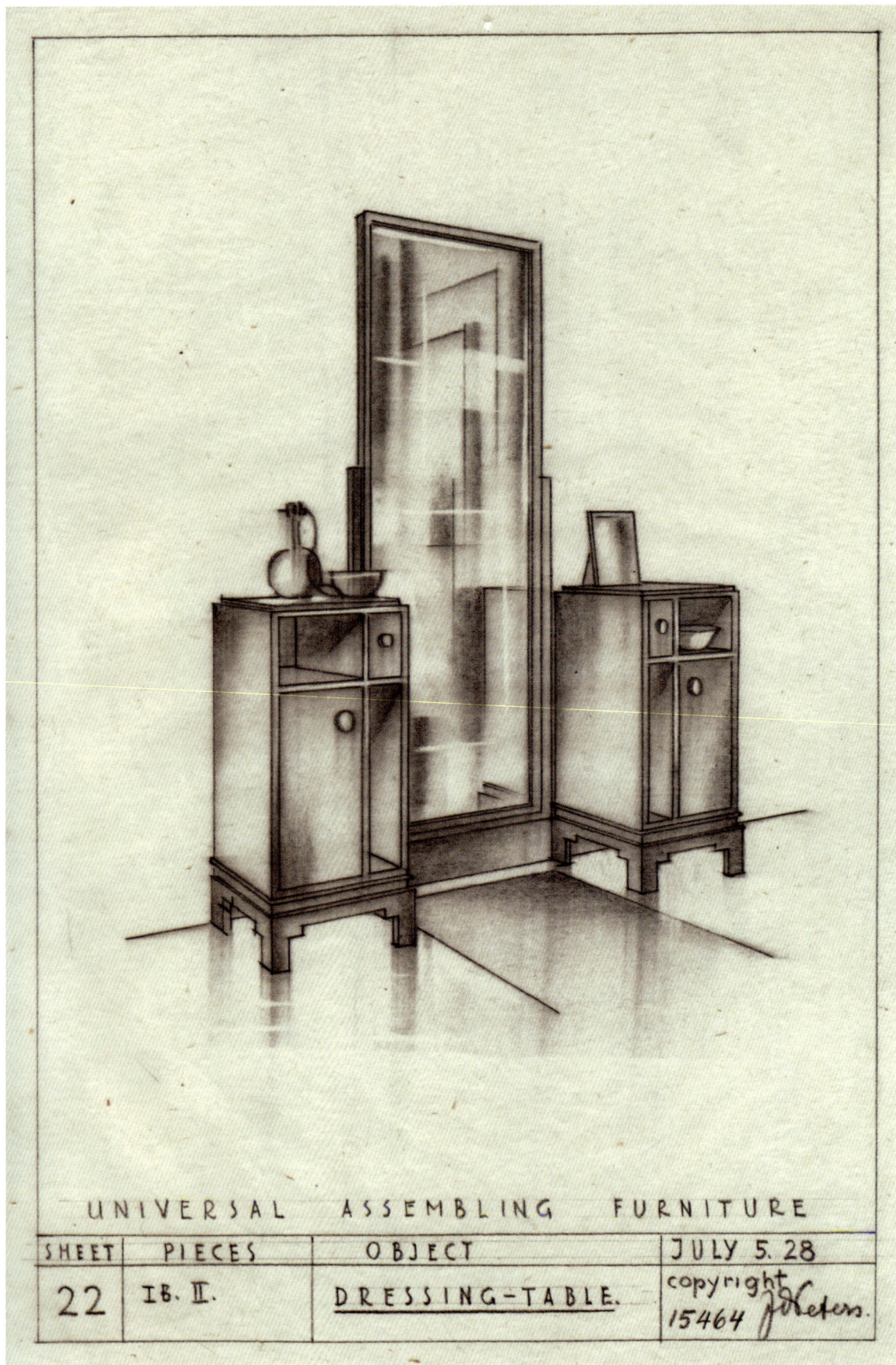

130. Jock Peters, Universal Assembling Furniture, 1928.
Dressing table. Pencil on paper. Collection Jock de Swart.

131. Jock Peters, Universal Assembling Furniture, 1928.
Stool and chair. Pencil on paper. Collection Jock de Swart.

One of the few American firms aggressively promoting modernism was the Modernage Furniture Company in New York City. Modernage had a very different sales strategy from the mass manufacturers in the Midwest. The company sold inexpensive versions of high-style pieces, occasionally made with the participation of the designer but more often as "facsimiles." Modernage, for example, brought out its own line of "Skyscraper" furniture, "borrowed"—which is to say, stolen—from Paul T. Frankl's line.[233]

Martin H. Feinman had founded Modernage in 1925. Born in Odessa, Russia, in 1899, Feinman began making his pieces in the mid-1920s, in a corner of his father's furniture factory in lower Manhattan. He aimed for a mostly middle-class consumer base, making the designs of individual modernists, like Frankl and Eugene Schoen (whose handcrafted pieces could be prohibitively expensive), accessible to those of more modest means—and turning a tidy profit in the process. The concept turned out to be surprisingly successful. Modernage marketed and sold its pieces nationally, becoming the first firm to break through with modernist designs.

Most of the other modernist furniture designs from this time were custom examples, made for, and installed in, specific settings. This was the case in Southern California, where individual designers—among them, Schindler and Neutra—produced furniture for their own residential commissions. The main exception was Barker Brothers, under Weber's direction. Starting in 1926, Barker Brothers sold original pieces, as well as custom and production furniture from Weber. Customers could purchase ready-made pieces or commission Weber to design individual pieces or full ensembles. Clients sometimes also mixed and matched, selecting furniture from the store floor—a great deal of it the work of the leading New York or Parisian designers—and pairing the pieces with those from Weber and other West Coast modernists.[234] The market, in any event, was tiny, confined largely to those from "artistic circles" in Hollywood and along the coast, in Malibu, Santa Monica, and Santa Barbara. The reality of a mass-manufactured modernism was still nearly a decade away.

After struggling for more than a year to secure clients and commissions, Peters found himself busier than he could have hoped or imagined. He was now designing furniture, interiors, textiles, and packaging for products, along with decorative accessories, including rugs and lamps. He had also taken on a teaching position at the recently founded Academy of Modern Art (fig. 132).[235]

The academy was one of three important private art schools established in the Los Angeles area in the late 1920s and early 1930s. (The others were Chouinard Art Institute and the Art Center School.) Founded in 1927, it was the creation of Franz K. Ferenz, a Viennese from a Hungarian family.

Ferenz arrived in New York before the war. He first operated a bookstore, gallery, and artists' supply store on MacDougal Street, in Greenwich Village; later on, he owned a bookstore and gallery on Madison Avenue, where he sold modern Viennese designs, art books, and prints.[236] Ferenz moved to Los Angeles in 1927, the same year he started the school, which at first was housed in the Fine Arts Building, where Peters had his office. He met Peters one morning in the elevator and hired him on the spot.[237]

Peters, already an experienced teacher from his time at the applied arts school in Altona, began teaching a few night classes each week. By early 1929, Ferenz made him the school's codirector.[238] Peters found himself in excellent company: several other prominent Angelino modernists, including Neutra, were teaching there, and among the school's students were Gregory Ain and Harwell Hamilton Harris, future stars of the local scene.

Peters loved the camaraderie he found at the school. He enjoyed the time spent with students and colleagues and the opportunity to explore new pathways for design without having to worry about acceding to his clients' wishes. Soon, Peters was expending a significant portion of his time and energy teaching and meeting with students. Had nothing else changed, he might well have gone back into education full-time.

But Peters's career was about to take a radically different direction. Greatly more important for him, in terms of both his visibility and his future prospects, was another side job he had taken on. It would alter the course of his professional life and bring him his first real fame. He began doing contract work for another local architectural office, Feil and Paradise.

132. Jock Peters, advertisement for the Academy of Modern Art, Hollywood. From *West Coaster*, 15 March 1928, 1. UCSB.

ANNOUNCING THE

ACADEMY OF MODERN ART
HOLLYWOOD CALIF.

SPRING AND SUMMER CLASSES
NOW FORMING

in MODERN
COMMERCIAL ART
LIFE DRAWING
INDUSTRIAL ART
INTERIOR
DECORATION

FOR FULL INFORMATION
AND REGISTRATION
APPLY TO OFFICE OF
SCHOOL 1517 N·WILTON
NEAR SUNSET · DAILY
9 · 10 A·M· OR 5·6 P·M·

Chapter 8 |
BULLOCK'S WILSHIRE

Outwardly, Peters's decision to accept Feil and Paradise's offer of work was a surprising one. Almost from the moment he set foot on American soil, he had dreamed of having his own independent practice. Peters had reluctantly taken the jobs with Neher and Famous Players-Lasky; in each instance, he was compelled to do so out of financial necessity. His brief time working with Kem Weber had been different: he genuinely respected Weber and enjoyed collaborating with him. But the lure of finally going his own way proved too strong for him. When he and George launched Peters Brothers Modern Furniture, he was determined never again to work for someone else.

His willingness to take up the offer from Feil and Paradise had everything to do with the seeming freelance nature of the work. The jobs he did for the firm were offered to him piecemeal, and he accepted each one in turn because it was work he wanted to do and because he believed he could preserve his independence. Despite his income from teaching and the increasing number of commissions he received, Peters was still having difficulties making ends meet. His feelings about the offer would soon change, but at the outset he was excited about the new arrangement.[239]

What Peters could not have known at the time was that his association with Feil and Paradise would lead to his creation of the interiors for Bullock's Wilshire, his first great success in America and the turning point in his career (fig. 133). He could also have had no inkling that his collaboration with Feil and Paradise would turn out badly.

In 1927, Feil and Paradise was an established Los Angeles architecture firm with a rising reputation. It was one of a handful of offices in the city specializing in commercial interiors, and one of an even smaller number consistently producing modernist designs. Joseph L. Feil, the first of the firm's two named principals, was the firm's founder, head, and guiding spirit. Born and reared in Dayton, Ohio, he was a year younger than Peters. He had moved out to Los Angeles in 1913. Not long after arriving, he opened his first office.[240] In those early years, Feil worked with an ever-shifting cast of architect partners on a comprehensive array of projects. As time went on, he became a specialist in store and interior design. The practice he opened around 1925 with Bernard R. Paradise concentrated almost exclusively on commercial and retail spaces.

133. Parkinson and Parkinson (John Parkinson and Donald B. Parkinson), Bullock's Wilshire, Los Angeles, 1929. UCSB.

Born in Russia in 1881, Paradise had immigrated with his family to the United States as a child. He lived in Racine, Wisconsin, for a time and, later, in Chicago; around 1916, he decided to seek his fortune in Southern California. He worked briefly in several local architectural offices before joining up with Feil.[241]

Feil became the public face of the firm, interacting with clients and securing commissions; Paradise assumed the role of contractor, overseeing the construction and finishing work. Both men had a hand in the design process, and in those first years they undertook all the work themselves. As they became ever busier, ever more challenged to meet the demands of a growing client list, they sought outside design help.

In the summer of 1927, Feil and Paradise were hired to design and execute the interiors for the Oviatt Building, a twelve-story structure for retail and artists' studios on South Olive Street in downtown Los Angeles. The client for the project, James Zera Oviatt, was co-owner of one of the most upscale clothiers in the city. The firm of Alexander and Oviatt would occupy the lower three floors of the building. Oviatt had recently been to Paris, where he visited the Exposition des Arts Décoratifs et Industriels Modernes. He returned to Los Angeles determined to build something that was just as au courant.[242]

Oviatt was a willful and demanding client, the work all-consuming. Feil and Paradise were soon falling behind with their other jobs and decided to engage another architect to help them. They knew Peters from the Fine Arts Building, where they, too, had their offices. Because of Peters's experience with modern styles, they thought him the ideal partner to contribute designs for two of their other commissions.

One of these was Desmond's, a local clothier chain. The company had commissioned Feil and Paradise to fit out their new premises on Seventh Street. Feil and Paradise, in turn, passed on part of the job to Peters.[243]

His main assignment was to design a new façade for the store. The exterior he came up with conveyed a crisp and monumental elegance. Following the trend of the moment, he appropriated a good portion of its language from the French pavilions at the Paris exposition. The spare, classical massing, oversized panels, decorative floral motifs above the windows, and coffered ceiling of the set-in porch he took more or less directly from the Parisian models (figs. 134, 135).

An advertisement that appeared shortly after the store opened in 1928 proclaimed: "Modernism is the keynote. Modernism without ever being garish or ultra-bizarre . . . a bit of Paris discovered in America."[244] What Peters gave his clients, however, was a budget version of the new style. The materials were modest: the exterior cladding, which at first reads as black marble, was actually terra-cotta and the trim around the doors and windows a dark-stained oak. Only the paving leading into the store was a luxe material: black and white marble, laid in strips.[245] Peters had supplied what was required: an upscale look at a decidedly lower cost. He had now mastered precisely the sort of visual fakery that he had decried when he first arrived in Southern California.

In the publications on the new Desmond's that appeared after it was completed, Peters is listed as the project's "designer," Feil and Paradise as its "architects." Yet there is little, if any, evidence of Feil and Paradise's participation in the façade. Peters apparently undertook the work alone. The interiors, on the other hand, to judge from the surviving photographs, were mostly the work of Feil and Paradise. The store's front sections, which included the Men's Department, reflect an updated traditionalism. They are sharply out of character for Peters. The women's section at the store's rear, though, is different: it is lighter, more aspiring—incontestably more modern (fig. 136). It was undoubtedly his work. What speaks for this is not only the more astringent cast of the built-ins and furnishings, but also the ceiling mural, which closely resembles his winning rug design for Mohawk Carpet Mills.

Around the same time—possibly earlier, because his drawings from this period are not precisely dated—Peters also started on a second commercial job for Feil and Paradise, a ticket sales office for Maddux Air Lines.

The company's founder was Jack L. Maddux, owner of a local Ford and Lincoln car dealership. Maddux had established his airline in the late summer of 1927, employing another of Ford's products, the 4AT Tri-motor airplane, to ferry passengers between Los Angeles and San Diego. Over the following year, he expanded the route, introducing service between San Francisco and the racecourse at Agua Caliente Casino in Ensenada, Mexico, with stops along the way in Oakland, Fresno, Bakersfield, and Tijuana.[246]

The façade Peters devised is reminiscent of those he made for Lingenbrink at Silver Strand Beach—hardly a surprise, since the projects were nearly concurrent. The front of the building was asymmetrically arranged, topped with a prominent cornice and clad with horizontal "speed lines" and vertical fluting (fig. 137). Framing the street-side door were large display windows. Above, Peters placed a transom faced in iron letters spelling out the airline's name, and on the upper right, he set a small modern bas-relief airplane and a neon "blade" sign.[247]

It was all very up-to-date—as modern as any commercial building in Los Angeles at that time. Yet more innovative still

134. Jock Peters, Desmond's, Los Angeles, c. 1928. Preliminary drawing for a façade and entry porch. Reverse print. UCSB.

135. Jock Peters, Desmond's, Los Angeles, 1928. Front façade. From William Lingenbrink, *Modern Art in Store Fronts* (Los Angeles, n.d. [1928 or 1929]), folio A, plate 4.

136. Jock Peters, Desmond's, Los Angeles, 1928. Women's section.
Mott-Merge Collection, California State Library, Sacramento.

137. Jock Peters, Maddux Air Lines ticket office, Los Angeles, 1928.
Mott-Merge Collection, California State Library, Sacramento.

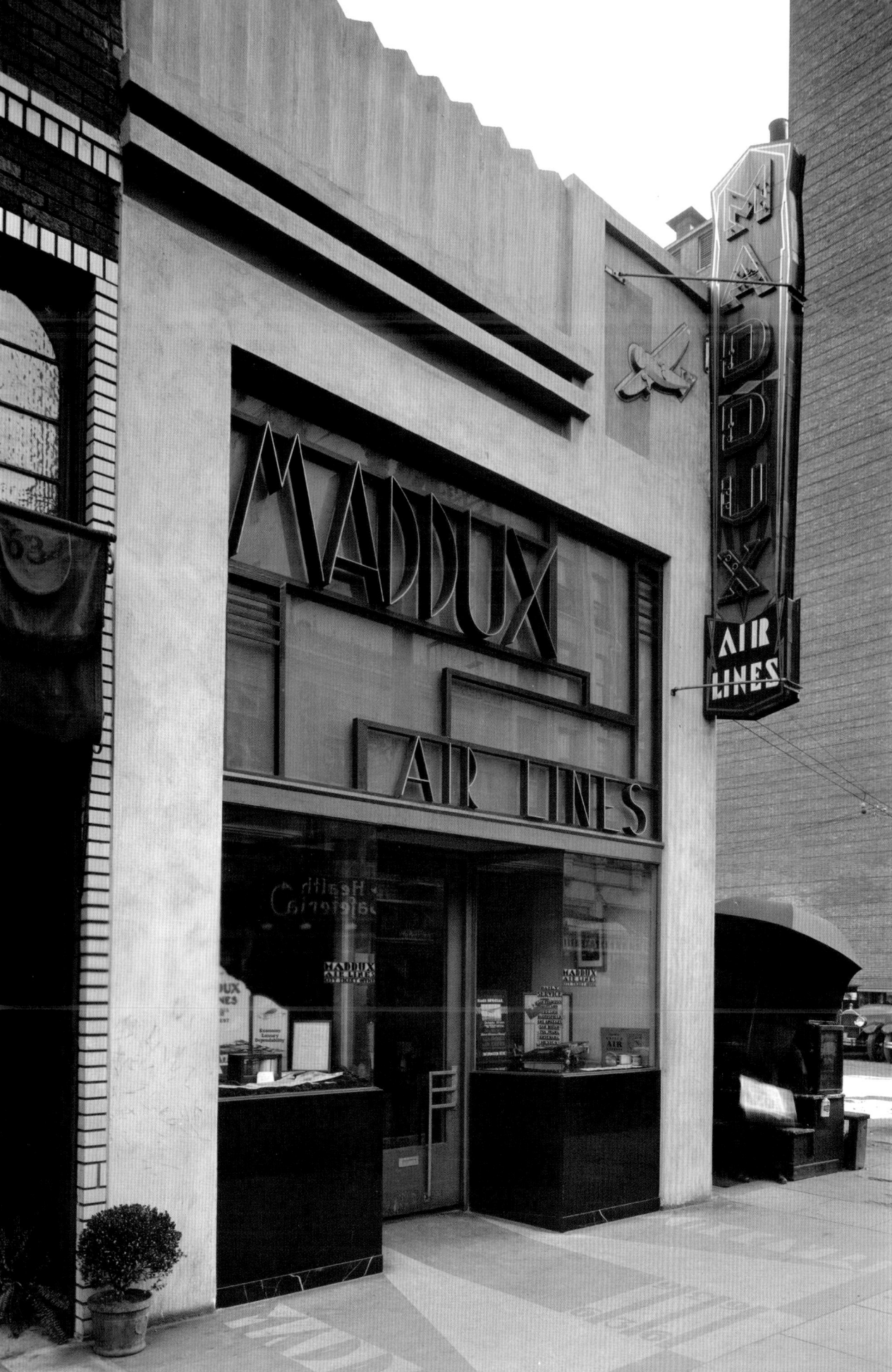

138. Jock Peters, Maddux Air Lines ticket office, Los Angeles, 1928. Interior. Mott-Merge Collection, California State Library, Sacramento.

were its interiors. In addition to a geometric counter and pared-down chairs and a table, Peters introduced several large murals, two on the sidewalls, the other on the ceiling (fig. 138). Prominently featured in them were side and bottom views of Ford Tri-motor aircraft, like those in Maddux's fleet. The office's exterior wall featured another, related mural, with imagery of flight and the names of the various stopping places along the airline's route (fig. 139).[248]

Peters's design expressed a sense of newness and possibility: it was very much in the spirit of what was then still a nascent industry. Maddux, with his fledgling airline, could scarcely have wished for more. The lifespan of both the office and the design, however, turned out to be exceptionally short, even for the rough-and-tumble of early modernist commercial architecture in Los Angeles. After a fatal crash of one of its planes in 1929, Maddux merged his company with Transcontinental Air Transport (TAT); afterward, it became part of Transcontinental and Western Air (T&WA), the future Trans World Airlines (TWA). The ticket office was altered, then closed.

For Peters, though, these first projects for Feil and Paradise brought an unexpected windfall. Not only did he receive a much-needed boost of cash for the work, but, even before the Maddux office was fully completed, his employers had passed on to him a far more important commission: the interiors of the new Wilshire branch of Bullock's department store.

Bullock's Wilshire was a revolutionary undertaking—even by Los Angeles standards. The store's founder, John G. Bullock, had established the company's original store in 1907 in downtown Los Angeles, at Seventh Street and Broadway.[249] Bullock was a retailing visionary, and the store soon earned a reputation for superlative service and high-quality specialty merchandise.

In 1912, Bullock bought the adjacent six-story building, demolished it, and replaced it with a new ten-story structure that doubled the size of the store.[250] In 1917, he enlarged the store again, leasing an eight-story building on Hill Street and connecting it to the main block via a pedestrian bridge. Two years later, he added another nearby eight-story structure to the complex. Bullock's thus became the largest retail establishment on the West Coast.[251]

Despite the store's already enormous size, Bullock enlarged it several more times in the early 1920s. But by the middle of the decade, he and his business partner, P. G. Winnett, decided to pursue a different course. Recognizing that Los Angeles was now expanding rapidly to the west, they decided to open a branch store on what they believed was destined to become a new retail hub on Wilshire Boulevard.[252]

Hailed as the "Fabulous Boulevard" and the "Fifth Avenue of the West," Wilshire had already become, in the words of one observer, "the most traveled corridor in the most motorized town on earth."[253] The street was lined—or soon would be—with some of Los Angeles's most fully chic establishments: the Ambassador Hotel and its renowned Cocoanut Grove nightclub, in the 3400 block; the refined I. Magnin department store, in the 3200 block; and numerous other upscale restaurants, bars, and retail outlets.[254] (In 1934, Paul T. Frankl opened his first Los Angeles gallery nearby.) Bullock and Winnett purchased a large lot in the 3000 block and hired John and Donald B. Parkinson, Architects to design the new store.

It was a sound and unsurprising choice. The Parkinsons had one of the city's leading architecture firms. They had built a great many of Los Angeles's early landmarks, including the mammoth Memorial Coliseum and the city hall. Moreover, Bullock already had a business relationship with them: English-born John Parkinson had designed the first downtown Bullock's store, and he and son Donald worked jointly on the many subsequent additions.[255]

But the new Bullock's was to be something altogether different. Winnett, who as vice president of the company saw to the store's day-to-day operations, had been formulating plans for it as early as 1925. His initial concept was essentially to reproduce the original store at a smaller scale. After a visit to Europe that summer to see the Paris exposition, he rethought his plans. He decided that he wanted something similar to the Paris pavilions: exuberant, luxurious, and sophisticated. He also wanted certain "practical" adjustments, including outsized display windows and a large tower that would serve to draw in passing motorists.

The Parkinsons, inspired themselves by the possibilities of the new French aesthetic, were only too happy to oblige. (Donald had joined the throngs of Americans who journeyed to Paris to view the exhibition that summer; he, too, had returned buoyed by the experience and with a new sense of what modernism might offer.)[256]

The design of the structure was well underway by the middle of 1928. Excavations were started in late autumn, and by March of the following year, the first three stories of the steel frame had been set up.[257] The Parkinsons early on recognized that they needed a partner firm to fit out the interiors, to reach the heights of sumptuousness that Bullock and Winnett envisioned. Their choice fell—naturally—on Feil and Paradise, whose recently finished Oviatt Building, with its stylish modern spaces, was then the talk of the town. Feil and Paradise, in turn, asked Peters to take on some of the design work.

Peters would not work on the project alone. Bullock's appointed a young interior designer, Eleanor H. LeMaire, to oversee the job. Together she and Peters would fit out most of the spaces.

Born in Berkeley in 1897, LeMaire attended courses at the University of California and the Columbia University School of Architecture. She graduated from the Parsons School of Design in New York City, becoming one of the first American women with formal higher education in the fledgling field of interior design. She began her career in 1926 as a stylist in Bullock's Home Furnishings Department. Winnett and Bullock soon recognized her talent and asked her to make over and modernize the entire downtown store. When the job was completed, they assigned her to coordinate the decorating scheme for the new Wilshire store.[258]

LeMaire had a keen sense of what the job required. She had a good understanding of the latest modernist currents, and she saw the project as an opportunity to do something on the cutting edge. She also saw it as a chance to make her name, which it did. Her collaboration with Peters might have gone terribly wrong, since both had more-than-resolute personalities. Instead, their working relationship turned out to be surprisingly harmonious: Peters respected LeMaire's abilities and taste; she found in him a willing, gifted, and agile designer. Their relationship, though close, remained formal—they always addressed each other as Mr. or Mrs.—but they came to deeply respect and trust each other.

What guided them was a shared sense that the new Bullock's store needed to be both fresh and distinctive. Winnett wanted the Wilshire branch to be less a traditional department store with a full band of merchandise, than a series of upscale specialty shops housed under a single roof. This was especially true of the lower floors, which were to offer the more expensive merchandise. Winnett and Bullock were mindful of their prospective clientele: a large segment of the Hollywood film community lived in the neighborhoods nearby or up in the northern hills, and the new Bullock's was to be very definitely swank, with more exclusive merchandise than the main store, and, also, modern to the minute—a place for the city's fashionable elite to shop and to be seen in just the right surroundings.

One of the novel features of the new store involved how customers would enter. Winnett decided early on that the street side facing Wilshire Boulevard was to have a standard main entrance from the sidewalk, as expected. Peters recognized, though, that in a part of town where nearly everyone drove to get anywhere, the majority of the store's customers would arrive by automobile. He decided to place another principal entrance in the rear, facing a parking lot. If they so wished, shoppers could motor directly to the rear entry and leave their cars with a valet. It was a novel idea at the time—a significant alteration to the way such buildings were normally arranged.[259]

The Parkinsons first imagined the rear entry as a simple double door, with a sweeping canvas awning.[260] Early in the design process, however, with input from Winnett and LeMaire, they instead introduced a massive porte cochere, which would establish a grand entrance into the building and shield the store's smart clientele from the sun or rain.

The decision to introduce a dual entrance would have significant consequences for the ground-floor plan. The Parkinsons, in what was standard practice at a time when Beaux-Arts planning principles still reigned, placed the front and rear entries on an axis, creating an exceptionally long and broad gallery linking them. Close to the building's rear was a second axis, set perpendicular to the first, which extended nearly the full width of the store, connecting the principal shopping areas on the first level (fig. 140).

Peters's first task was to come up with a way to arrange and articulate the great entry hall. He sat down—straightaway after Feil and Paradise had asked him to work on the project—and, according to their instructions, rendered a more or less conventional version of a grand concourse (fig. 141). Exactly what happened next is not clear. Winnett and LeMaire apparently rejected the design out of hand and threatened to fire Feil and Paradise on the spot. Peters came to the rescue. Recognizing that the space had to be both appealing and functional—and very much more up-to-date than what Feil and Paradise had had in mind—he redesigned it, making it considerably more modern in look and feel, and inserting sales counters for perfumes and cosmetics along either side (fig. 142 top). Winnett and LeMaire loved the new design and insisted that much of the lower two floors be turned over to Peters, essentially sidestepping Feil and Paradise.

Peters immediately started work on most of the spaces on the lower two floors. The remaining areas, especially those on the third and fourth floors, were divided among several other designers. The plan was for Feil and Paradise to devise a portion of the ground floor housing the Accessories Department. LeMaire also engaged two other local

---

139. Jock Peters, Maddux Air Lines ticket office, Los Angeles, 1928. Side view with mural (photographed before the installation of the corner neon sign). Photography Collection, University of Southern California Library.

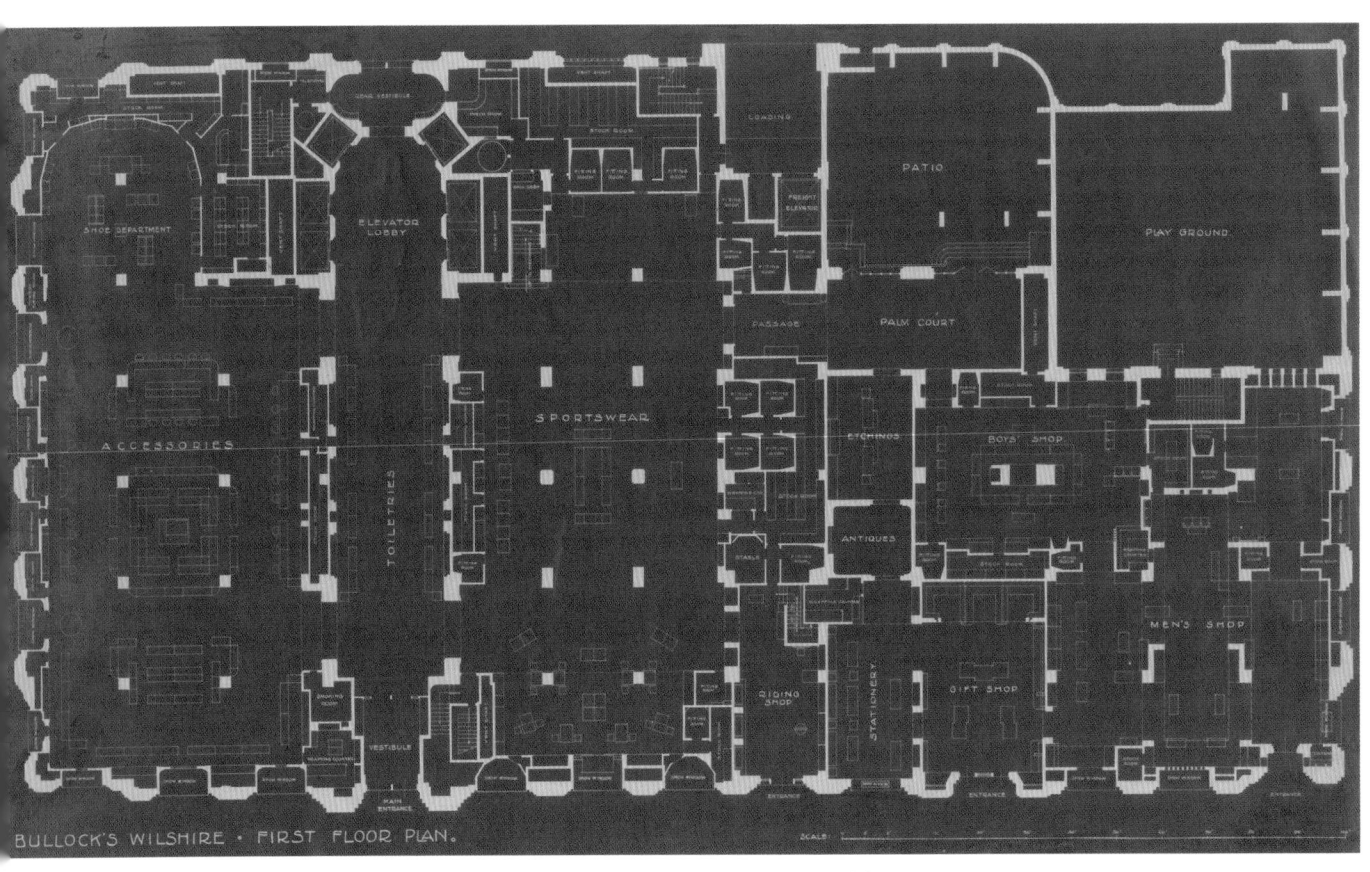

140. Parkinson and Parkinson, Bullock's Wilshire, Los Angeles, 1929. Plan, Print. UCSB.

141. Jock Peters, Bullock's Wilshire, Los Angeles, 1929.
Preliminary design for the lobby concourse.
Pencil on paper. Collection Jock de Swart.

143. Jock Peters, Bullock's Wilshire, Los Angeles, 1929.
Lobby concourse with the perfume area. UCSB.

142. Jock Peters, Bullock's Wilshire, Los Angeles, 1929.
Design for the lobby concourse. Print. Collection Jock de Swart (top).
Color photograph, 2007. Tim Street-Porter (bottom).

145. Jock Peters, Bullock's Wilshire, Los Angeles, 1929. Design for the elevator doors. Pencil and colored pencil on paper. Collection Jock de Swart.

144. Jock Peters, Bullock's Wilshire, Los Angeles, 1929. Elevators in the lobby concourse. Color photograph, 2007. Tim Street-Porter (top). Archival photograph. UCSB (bottom).

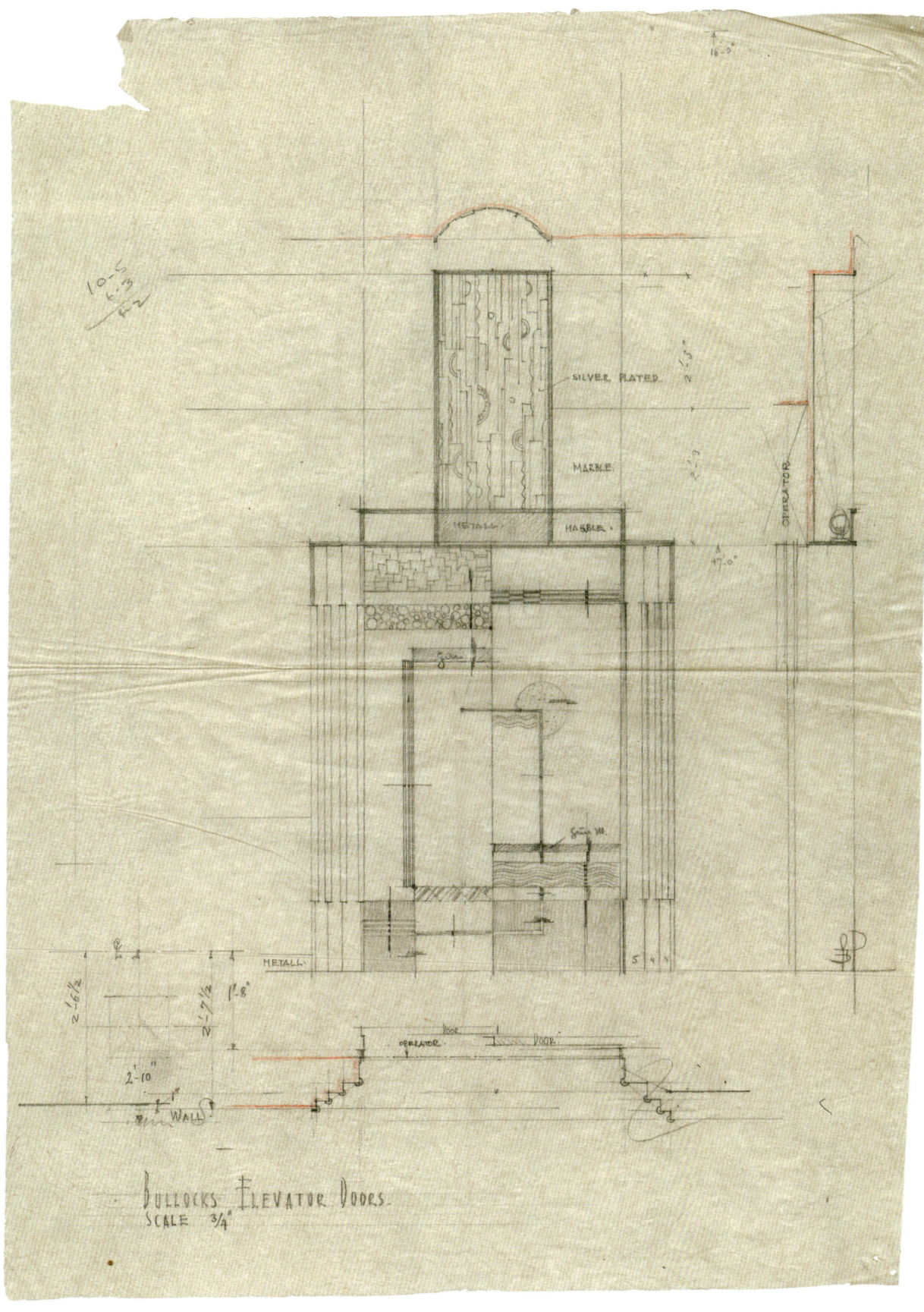

designers, John Weber (a recent Swiss-born immigrant) and David Collins, to create a few of the second-floor interiors, including the beauty salon.[261] Peters worked closely with LeMaire to plan the remainder of the interiors. Others, including LeMaire herself, were to decorate the remaining rooms, most of them on the upper floors.

The logic of dividing up the spaces among various designers was in part due to the short time available to complete the task. The decision was also a response to Winnett's insistence on making the sales areas as varied as possible: each designer was to bring his or her individual sensibility to the work. LeMaire also had the idea of engaging some of Los Angeles's leading artists to install original artworks throughout the store. Those she hired were mostly European-born immigrants recently arrived in Southern California, including Serbian-American painter and muralist Gjura Stojana and German artists Herman Sachs and Eugene Maier-Krieg.[262] LeMaire also purchased works from several artists living abroad, notably rugs from Russian émigré Sonia Delaunay and furnishings from Parisian designers Léon and Maurice Jallot.[263]

From the outset, LeMaire's overriding concern was to have each department reflect the character of the goods it was selling. She directed Peters and the other designers and artists to devise spaces and built-ins that related a visual narrative about the "emotionality" of the goods for sale in each area. Peters quickly grasped her concept: the nine rooms he came up with were fully differentiated—and evocative in just the way she intended.

His main entry hall, dominated by the Perfume Department, was a perfect response to the idea. It was open, welcoming, and unexpectedly incandescent (especially given the small size of the doors at either end; much of that brightness was achieved through Peters's assertive use of electric lighting in the display cases and on the walls and ceiling). The hallway was also, with its impressive monumentality, an immediate beacon of the store's ambitions (figs. 142 bottom, 143). The marble-clad walls (fashioned from a western stone called St. Genevieve Rose Marble) and the polished wood and glass vitrines Peters installed yielded an impression of refinement.[264] Even more, the elevators at the far end of the hall—immediately adjacent to the motor entry—underscored the store's intended aura of sophistication. Peters worked for some time on their design, eventually coming up with a scheme that combined various geometric forms with inlays and sumptuous materials (figs. 144, 145).

The speed of design and construction—the entire building and its full complement of interiors were completed in just over twelve months—necessitated changes to the usual working procedure. Rather than relying on outside fabricators, LeMaire and Peters set up an on-site workshop staffed with nearly a hundred artisans—experts in wood, glass, leatherworking, and tapestries—to craft what was required.[265] Peters personally oversaw the making of nearly every article for his designs.[266]

Once the project began, Peters worked on it continuously—to the exclusion of almost all else coming into his office. A great deal of his time was directed toward finding individual looks that resonated with what was being offered in each department. He did so in some instances with grand gestures, sometimes through the configuration of the spaces (large versus small, closed versus open), and also through fine-tuning their details. He made recourse to sundry palettes of forms and materials (differing woods, or woods contrasting with metals, for instance) and varied ways of displaying the merchandise (on open shelves or in closed vitrines). And in each department, he used specific imagery associated with what was being sold.

He was concerned, too, with fostering a sense of continuity and movement. In a large building made up of rooms for different purposes and of varying shapes and sizes, he was careful to indicate the pathways and transitions. Evidence of this can be seen at the intersection between the store's two main axes. Peters introduced noticeable alterations in the floor patterning—he set elongated rectangles perpendicular to those in the main hall—to draw shoppers' attention to the change in direction (fig. 146). Above, a light fixture extending in inverted stair-step fashion from the ceiling to the upper wall similarly presented a visual signal of changeover.

Just beyond the main concourse was the Sportswear Department, one of the three main spaces on the ground floor. It was perhaps Peters's most successful design. He gave it a soft, muted, and clubby look (fig. 147). Extending along nearly the full length of the west sidewall was a massive installation by Stojana, part mural, part abstract relief. Titled *The Spirit of Sports*, the work (still extant) was intended as an expression, as Pauline Schindler (R. M. Schindler's wife and frequent writer on local modern architecture and design) described, "of action, speed, movement."[267] Stojana assembled it out of a hodgepodge of techniques and materials, including colorful frescoes and thin strips of wood veneer with silvered highlights.[268]

To one side of the room, Peters placed an ample seating area, complete with cozy sofas and chairs. Much of the merchandise was displayed in glazed niches set into the walls and executed in sycamore, in a warm brown tone, and

146. Jock Peters, Bullock's Wilshire, Los Angeles, 1929.
Lobby concourse looking toward the Sportswear Department.
UCSB.

148. Jock Peters, Bullock's Wilshire, Los Angeles, 1929. Sportswear Department with vitrines and Gjura Stojana's mural on the left. UCSB.

147. Jock Peters, Bullock's Wilshire, Los Angeles, 1929. Sportswear Department with Gjura Stojana's mural. UCSB.

150. Jock Peters, display table from the Sportswear Department, Bullock's Wilshire, Los Angeles, 1929. Mahogany, zebrawood, sycamore, and other woods. Gift Decorative Arts and Design Council Fund in honor of Rose Tarlow and others receiving the 2010 Design Leadership Award. Los Angeles County Museum of Art.

149. Jock Peters, Bullock's Wilshire, Los Angeles, 1929. Accessories area in the Sportswear Department. UCSB.

edged with copper. There were also frameless vitrines set on wooden bases (figs. 148, 149). To highlight the merchandise and generate a warm ambience, Peters took advantage of varied ways of bringing light into the room: lamps, sconces, partially illuminated columns, and inset ceiling fixtures.

His multilayered approach served to make the opulent materials look even richer. It also allowed him to differentiate the space, cutting it into discrete sections. The individual furnishings extended the play of geometric forms in Stojana's mural. Peters also designed several wood display tables with inlays that repeated his language of restless dynamism (fig. 150).

From the Sportswear Department, one could enter directly into the Riding Shop through one of several portals "signed" with a wood inlay of a horse head (fig. 151). This space was smaller, and it was considerably brighter. The walls were chalk white, and the room was illuminated by large street-side windows and continuous cove lighting (fig. 152). On the walls were plaster reliefs fashioned by Maier-Krieg (who executed them free-form) depicting scenes of horsemanship and hunting. Most of the other architectonic elements were sharply formed and reduced.

In what was surely a deliberate gesture on Peters's part, the Riding Shop had an almost domestic feel (fig. 153); its more intimate scale stood in marked contrast to the much bigger sportswear and lobby areas. It was perhaps a nod to the idea that visitors needed a sense of relief and quiet after strolling through the larger rooms. A staircase along the west wall led up to a loggia, as in a villa; in the small space above, Peters installed the "Doggery," dedicated to pricey accessories for canines.

Immediately adjacent to the Riding Shop (but closed off from it) were the Stationery Department and Gift Shop, the latter accessible directly from the street. Here Peters opted for yet another design palette, one that relied largely on primary forms—circles, squares, triangles, and spheres (fig. 154). The furniture and vitrines—direct and regular—suggested an upscale office environment. More than the other downstairs sales areas, the space also conveyed the impression of a small, independent specialty shop.

The large Menswear and adjoining Boys' Departments, which occupied most of the building's west end, were again different in look and feel. A double door led in from Wilshire Boulevard past one of Peters's most extraordinary installations: a pair of massive radiator covers (figs. 155, 156). Executed in wood and metal, with display stands and towering light fixtures set on them, they were fully in accord with his personal vision, a lively assemblage of solids, voids, and continuous lines.

Everything in the space, whether built in or freestanding, offered examples of modern form-making (fig. 157, 158). There were the "textile blocks" arrayed along the upper walls' edges (an homage to—or perhaps more accurately, an unabashed "borrowing" from—Frank Lloyd Wright's Southern California houses); light fixtures, with a recognizably De Stijl arrangement; and tubular steel chairs à la Marcel Breuer (if moderated through the application of brightly colored upholstery).

The fact that so many of the space's features were in some way "appropriated" does not obscure the novelty of Peters's achievement. It was not just that he brought all these diverse sources together, recasting them and contriving thereby an improbable modernist concoction, eclectic yet also somehow holistic; he also produced many individual elements that were, in their own way, powerfully expressive of the contemporary aesthetic.

A display table he designed for the Menswear Department offers a telling example of his ideas (fig. 159). It is tightly composed and well proportioned. In stylistic terms, it is, like the adjoining larger space, splendidly mingled: the continuous linear pulls of the drawers are a pure modernist gesture befitting the leading contemporary German designers' penchant for primary forms; the tabletop, with its set-back edge, resembles the works of Émile-Jacques Ruhlmann; and the metal striations separating the drawers, and the curved, banded leg have an American look, taken perhaps most nearly from Donald Deskey and Eugene Schoen. The desk is as composite as the room.

Peters did not disregard the practicalities of designing in the commercial sphere. He paid close attention to how things worked, how customers could be enticed to buy. Lost to some degree in the old photographs is the sheer novelty of how the displays worked. Because LeMaire and the store's bosses placed such priority on the customers' experience, Peters and the other designers were challenged to come up with new ways to present the wares, especially clothing and larger accessories. Often, Peters placed objects

151. Jock Peters, Bullock's Wilshire, Los Angeles, 1929. Entry to the Riding Shop from the Sportswear Department. UCSB.

Following pages – left:
152. Jock Peters, Bullock's Wilshire, Los Angeles, 1929. Riding Shop. UCSB.

Following pages – right:
153. Jock Peters, Bullock's Wilshire, Los Angeles, 1929. Stair to the mezzanine in the Riding Shop. UCSB.

in flat glass cases or on rosewood stands. (The store, following the traditions of Parisian couture, also presented the clothes on live mannequins.) What he painstakingly avoided were standard clothes racks, which would have interfered with the sight lines and rendered the whole ordinary. Peters was particularly inventive when it came to the display of individual objects. At times, he simply draped pieces on surfaces or wove them through hoops attached to a vertical pole (see fig. 155). In the men's shoes area, he devised an elegant, three-tiered stand that could display not only the shoes, but also matching socks and gloves (fig. 160). One of his most ingenious devices was an adjustable, wall-mounted clothing hanger (figs. 161, 162). A horizontal rod could be extended outward to hang multiple articles. There was a hook below and a rounded-over "button" on the top to hold a hat or a cap. Peters also designed an impressive range of vitrines, some wall mounted, others set on stands or solid bases. Every piece was custom-made—even the dressing mirrors. A large freestanding mirror with chevrons was one of the standouts (fig. 163).

And yet, despite the ebullience of the installations, what is most striking is the extent to which Peters relied more on reduction than excess. The design of the Shoe Department on the ground floor is notable precisely because so few shoes are visible (fig. 164). A great deal more prominent were the sophisticated chairs and settees that filled most of the space.

Upstairs, on the second and third floors, were several additional areas Peters designed or contributed to. They were, on the whole, more functional in appearance. The large Lingerie Department, for example, retained a degree of elegance, but it was more conventional in its presentation of merchandise (fig. 165). And the same was true of the Collegienne Shoe Department, which featured less expensive footwear for younger women (figs. 166, 167). Peters collaborated with LeMaire and John Weber on one of the most arresting spaces, the second-floor "Salon of Beauty." Like the Collegienne Shoe Department, it had tubular steel furnishings (among the earliest installed in a commercial space in the United States). Peters designed the overscaled couches, the floor pattern, and some of the detailing (figs. 168, 169).

It is tempting to say that the hybrid nature of the installations is pure Peters—boldly eclectic and compelling. In a sense, of course, that is true. At the same time, they were a reflection of the company's ambitions to be modern and appealing, a set of stylistic gestures intended to be so exuberant and so varied as to please everyone—a very smart retailing strategy. They spoke to a wider enthusiasm for the new, which was especially evident in Los Angeles, a city where novelty was as firmly and happily embraced as anywhere in the nation.

Still, this misses something essential: Peters's design was not merely a commercial gesture or an echo of the city's vital modernity. The store's lower floors—even those spaces for which he was not responsible—formed a complete tableau. The interiors were for him a discourse about the very nature of modernity. By this time, he had come to view contemporary life as a fête of possibilities, a new world in which very much was now possible, and any attempt to limit it misguided. In Bullock's, Peters fulfilled the exigencies of retailing; even more, though, he expressed his belief in a splendid multifariousness. Modern life, he again seems to be saying to us, is too diverse and too rapidly changing to be expressed as one note.

His ambitions for the design were not lost on contemporary commentators. Arthur Millier, the art and design critic for the *Los Angeles Times*, commended Peters for his "interplay of thoughts and needs"—his understanding, in other words, of the need to ally function and form in a manner befitting an upscale retailer.[269] The most insightful and far-seeing commentary, though, came from Pauline Schindler, writing in *California Arts and Architecture*:

> Bullocks [sic] Wilshire is a significant contribution to the culture of our generation. . . . The interior shows an amazing fecundity of creative vitality. . . . [T]he countless units so good that they are arresting, there [are] only architectural forms moving with dignity and superb flow into one another; lighting fixtures, chairs, units for the showing of wares—every detail designed for its place . . . a fine integration, a harmony of a thousand individual parts.[270]

---

154. Jock Peters, Bullock's Wilshire, Los Angeles, 1929. Stationery Department and Gift Shop. UCSB.

155. Jock Peters, Bullock's Wilshire, Los Angeles, 1929. Entrance to Menswear Department. UCSB.

156. Jock Peters, radiator cover in the Menswear Department, Bullock's Wilshire, Los Angeles, 1929. Mahogany and metal. Courtesy Thanks for the Memories (hereafter TFTM), Los Angeles.

BULLOCK'S WILSHIRE 181

157. Jock Peters, Bullock's Wilshire, Los Angeles, 1929. Menswear Department. UCSB.

159. Jock Peters, display table in the Menswear Department, Bullock's Wilshire, Los Angeles, 1929. Mahogany and metal. Courtesy TFTM, Los Angeles.

158. Jock Peters, Bullock's Wilshire, Los Angeles, 1929. Menswear Department. UCSB.

161–162. Jock Peters, clothes display device (closed and extended), Bullock's Wilshire, Los Angeles, 1929. Brass and nickel. Courtesy TFTM, Los Angeles.

163. Jock Peters, mirror, Bullock's Wilshire, Los Angeles, 1929. Painted wood, metal, and glass. Courtesy Historical Design, Inc., New York.

160. Jock Peters, Bullock's Wilshire, Los Angeles, 1929. Shoe display and fitting area in the Menswear Department. UCSB.

164. Jock Peters, Bullock's Wilshire, Los Angeles, 1929.
Shoe Department. Perspective. Print on paper. UCSB.

165. Jock Peters, Bullock's Wilshire, Los Angeles, 1929.
Lingerie Department on the second floor. Perspective.
Print on paper. UCSB.

166. Jock Peters, Bullock's Wilshire, Los Angeles, 1929.
Collegienne Shoe and Millinery Departments.
Plan and elevations. Print on paper. UCSB.

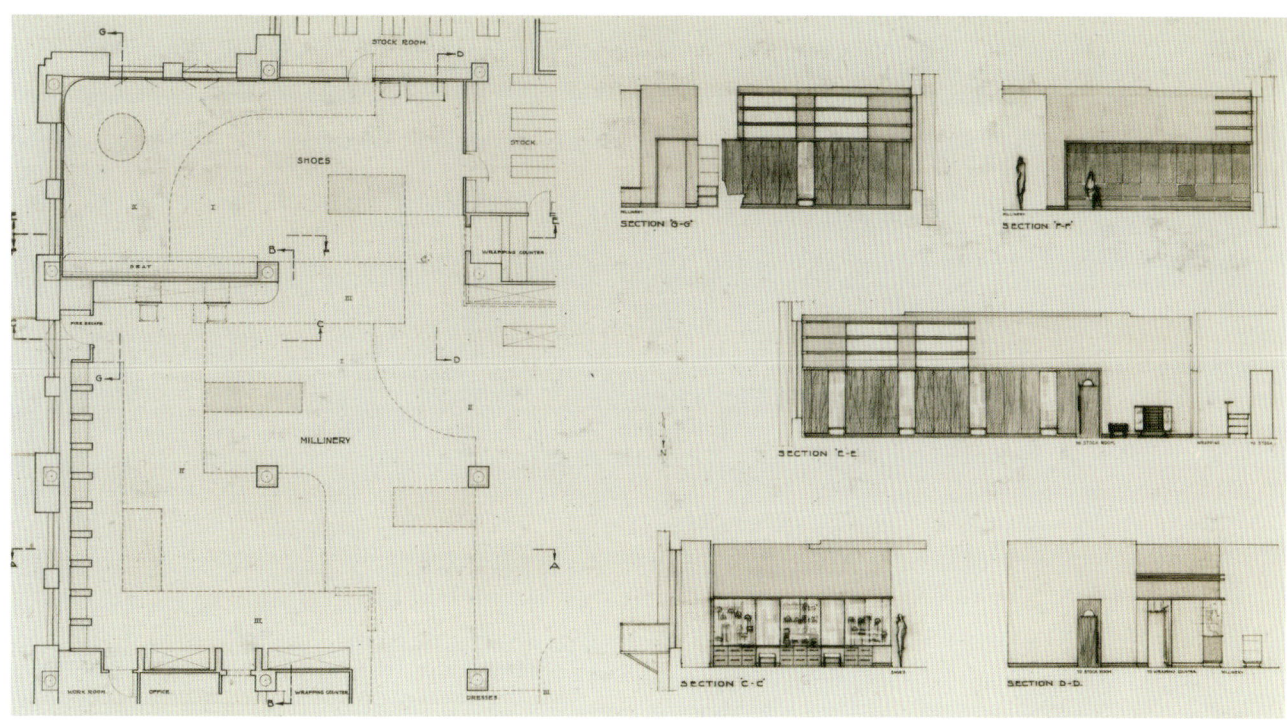

167. Jock Peters, Bullock's Wilshire, Los Angeles, 1929. Collegienne Shoe Department. UCSB.

168. Eleanor LeMaire and John Weber, with Jock Peters, Bullock's Wilshire, Los Angeles, 1929. Salon of Beauty. UCSB.

169. Jock Peters, Bullock's Wilshire, Los Angeles, 1929. Preliminary sketch for the sofa in the Salon of Beauty. Colored chalk on paper. Collection Jock de Swart.

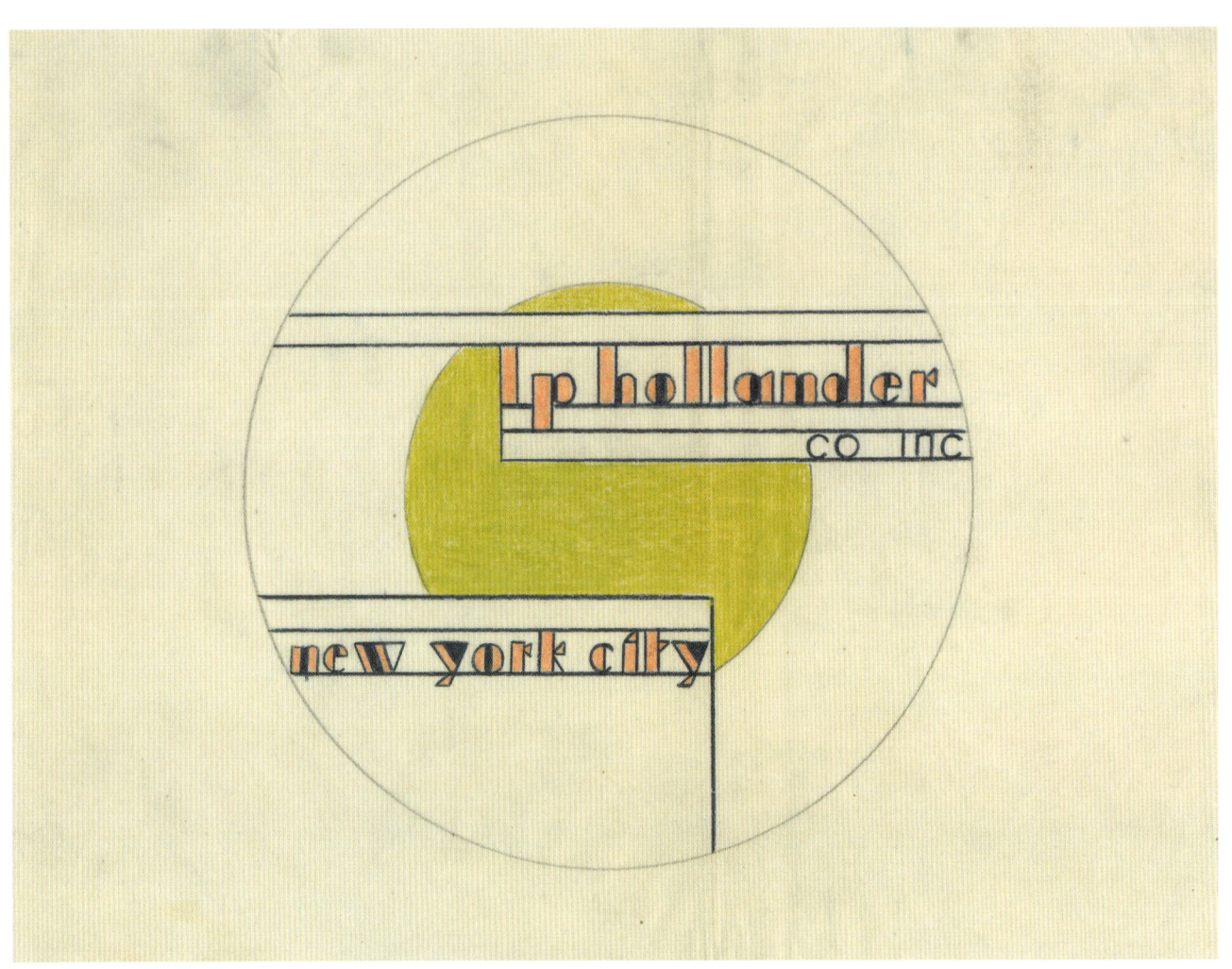

Chapter 9 |
HOLLANDER

The opening of Bullock's Wilshire in the fall of 1929 did much to burnish Peters's local reputation. For the first time, too, he began to be known nationally. His winning entries for S. Karpen & Brothers and Mohawk Carpet Mills had lent him a small degree of prestige. But the many feature stories about Bullock's Wilshire that appeared in major publications soon after the store's completion finally brought him some renown among the general public and real fame within the narrow world of modern designers.[271] Peters wanted very much to build on his success.

Even while work on Bullock's was ongoing, he had been making efforts to put his creative products and ideas before the public. In the late fall of 1928, he had a small exhibition of his designs at Frank Lloyd Wright's Hollyhock House, where the California Art Club regularly mounted shows.[272] That same fall, Peters's designs were also included in the ambitious *Decorative Arts of Today* exhibition at the Bullock's downtown store. The show featured works by most of the leading Los Angeles modernists, including Neutra, Schindler, and Kem Weber.[273] The exhibition was covered extensively in the local media, and it drew throngs of viewers eager to see the latest trends.[274]

The downtown Bullock's exhibition and the opening of the new Wilshire Boulevard store were a coming-out of sorts for Peters; from that time on, he was part of the Los Angeles modernist scene. He relished belonging to a larger community of artists. He accepted offers to speak whenever he could, and he enjoyed having his work shown alongside that of other modernists. It was a sign, Peters thought, that he had made it at last.

Socially, however, he remained apart. He met up occasionally with Weber and Lloyd Wright, but he kept his distance from most of the other local architects and designers. He and Herta were never comfortable in the smart crowd of artists and intellectuals that gathered at Schindler's Kings Road house, and they avoided Neutra and his wife, Dione, whom they found haughty and distant.[275] They saw Jacob Asanger and J. R. Davidson—both German émigrés—from time to time, though never on a regular basis. Peters also met Frank Lloyd Wright during one of his visits to the area, but Peters was not part of that world, either. When most of the local modernists went for after-work drinks at Jake Zeitlin's downtown bookstore, the main gathering space of the

170. Jock Peters, drawing for a hatbox, L. P. Hollander Company store, New York, 1930. Pencil and colored pencil on paper. UCSB.

Los Angeles avant-gardists, or at nearby watering holes, Peters usually headed home. He was not antisocial; he simply preferred to spend time with Herta and the children.[276]

He and Herta were especially devoted to each other. They enjoyed every quiet moment they could sit together and talk. Their conversations ran the full spectrum, recounting the day's events and gossiping about people they encountered. They had long discussions about art, music, and literature. Herta more than matched her husband's bent for aesthetic topics, and they shared a love of all things cultural. Despite her rationed early education, Herta read incessantly and was acutely curious. The two were usually happy to be on their own, away from the larger modernist scene.

Peters's health also must have played some role in his self-chosen isolation. His lungs had improved since his arrival from Germany, but he still tired easily. He was often exhausted by the end of the workday. He never openly complained about his health problems, but their impact was obvious to anyone who knew him.

Through the first half of 1929, Peters was working feverishly to complete the Bullock's project. The publicity for the new store meant that more commissions were now coming into his office. Peters tried to manage by himself, but the volume of work made it impossible. He knew he needed help. After some thought, he decided to form a partnership with a local architect by the name of W. F. Ruck.

William Frederick—originally Wilhelm Friedrich—Ruck was yet another German émigré. He had arrived in Los Angeles in February 1924, not long after Peters. He bounced around the local architectural scene for several years, working in various offices.[277] Peters knew him from the German-speaking art and design community; he thought that joining forces with Ruck, a capable and serious-minded practitioner with rigorous German training and a kindred outlook, made good sense. They agreed to establish a partnership in August 1929.[278]

Ruck moved into Peters's office in the Fine Arts Building. But after toiling for years to earn a reputation, Peters was hardly willing to give Ruck equal billing. Peters's logo—his initials entwined with an ankh—remained on the door, and his name stayed at the top of the firm's letterhead (figs. 171, 172). He did make one concession: Peters listed both his and Ruck's names on the same line as partners on the firm's Christmas card he designed for 1929 in a bid to advertise their new partnership (fig. 173).

The timing for their new venture, as it turned out, was hardly auspicious. The collapse of the stock market on Wall Street occurred just days before the new partners began

171. Interior of Jock Peters's office in the Fine Arts Building, downtown Los Angeles, c. 1929. Collection Jock de Swart.

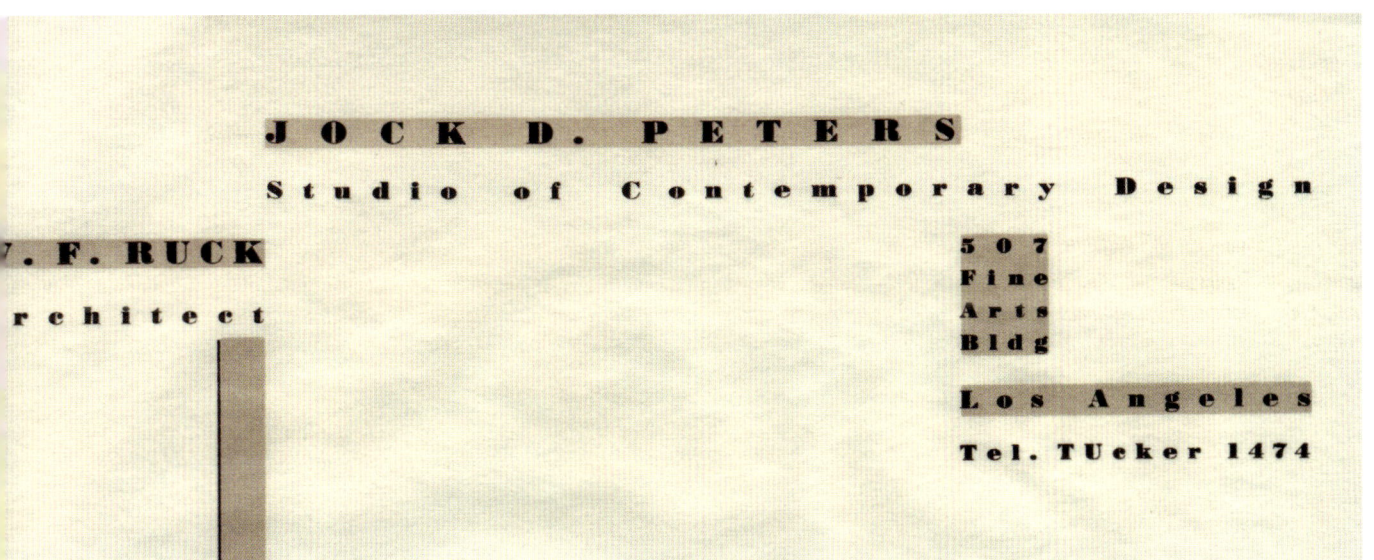

172. Letterhead for Jock Peters's Studio of Contemporary Design, 1929. Collection Jock de Swart.

mailing out their Christmas cards. At first, Peters barely noticed. At the time of the Wall Street crash, there was an exhibit of his drawings at the new Bullock's Wilshire, putting him in the spotlight once more.

Los Angeles Times critic Arthur Millier gave his work a full-column rave review. Included in the exhibit were Peters's renderings for the store's interiors, as well as some of his film sets, among them those he had created for *The City of the Future* and *Mars*. Millier, though, was especially drawn to a group of six drawings "for an art education center," which, he thought, might form the locus of an "outstanding scientific and artistic institution" yet to come.[279] Millier was unaware that the drawings for the futuristic complex were those that Peters had prepared in 1921 for the school in Altona, with new labels in English glued over the original German ones (fig. 174). Peters's Mendelsohnian streamlined forms from eight years before still looked fresh—at least in the American context.

But there were darkening skies in the distance. After the completion of Bullock's Wilshire, Peters had terminated his agreement of cooperation with Feil and Paradise. The move was not entirely cordial, because Peters had resented their meddling while the work was ongoing. He was also more than a little miffed when he learned from Eleanor LeMaire that Feil and Paradise, in a bid to harvest all the credit for Bullock's, were conducting a whispering campaign around town implying that the store's interiors had been largely their work and that Peters had, in their telling, only a minor role in their realization.

173. Christmas Card for Jock Peters's Studio of Contemporary Design, 1929. Collection Erika Plack.

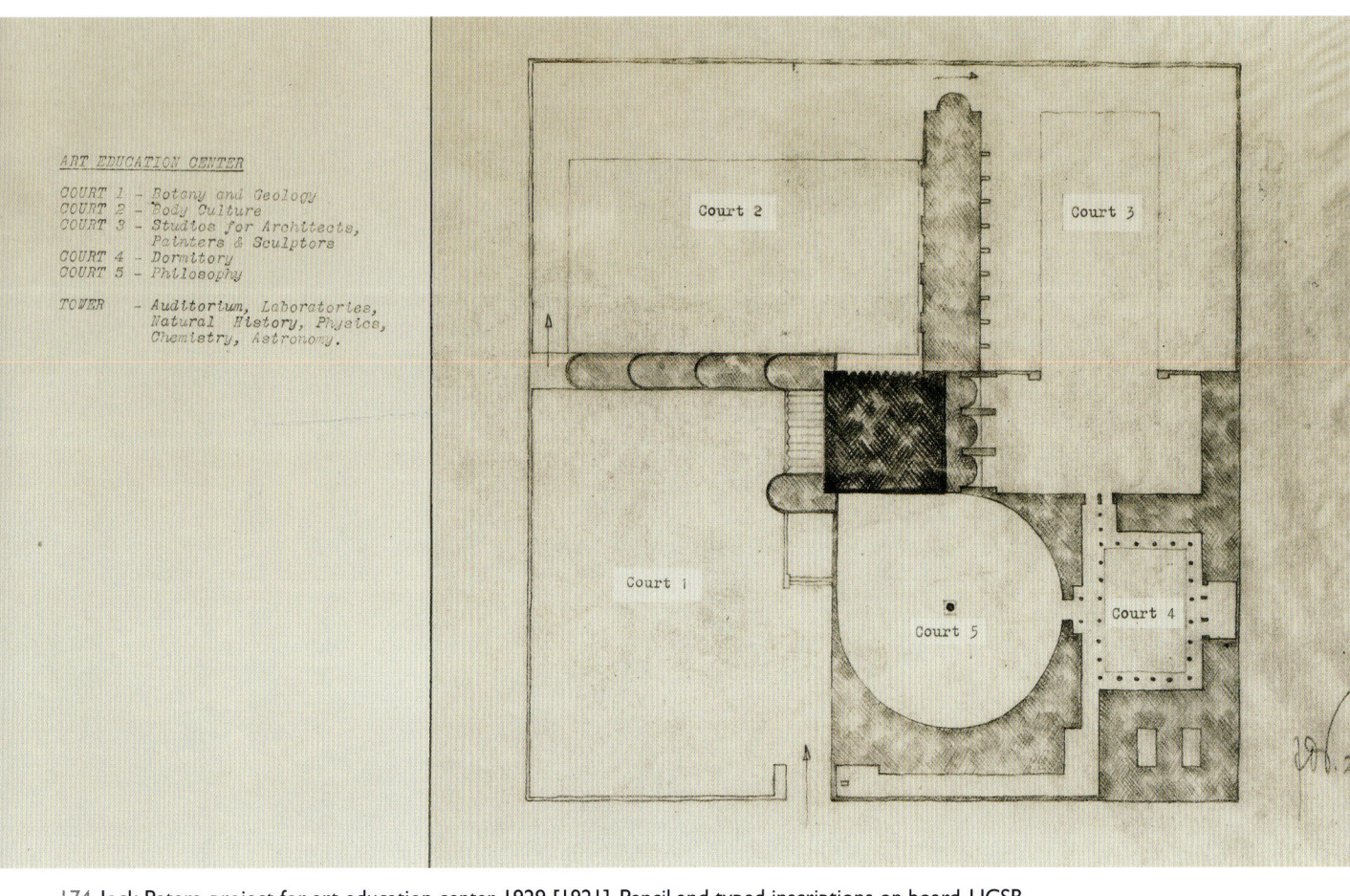

174. Jock Peters, project for art education center, 1929 [1921]. Pencil and typed inscriptions on board. UCSB.

Even worse for Peters, suddenly there was almost no new work coming into his office. The freewheeling days of the late 1920s, when finding clients had, at last, become relatively easy for him, were over. And neither he nor anyone else knew how long the economic slump would last.

The single beacon of good fortune was a new commission, which sustained him through most of 1930 and helped to cement his reputation: the design of the interiors for the decidedly upscale L. P. Hollander women's clothing store in New York City.

The lead came from LeMaire. After the opening of Bullock's, she had decided to move to New York City and launch her own practice, specializing in store interiors. Before leaving, she and Peters, who had both enjoyed their collaboration, made an informal agreement to work together on any new retail projects that either one might secure. For Peters, it turned out to be a very good arrangement.

Almost immediately after LeMaire arrived in New York, in early January 1930, she caught wind of an announcement that the L. P. Hollander store was erecting a new building in Manhattan at 3 East Fifty-Seventh Street. She made an appointment with the store's president, a man named Clarence G. Sheffield, to pitch the idea that she and Peters might do the interiors.[280] Their prospects seemed unlikely: Hollander, as she wrote to Peters, was "an old conservative firm originally from Boston," not at all disposed to modern design.[281]

The L. P. Hollander Company, at first glance, did seem an unlikely client. Dressmaker Mrs. Louis P. Hollander (née Maria Theresa Baldwin) had founded the firm in New York City in 1848, after her husband's business had failed. Together, they moved the store to Boston. There Hollander and her sons (who soon replaced their father in the day-to-day running of the shop) expanded the business to include imported European fashions, and, beginning in the 1890s, they opened branches in New York, Palm Beach, and Pasadena.

The company remained a bastion of old-money respectability until 1929, when Theodore, the last of the surviving sons, sold his interest. Sheffield became the store's president, and he immediately began to consider ways to update the store's image and enhance its profitability.

175. Jock Peters, L. P. Hollander Company store, New York, 1930. Presentation drawing for the first floor. From *A Folio of Pictures Showing the L. P. Hollander Co. in Its New Home at 3 East 57 Street* (New York: L. P. Hollander, 1930), n.p. Collection Jock de Swart.

He decided to move the New York store to East Fifty-Seventh Street, then developing into an upscale shopping district. He signed a commercial lease for the site of the former August Van Horne Stuyvesant House and hired Shreve, Lamb & Harmon—who shortly thereafter would begin work on the Empire State Building—to design the new structure.[282]

Despite engaging a progressive firm to create the shell of the new retail outlet, Hollander's had an established and long-standing reputation for traditionalist fashions and elaborate period showrooms. It seemed doubtful the company would opt for modern interiors. At her first meeting with Sheffield, however, LeMaire learned that he was thinking about breaking with the company's past. He was, he told her, "very much interested in having an artistic job done," and modern was, in his word, a "possibility." LeMaire wrote excitedly to Peters on January 13, giving him the details of the planned layout and asking him to draw up some proposals.[283]

They began a furious back-and-forth correspondence, with LeMaire offering rapid-fire suggestions and cautions. In one telegram, she wrote,

AVOID ANY REFERENCE TO OR REPETITION OF DESIGN AND MATERIALS USED IN [Bullock's] WILSHIRE WHEN CONSIDERING SIMILAR DEPARTMENTS HOLLANDERS STOP FOR COLLEGIENNE HAVE IDEA OF SAND BLASTED GLASS PARTITION STOP BELIEVE IT WILL BE NECESSARY TO APPEASE HOLLANDERS CONSERVATISM BY BEING PREPARED TO DO THIRD FLOOR DRESS PERIOD STYLE.[284]

As quickly as he could, Peters drew up a series of presentation boards for the proposed seven floors of retail space. LeMaire presented them to Sheffield in a meeting in mid-February (figs. 175–177).

On February 19, while Sheffield was still considering their proposal, Peters wrote to LeMaire—in his still not fully idiomatic English—that he was concerned about the very short time line given to complete the job:

When I read your letter of February 13th where you mentioned the completion date of September 15th and the completing of designs by May 1st, I nearly fell down from my chair because if you want to do seven floors in this length of time—March to April—you just have one week for each floor. Considering long distance, mailing of sketches, some misunderstanding and full size detailing it seems to be almost impossible for this work to be accurate and sincere, the way we did it at Bullock's, so we really have to think of some short cuts.[285]

176. Jock Peters, L. P. Hollander Company store, New York, 1930. Presentation drawing for the fifth floor. From *A Folio of Pictures Showing the L. P. Hollander Co. in Its New Home at 3 East 57 Street* (New York: L. P. Hollander, 1930), n.p. Collection Jock de Swart.

Peters suggested that he might travel to New York and produce some additional drawings, which they could present to Sheffield for immediate approval.[286] LeMaire, ignoring for the moment Peters's concerns, responded that the drawings he had prepared—which by then had arrived in New York—"look like a million dollars" and that "even the . . . conservative . . . [Sheffield] felt the sincerity of their design and he is opposed to all 'things modern.'" She also reported that the budget for the job was "not to exceed $250,000" for the twenty-eight-thousand square feet of space, putting the cost per square foot at "about $10," nearly double the standard construction budget for retail in New York.[287]

Three days later, on February 24, LeMaire jubilantly wired Peters that they had won the job:

MR. SHEFFIELD HAS DECIDED THAT HE WANTS YOU TO DO THE DESIGNING FOR AT LEAST THE MAJORITY OF THE FLOORS AND I BELIEVE IT IS DESIRABLE FOR YOU TO COME TO NEW YORK AT ONCE STOP.[288]

Peters caught the next cross-country train, arriving in Manhattan just three days after receiving the news, despite a long delay in Chicago due to a snowstorm. Over the next several weeks, he and LeMaire worked closely on every detail of the project. Ruck, whom Peters had left in charge of the office in Los Angeles, began working on the detail drawings. They also hired John Weber, whose work on the Bullock's project had impressed them both, along with another man, to assist them.[289]

Peters remained in New York for nearly a month, collaborating with LeMaire on the ideas for every area of the store. After they had tackled most of the conceptual work and some of the detailing, Peters returned to Los Angeles to complete the final drawings. He was again delayed for hours by snow in Chicago and finally arrived home, tired but relieved, on the evening of March 27.[290]

While he was still in New York, Peters had received word from Ruck that they were under consideration for another commission, the design of a Chevrolet automobile dealership in the Los Angeles suburb of Wilmington, near Long Beach.[291] Peters and Ruck hastily drew up a proposal, which got them the job, and they began working on it on the side.

With so much to do for the Hollander store and the time short, Peters and LeMaire decided to farm out a portion of the work, especially for the furniture and display cases. They contracted with several Los Angeles manufacturers, including the Vernon Fixtures and Cabinet Company, to make the

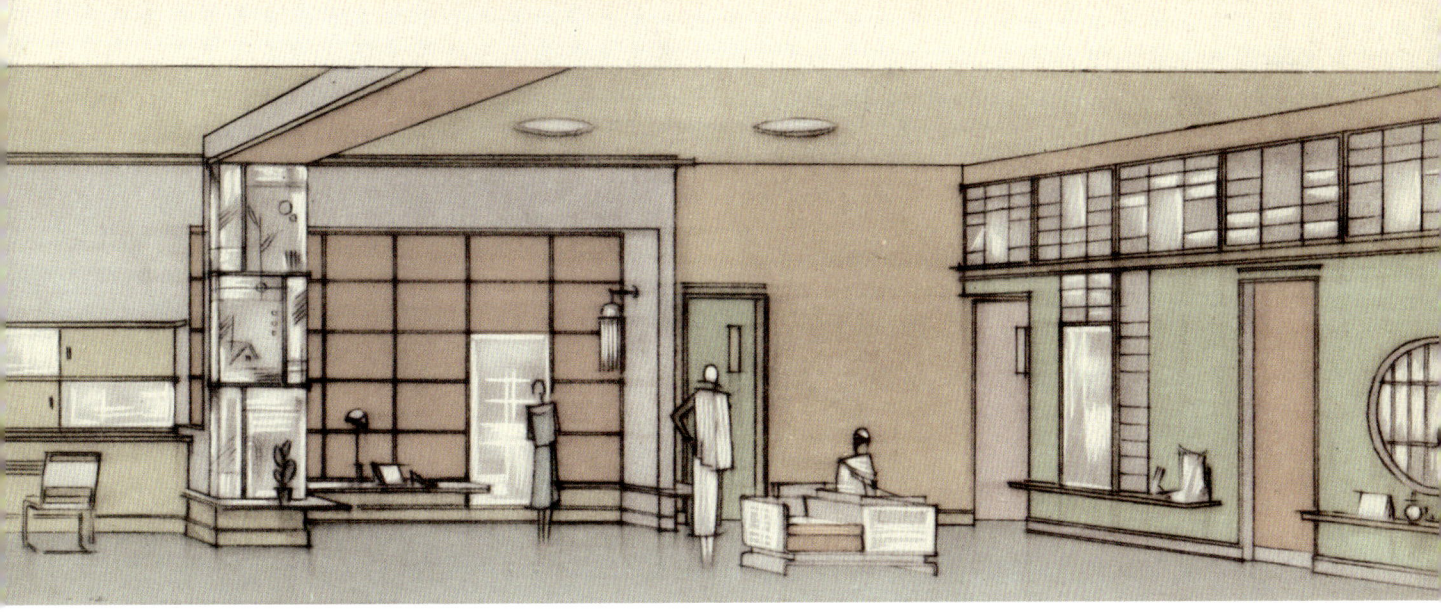

177. Jock Peters, L. P. Hollander Company store, New York, 1930. Presentation drawing for the seventh floor. *From A Folio of Pictures Showing the L. P. Hollander Co. in Its New Home at 3 East 57 Street* (New York: L. P. Hollander, 1930), n.p.
Collection Jock de Swart.

pieces. LeMaire also wrote to the architect Paul R. Williams, asking him if he would consider designing some chairs "that are fine enough for sophisticated New Yorkers."[292] Williams responded that he would deliver some sketches. On April 15, LeMaire sent Williams instructions for carrying out an array of seating models for the different floors, as well as several tables.[293] The Vernon Fixtures and Cabinet Company quickly fabricated the designs.

Throughout April, Peters and LeMaire worked on design ideas for the building's lower façade. Neither was happy with Shreve, Lamb & Harmon's design. They were particularly concerned about the street-level display windows, because they lacked awnings and were open on the inside. But those were only some of the many problems they would face; over the following weeks and months, while separated by a full continent, they corresponded almost daily, seeking solutions for the large, complex project.

Their letters are remarkable, filled with day-to-day observations about the contemporary design scene, things they saw or people they met—a time capsule of American modernism's early days. LeMaire, in one letter written in late April, mentions that she had just visited an exhibition of the work of Peter Behrens at the Brooklyn Museum, curated by the young American modernist William Muschenheim. She asks Peters whether he might want to help bring the show of his one-time boss to Los Angeles.[294] (He was at first enthusiastic but nothing came of the idea.) Later, on May 15, LeMaire informs Peters that a new booklet put out by Feil and Paradise documenting "their projects" included "a complete set of Bullocks-Wilshire photographs," which served only to infuriate him further.[295]

In another letter, LeMaire tells Peters that she had dinner with Muschenheim and a mutual friend and that, afterward, they went together to a meeting of AUDAC, the American Union of Decorative Artists and Craftsmen.

Started by Paul T. Frankl, Frederick Kiesler, and others two years before, the organization was an effort to bring together the country's modernist designers and manufacturers. LeMaire reports to Peters that she was "not very favorably impressed." She adds, "It seems that three or four of the leading spirits have plans of their own to carry out and I do not believe that any of the other members would have very much of a chance. Of course, I may change my opinion but I will keep you informed. Meanwhile I think it is best for us not to join this Association."[296]

Peters and LeMaire continued debating the merits of the organization, especially in light of AUDAC's campaign involving the 1933 Century of Progress International Exposition in Chicago, but their correspondence after that time was mostly consumed with the minutiae of getting the Hollander job done.[297] To aid LeMaire with the detail drawings and installation, they decided that Weber should go to New York. He flew east in late April and took up residence in LeMaire's small office on lower Fifth Avenue.[298]

Peters and Ruck, putting in long hours in Los Angeles, completed the first, fifth, and seventh floors by the end of June. Weber and LeMaire were doing all they could to oversee the contractors and craftspeople hired to fabricate and install the furnishings and built-ins. Peters engaged his brother George, with his cabinetmaker's eye, to check the details and to coordinate with the Vernon Fixtures and Cabinet Company to ensure that the designs being made there were executed properly.[299] The speed with which they were working created innumerable problems. Weber spent a great deal of his time simply trying to keep the contractors on schedule and seeing to it that the work was up to the quality they wanted; LeMaire was constantly called on to mediate between suppliers and fabricators.

Despite the many snags, most of the design work was completed by mid-August. Peters and Ruck rendered every facet of the complex installations in exhaustive detail, dispatching each drawing to LeMaire by express courier as soon as it was finished. She, in turn, made small changes before handing them off to Weber, the artisans, and workmen. Finally, in early September, Peters traveled back to New York to attend to the last details. Three weeks later, on September 24, the store had its official opening.

What visitors saw that evening was one of the most lavish modern commercial interiors in the United States—very much on par with what Peters and LeMaire had accomplished for Bullock and Winnett. But while they had worked in the spirit of their Bullock's design, the new Hollander store was not, as LeMaire had insisted early on, a full recapitulation of their previous work. It was emphatically different in look and feel. The rooms were more reticent, with a greater openness and fewer elements. Their spare and understated elegance also carried over to the individual objects, including the furnishings and vitrines.

Peters and LeMaire had significantly altered Shreve, Lamb & Harmon's original scheme for the lower façade and entry spaces. They had modified the display windows and had added awnings. They had also redesigned the entry doors, enlarging them and making them more elaborate (figs. 178–180). Just inside the doors, Peters and LeMaire introduced a small foyer (figs. 181, 182), and beyond, they widened the central hall. The overall result was a summary of the great ground-floor concourse at Bullock's, right down to the display counters that extended along the walls. The Hollander arrangement, however, was considerably condensed, because the building footprint was so much smaller. The main entry hall at the New York store also relied on strong horizontal lines on the outer surfaces rather than the vertical ones they had used for the Bullock's concourse (fig. 183). Very different, too, was the perfume area, which was confined to a single small space set off from the hall (fig. 184).

At the far end of the entry passage were the elevators. Peters had experimented with a number of variant designs for the doors and the interiors of the cabins, ultimately coming up with a look that merged the new language of purism (which was coming into vogue in America by then) with late Expressionist floral motifs (figs. 185, 186). As was the case throughout, he had employed a palette of deluxe materials. One of the novel ideas Peters had had for the Hollander store was to design unique exteriors for the elevator doors on each floor, matching the framings and surfaces to their surroundings. These were intended to provide customers with a visual reference to indicate where they were in the store. For the ground floor elevator doors, he had specified a fine pearwood veneer and Benedict nickel metal framing. The displays were similarly elegant, featuring a magnolia-wood backing, with aspen, madrone, burlwood, and ebony veneer detailing.[300] By contrast, the elevator doors on the fourth floor (housing the millinery and fur sales areas), were very different, highly simplified—even minimal (fig. 187).

Peters and LeMaire's effort to design each floor differently resulted in an exceptional presentation of modernist ideas. The second floor, which housed the Lingerie, Boudoir Accessories, and Decorative Arts Departments, was especially luxurious. The space was subdivided into three distinctive zones, according to the wares offered. The section offering accessories for the boudoir (ceramics, art glass, lamps, dressing tables, decorative bottles, and the like) was a neutral gray (fig. 188). Whereas, in the decorative arts area, the walls were decorated in bold geometric patterns in many colors (figs. 189). One wall was built out to create a display alcove for the furniture; decorative metal screens covered the vents below deeply set windows; and the

178. Jock Peters, L. P. Hollander Company store, New York, 1930. Exterior perspective. Print. Collection Jock de Swart.

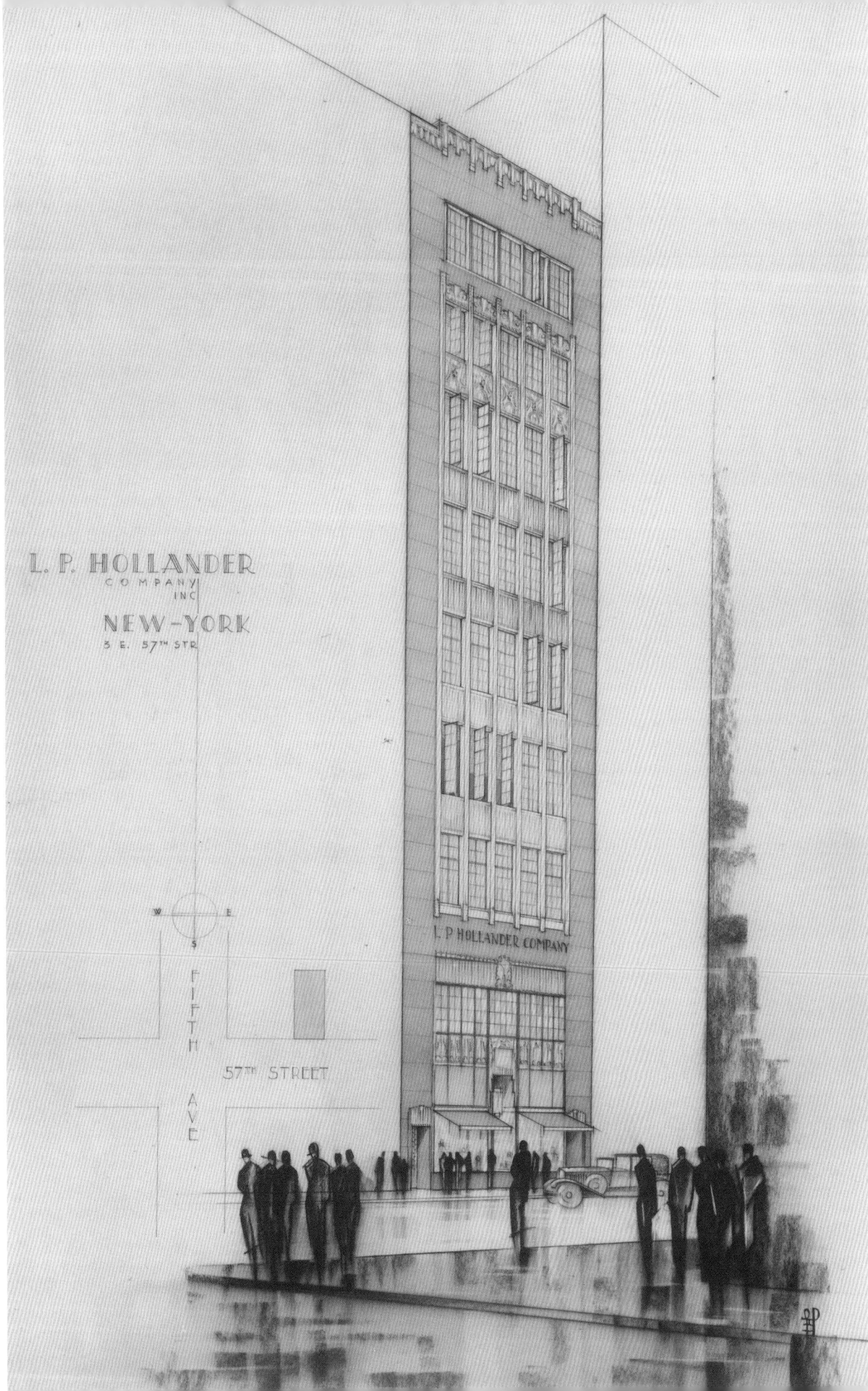

179. Jock Peters and Eleanor LeMaire, L. P. Hollander Company store, New York, 1930. Ground floor display windows. Collection Jock de Swart.

180. Jock Peters and Eleanor LeMaire, L. P. Hollander Company store, New York, 1930. Ground floor display window. Collection Jock de Swart.

181. Jock Peters, L. P. Hollander Company store, New York, 1930. Foyer. Collection Jock de Swart.

THE NEW HOLLANDER BUILDING AT 3 EAST 57

IS DESIGNED IN THE CONTEMPORARY SPIRIT

Entrance Foyer — Warm and inviting with panels of colorful pearwood

NATURALLY our new building is designed in the contemporary spirit. Since our modern life does not express itself in periods either classic or rococco, so in our architecture, too, we disregard the fragile circumlocutions of other years. Nor is our new building "modernistic" as that word has been misused to mean a restless striving for the bizarre.

It is, we much prefer the word, contemporary in design and decoration. Planned as a building for the display and sale of fine merchandise, our aim has been to combine harmoniously only what is basically sound in design with what is basically sound in merchandising.

184. Jock Peters, L. P. Hollander Company store, New York, 1930. Perspective sketch of perfume room. Pencil on paper. Collection Jock de Swart.

182. Jock Peters, L. P. Hollander Company store, New York, 1930. Drawing of the foyer. From *A Folio of Pictures Showing the L. P. Hollander Co. in Its New Home at 3 East 57 Street* (New York: L. P. Hollander, 1930), n.p. Collection Jock de Swart.

183. Jock Peters, L. P. Hollander Company store, New York, 1930. Ground floor concourse. UCSB.

185–186. Jock Peters, L. P. Hollander Company store, New York, 1930. Ground floor elevator doors and interior of elevator cabin. UCSB.

187. Jock Peters, L. P. Hollander Company store, New York, 1930. Millinery and Fur Department on the fourth floor. UCSB.

188. Jock Peters, L. P. Hollander Company store, New York, 1930. Boudoir Accessories section on the second floor. UCSB.

189. Jock Peters, L. P. Hollander Company store, New York, 1930. Decorative Arts Department on the second floor. UCSB.

190. Jock Peters, L. P. Hollander Company store, New York, 1930. Furniture displays on the fifth floor. UCSB.

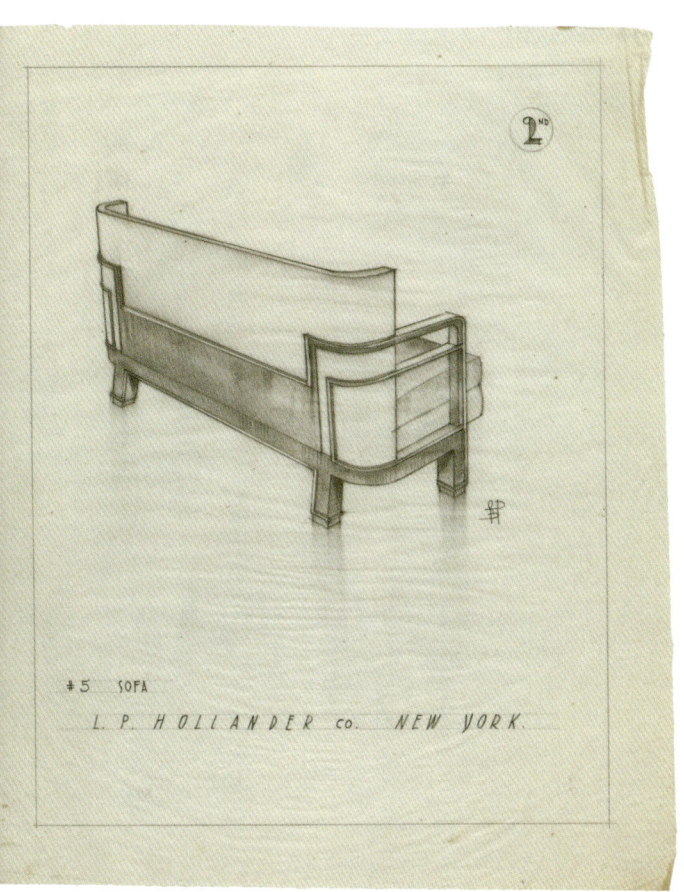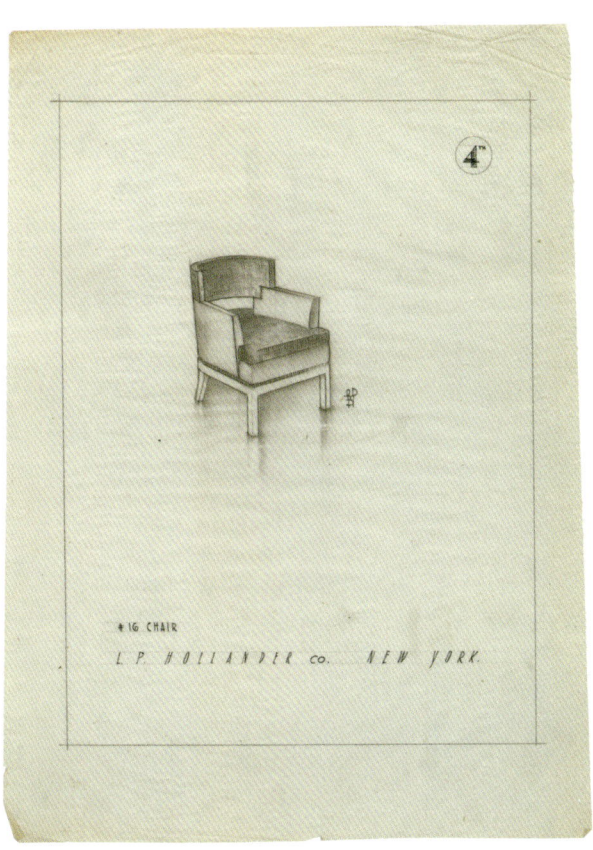

191–193. Jock Peters, L. P. Hollander Company store, New York, 1930. Drawings of sofa and chairs. Pencil on paper. UCSB.

sidewalls had flat lighting fixtures that seamlessly connected to the recessed lighting in the ceiling. On display there, as elsewhere, was a broad selection of furnishings, many of them of Peters's own designs (figs. 190–193).[301]

For the fourth floor—the Millinery and Fur Department—Peters created a unified set of richly articulated spaces, employing satinwoods and soft green lacquer trim (figs. 194–196).

The most conspicuously modern space was the Debonair Shop on the seventh floor, which had up-to-date furnishings and was especially understated (figs. 197–200). The open screen and horizontal span of lights, which appear repeatedly in his interiors, gave the room a Japanese quality.

Peters and LeMaire described their approach in the brochure celebrating the store's opening:

> We have done it in studio style, freeing it from the formality of definite partitions. The walls and furniture are black and white, precise and definite, relieved by color notes. The woodwork is of natural oak and black lacquer. The furniture is of metal. On this floor alone we indulged ourselves in choosing the pattern for the interesting carpet, gray-green shading softly to black.[302]

The standouts on the seventh floor were the metal chairs, stools, and tables. Peters and LeMaire acquired most of them from the Vienna-based J. & J. Kohn Company's New York City showroom; the pieces were very much on the cutting edge of European furniture design.

Equally innovative was the wide array of built-in lighting sources and fixtures Peters introduced throughout the store (fig. 201). In one instance, he sandwiched fluorescent tube lights between a backing and a panel of frosted glass through which the light glowed (fig. 202).

Seen as a whole, the Hollander's interiors represented a sort of early 1930s modernist *Gesamtkunstwerk*, or total work of art. And Peters's efforts to produce a complete and captivating world of shopping did not stop with the store itself. He designed a special delivery car, with its own color scheme, graphics, and elegant livery for the driver (fig. 203). He even came up with various designs for the shoe- and hat-boxes. The results, with their austere forms and clean language, were at the leading edge of American packaging design (figs. 170, 204–206).

The responses to the new Hollander store in the New York professional press were universally positive.[303] Noted design authority Alfred Auerbach commended the store's "individuality and novel expression" and its "intimate air. A tour through the Hollander store," he pronounced, "reveals that it is . . . a striking fusion of interior decorating and commercial retail requirements."[304] Ralph Flint, another prominent New York design critic, wrote in *Creative Art*, "in the matter of lighting, proportions, interlacing of parts, and in general inventiveness of detail, I venture to believe Mr. Peters is hardly to be matched in this country."[305]

Peters, for his part, was far less impressed with New York City. On his return trip for the gala opening he spent time wandering the city. He told Flint he found, "to his great amazement, Manhattan singularly devoid of the modern touch, with the exception of a few notable skyscrapers and a few smart shop fronts on Fifth Avenue."[306]

Peters returned to Los Angeles a little less than two weeks later, on October 8, bringing with him eight trunks of drawings, samples, and merchandise from the store. He immediately returned to work, designing and completing several other projects.[307]

One of them was the Chevrolet dealership in Wilmington (figs. 207, 208). Peters had already made the conceptual renderings, but he left most of the detailing to Ruck. The result was a disappointment, well below Peters's customary standard. The exterior of the finished building merged the language of streamlining, which was then just gaining popularity in Southern California, with vertical stringcourses. But the combination, carried out in brick, did not work particularly well, and the façade, as a result, was awkward and unsettled. The one redeeming part of the design was the showroom, with its dramatic staircase and upper-floor gallery, which was mostly Peters's work.

Peters and Ruck also collaborated on a second architectural project around this time, a house for William Lingenbrink in Whitley Heights.

Lingenbrink, who always had his finger on what was newest and trendiest, had hoped that his house would be a consummate example of the latest ideas. He told Peters that he wanted a house in the spirit of the "modernistic" storefronts that he had celebrated in his self-published folios of the late 1920s. What Peters gave him instead was a much reduced, purist design—more closely aligned with the German modernism of the day than the American Art Deco (fig. 209). It was an early premonition of what was to come in Los Angeles—a set of large volumes made light with wide openings. The two architects' use of corner windows and intricate mullion patterns, along with the dominant front window, the integrated garage, and the tiling along the cornice (a nod to the Spanish Colonial Revival), were all harbingers

194. Jock Peters, L. P. Hollander Company store, New York, 1930. Millinery and Fur Department on the fourth floor. UCSB.

195–196. Jock Peters, L. P. Hollander Company store, New York, 1930. Millinery and Fur Department on the fourth floor. UCSB.

197–200. Jock Peters, L. P. Hollander Company store, New York, 1930. Debonair Shop on the seventh floor. UCSB.

201–202. Jock Peters, L. P. Hollander Company store, New York, 1930. Fluorescent lighting fixtures. UCSB.

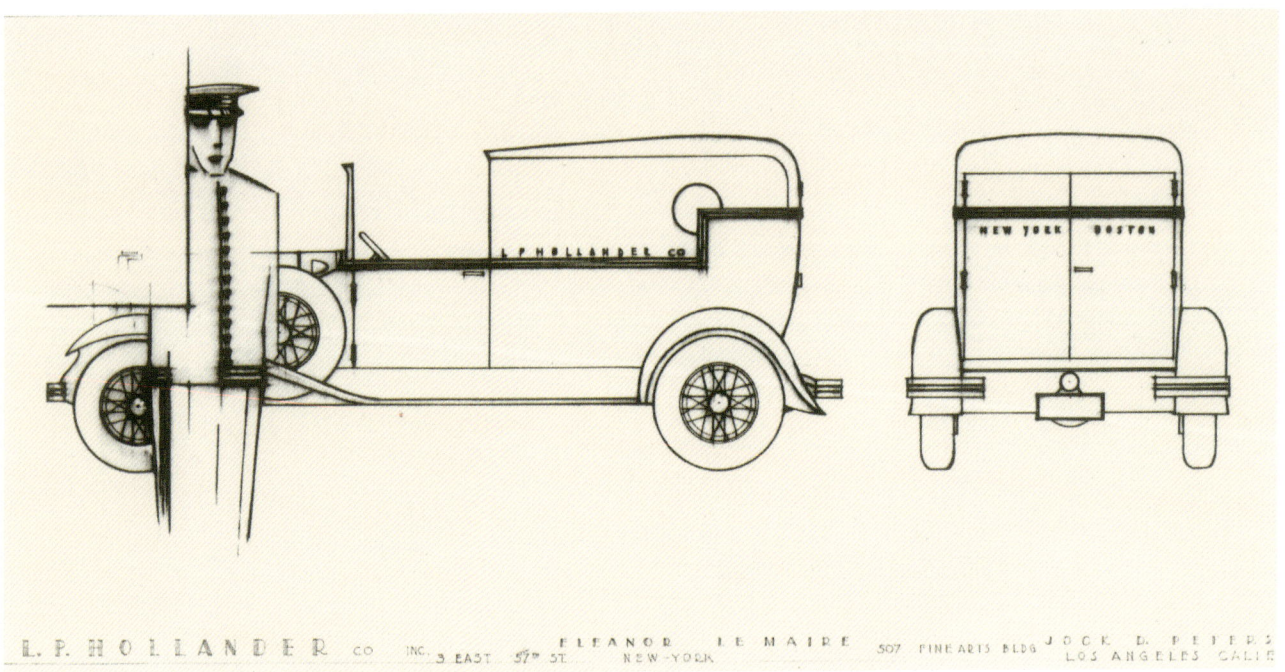

203. Jock Peters, design for a delivery car, L. P. Hollander Company store, New York, 1930. Print on paper. UCSB.

204–206. Jock Peters, drawings for a shoebox, L. P. Hollander Company store, New York, 1930. Pencil and colored pencil on paper. UCSB.

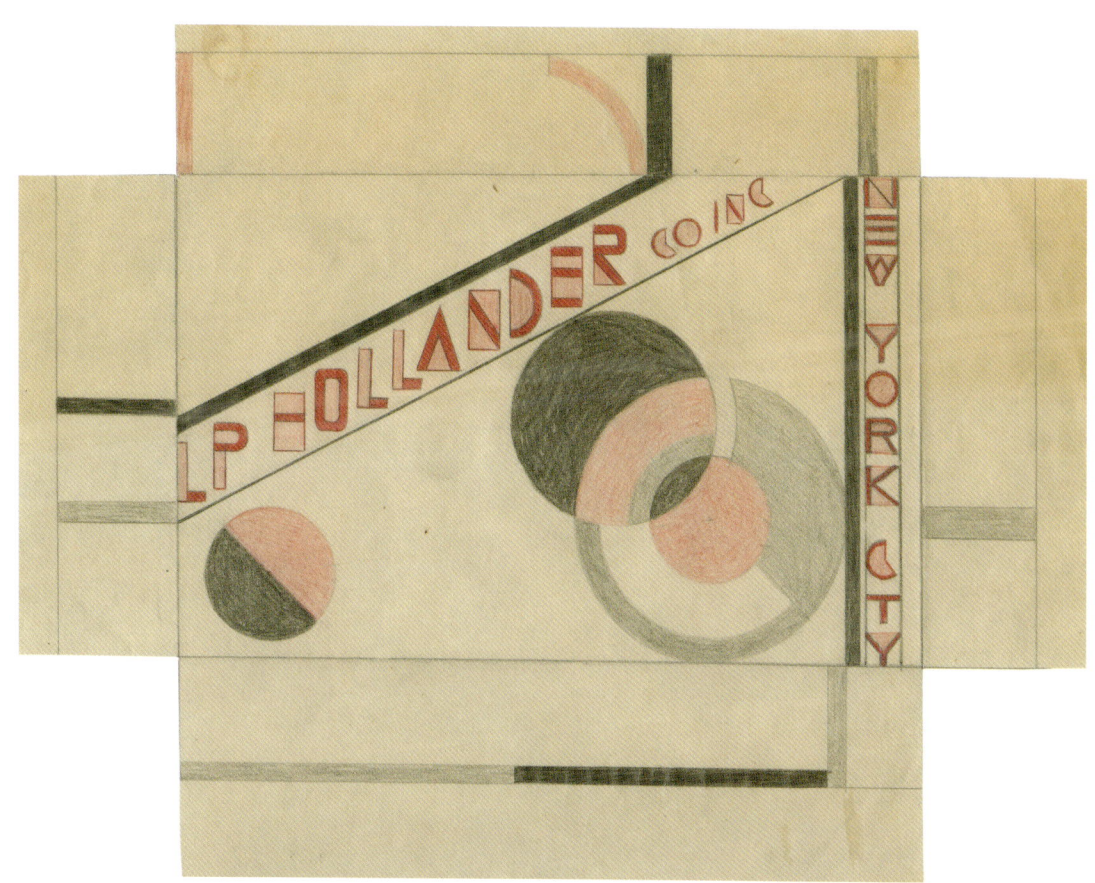

207. Jock Peters and W. F. Ruck, Harbor Chevrolet automobile dealership, Wilmington, California, 1930. Mott-Merge Collection, California State Library, Sacramento.

208. Jock Peters and W. F. Ruck, Harbor Chevrolet automobile dealership, Wilmington, California, 1930. Showroom. Mott-Merge Collection, California State Library, Sacramento.

209. Jock Peters and W. F. Ruck, House for William Lingenbrink, Whitley Heights, Hollywood, 1930.
Photograph courtesy Andrew B. Hurvitz, Los Angeles.

of the late-1930s and early-1940s aesthetic. What is also notable is the extent to which the house is recognizably *of* Southern California—especially in the manner in which it seemingly grows out of the landscape. It is not so much set upon the hill as it is joined to it—as if terrain and building were one.

Peters and LeMaire continued to work together after completing the Hollander project. He assisted LeMaire on the design for her new office in Manhattan, and they had continuous discussions about the possibility of further store commissions.

Nothing immediately came of their efforts, in large measure because Peters had already moved on to a new undertaking. On his return train journey from New York after the Hollander opening, he had received a wire from Paramount (the former Famous Players-Lasky Corporation, now renamed) asking him to return to Los Angeles "right away."

At first, Peters was unsure about what he should do. Before he left New York, Clarence Sheffield had asked him to make his return trip via San Francisco to confer with Joseph Magnin about renovating his store there. After receiving the telegram from Paramount while waiting to change trains in Chicago, Peters thought over the offer for several hours. He decided to investigate the Paramount lead and canceled the meeting with Magnin. He took the train directly to Los Angeles and, immediately upon arriving, went to the studio to meet with the company's heads.

They spoke to him about a position as an art director and "made [him]," he told LeMaire, "a good offer." Peters insisted, though, that he did not want to work for the studio exclusively; his experiences in the mid-1920s, especially what he felt was a loss of his creative freedom, made him reluctant to sign on as a regular employee. He proposed instead to work part-time "on the basis of a $10,000 retaining fee per year and an additional $10 per hour."[308]

Peters thought that the studio managers would balk at such an audacious proposal. To his surprise, they accepted his terms. He declined the offer nonetheless. He simply had no desire to return to what he considered a form of indentured servitude. But days later, after several prospective jobs fell through, and after mulling over Paramount's more than generous terms (no doubt with an eye on the weakening economy), he reconsidered, offering to work for the studio on a part-time, freelance basis.

He signed a contract with the studio and worked on a few projects. Neither he nor the studio heads were satisfied with the arrangement, and by early 1931, Peters decided to take on a full-time role with the company.

Peters rationalized his decision to work full-time for Paramount, telling LeMaire in a letter that he was "going to do this for one year." He believed that the step-up in income would allow him to do what he had hoped to accomplish for some time—namely, to build his own house in Eagle Rock and to become financially independent. When the year was out, he wanted to visit his parents in Germany and take his eldest daughter, Ursel, so that she could continue her education there.[309]

To his own surprise, he found himself working for the studio once more. Upon hearing the news, LeMaire reported to Peters that she "had 'a little lost' feeling when I realized the movies were going to gobble you up again."[310] But what Peters thought was a Faustian bargain on his part turned out—in light of the ever-worsening Depression—to be a stroke of good luck. Unlike most of his fellow modernist designers in Southern California, who had faced tough economic sledding after the early months of 1930, he would weather the financial storm with far less exertion. He was even able to aid some of his colleagues and friends, including Kem Weber, whom Peters helped find temporary employment in Dreier's art department at Paramount.[311]

Even with his hefty income from the studio, Peters was not entirely immune to the effects of the Depression. He discovered that Hollander was having difficulty coming up with the money to pay him for his last few months of work. A little more than a year after the store's opening, the company, beset with the same problems that all the nation's retailers were facing, declared bankruptcy. The expensively installed fittings were torn out, and anything of value was sold off. Peters would never receive all the money that was owed to him.

At the end of August 1931, with little work coming in, Peters and Ruck decided to end their partnership.[312] Peters elected to keep his office open, and he continued to pursue his own projects—despite his contract with Paramount—to the extent that his time would permit.

The effort, though, remained a struggle. Peters learned that autumn that the Joseph Magnin store project in San Francisco had fallen through. But he was at least able to report to LeMaire, with some satisfaction, that Feil and Paradise were having little luck finding their own commercial projects.[313]

LeMaire, meanwhile, was in discussions to renovate the Mary Sachs department store, in Harrisburg, Pennsylvania; by the late spring of 1931, she was fully engaged with the project. In keeping with their earlier agreement, she asked Peters to aid her with the design. He did so, though he was often late in delivering the drawings, because by now he was

210–211. Jock Peters with Eleanor LeMaire, Mary Sachs department store, Harrisburg, Pennsylvania, 1931. Elevation of ground floor and mezzanine. Pencil and watercolor on board.
Hagley Museum and Library, Wilmington, Delaware.

212. Jock Peters, Bullock's department store, Los Angeles, 1931.
Proposal for first-floor renovation. Print on paper. UCSB.

tied up with his work for Paramount. In spite of the delays and a considerably smaller budget, he was able to complete the presentation boards of the store's ground floor and mezzanine (figs. 210, 211).

Beginning in early December of 1930, Peters was also working for Bullock's, exploring a possible redesign of the downtown store's lower floors.[314] He had mostly completed his conceptual designs for the renovation by mid-February of 1931.[315]

His ideas for the new spaces were a decided departure from his sumptuous ground-floor concourse for the Wilshire branch (fig. 212). The designs were vastly more understated; the focus was squarely on the merchandise. The redesign was made to appeal to the ordinary shopper, who, faced with the growing economic uncertainty, wanted something up-to-date yet reassuring. Peters's interiors were also a clarion avowal of simplicity and repetition—rather than luxurious detailing and upscale materiality—very much in the spirit of what was then taking place in Germany.[316]

Peters was well aware of the latest trends in his homeland. Whenever he could, he read the German architecture and design magazines and books. He had some of the publications sent to him directly from Germany; others he acquired from the Westermann Company in New York City, including copies of El Lissitzky's *Russland* (Russia) and Richard Neutra's *Amerika*. His friends and former colleagues in Germany also mailed him issues of various professional journals—especially those that featured their own works.[317]

Peters's drawings for the new downtown Bullock's interiors borrowed elements from what he was seeing in the magazines. In a word, they were significantly more "democratic" than what he had installed in the Wilshire branch, and, in that sense, they reflected the more realistic temper of the time.

Despite their inherent practicality, Peters's proposals were never carried out. The specific reasons are not known. Continuing pessimism about the economy must have played some part. But the main reason was likely that Bullock's management found the design too far in advance of public taste.

What speaks for this are several sketches Peters made for updated façades for the store's downtown branch. Because Bullock's had grown up piecemeal over several decades, combining or adding a number of different structures, the store had a decidedly "assembled" appearance. It also looked very much out-of-date, since the original buildings reflected the commercial aesthetic of the early part of the century. Whether Peters took it upon himself, or whether Winnett and the other members of the management team commissioned him to do so, he produced several quick sketches of how the exterior of the store might be reclad to present a more modern and contemporary guise.

He came up with three different solutions to unify and update the buildings—all reproducing the emerging commercial aesthetic as it was developing in Europe by that time: large simplified masses, flowing horizontal contours, and the addition of super graphics. One of the schemes was a more or less undifferentiated rectangular block; a second showed a similar block but with speed lines; and the third had a prominent sign and vertical striations (figs. 213–215).

Whether Winnett or anyone else at Bullock's saw these sketches is unknown. In any event, it is evident from their subsequent actions that they had something very different in mind. When Bullock's constructed its next branch, in Westwood near the new University of California, Los Angeles, campus, they again hired the Parkinsons, who devised a vaguely modernized Spanish Colonial design. Only after World War II would the Bullock's management adopt the language of high modernism for its stores.

Despite the rejection of his Bullock's designs, Peters was earning enough from Paramount at the beginning of 1931 to keep him afloat. He was still actively taking part in exhibitions in and around Los Angeles—even while they cost him more to mount than what he received in return. The previous year, in April 1930, he had participated in the exhibition of Southern California modernists at the UCLA campus.[318] Once again, he had been in good company; among those whose works were shown were Neutra, Schindler, J. R. Davidson, and Kem Weber. Peters followed this with several other exhibitions of his work in 1931, including shows at the Stickney Memorial School of Fine Arts, in Pasadena; at the Little Studio-Gallery, in Monrovia; and at the Annual Art Exhibit, in Eagle Rock.[319]

The few designs he did manage to complete displayed, as before, his penchant for a modernist eclecticism. Not only were they stylistically mixed, but they reflected an unsteadiness about how forms, materials, and practical considerations could be effectively brought together.

In January 1931, Peters created a room for a "young lady with a bed with side table, a combined cabinet for negligees and toilet articles and a full-length mirror, a combination book shelf and writing desk [and] one easy chair" for an international exhibition in Cologne, Germany.[320] He came up with a suite with a vaguely neoclassical couch in three sections featuring an unusual blue-and-orange color scheme (fig. 216). Around the same time, he also produced a drawing for a mahogany and polished-brass smoking table for an unknown

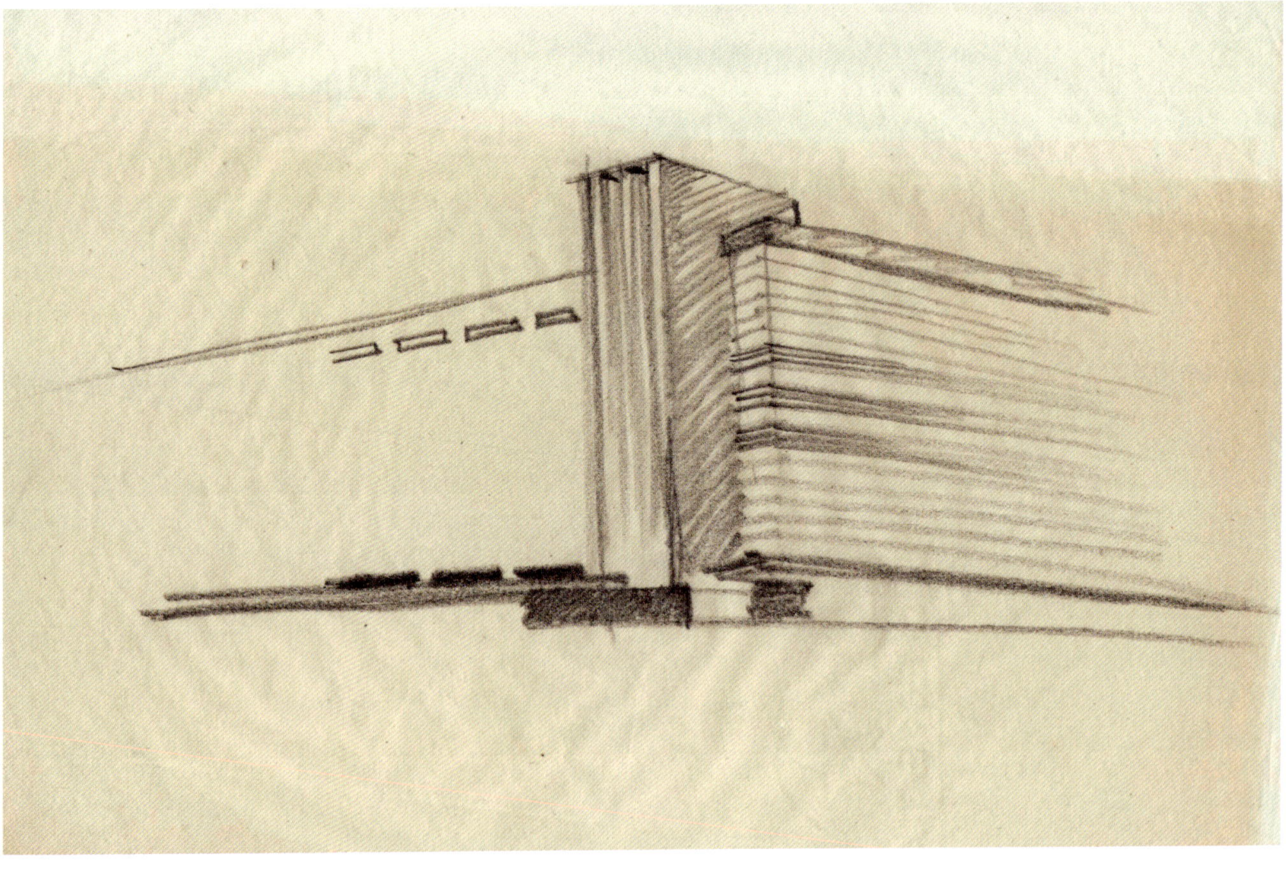

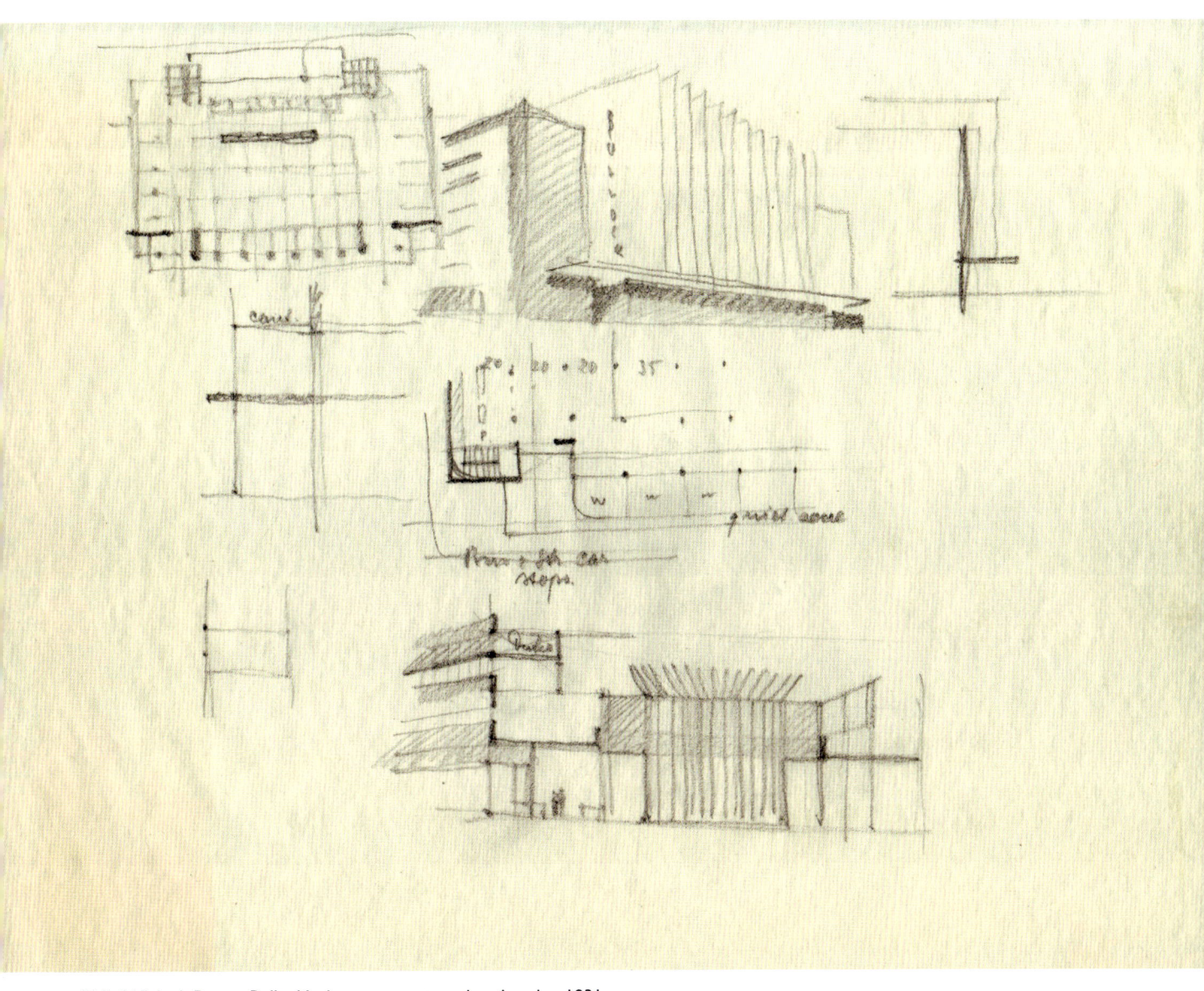

213–215. Jock Peters, Bullock's department store, Los Angeles, 1931.
Proposals for a new façade. Pencil on paper.
Collection Jock de Swart.

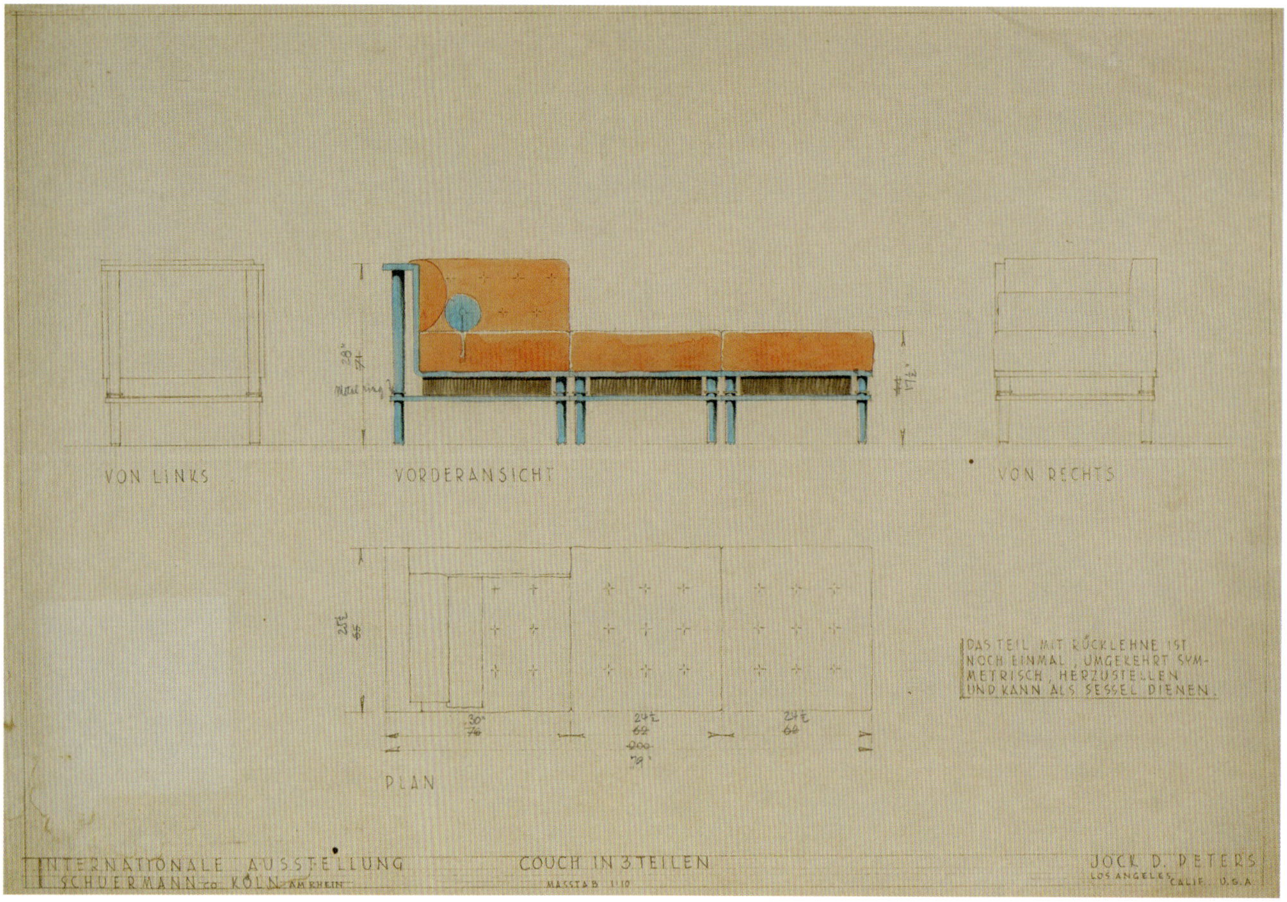

230 JOCK PETERS

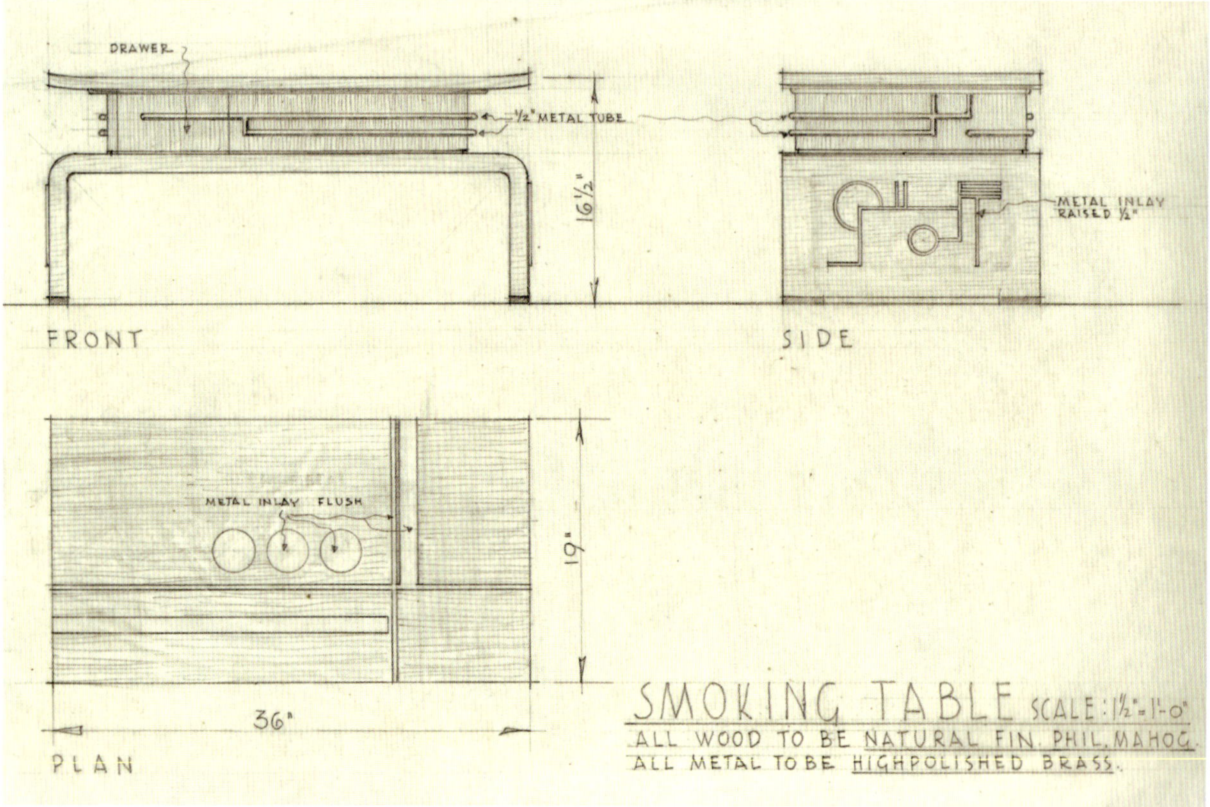

client that made direct reference to the geometric form-language of the late Art Deco as well as Chinese traditional furnishings (fig. 217).

Throughout this time, Peters and LeMaire had continued their discussions concerning AUDAC. Peters was less pessimistic than LeMaire about the organization. He thought that it might do some good, especially in light of many of the members' economic woes.

In the summer of 1930, when the Los Angeles modernists had finally formed their own "western chapter" of AUDAC, Peters was among the founding members, along with Kem Weber, Lloyd Wright, J. R. Davidson, photographer Will Connell, and Jacob Asanger. Asanger was chosen as temporary chairman, Connell as secretary. They described their aims (in heavily German-inflected English) "to lessen the discrepancy between the spirit of the modern age and its setting through the encouragement of designs that are in harmony with modern life."[321]

LeMaire remained unconvinced. When AUDAC was planning its exhibition at the Brooklyn Museum in 1931, she told Peters that she had "withheld from joining due to several reasons, the most important one being that I object to many of the members and these are the members who seem to be directing all their activities—Frankl, Keisler [sic], etc., but I may change my mind and join later on, depending."[322] She never did.

Little came of the West Coast chapter of AUDAC. The group met a few times, but any thought of mounting exhibitions or putting out a publication fell prey to the economic circumstances. The Los Angeles designers, moreover, were too preoccupied with keeping their practices—and themselves—afloat. When the New York branch dissolved in 1932, they simply dropped the effort.

Peters by this time was working on sets for Paramount several days a week. His assistant, Walter Holscher, was also able to report to LeMaire that Peters had found a few other commercial jobs.[323] One was a Los Angeles showroom for Mabel Skinner, who represented Rena Rosenthal, the New York maven of new design retailing, selling Rosenthal's full line of American-made and imported decorative articles out of a space in the Fine Arts Building, one floor below where Peters had his office.[324]

More important, though, were the interiors he designed for Irene Ltd., the fashion house of Irene Maud Gibbons (née Lentz).

Gibbons was married to Eliot Gibbons, brother of MGM art director Cedric Gibbons. After a brief career as an actress, Irene, as she was universally known, began sewing dresses for the Hollywood elite and for many of the studios. She purchased an existing building at 9000 Sunset Boulevard, in what is now West Hollywood, and asked Peters to redesign the exterior of the structure, the interiors, and all the furnishings.[325]

What Peters gave her was very much in the spirit of the Hollander store. Throughout, he recreated the same elegance, spaciousness, and modern touches (figs. 218, 219). The same was true for the seating pieces, including a corner chair and Irene's own desk, which he set into a nook (figs. 220, 221). New for Peters, however, was the telephone bench with built-in table, which he specially devised for the room adjacent to the entry vestibule (fig. 222).

The Irene shop was "modern-to-the-minute," as the saying went at the time. It was the quintessential expression of a new style epitomizing Hollywood glamour—one soon to appear in innumerable films. But in terms of the architecture of the best Los Angeles modernists, it stood apart. It had none of the refined and transparent eloquence that Neutra was developing in his houses, none of the sophisticated massing and complex geometries of Schindler's works. It was also less spirited than Weber's interiors and individual furnishings. It retained an element of traditionalism, of bourgeois propriety that the others had already abandoned. Still, it represented a fresh and original voice. Even if Peters took over elements from past designs, he altered and recombined them in ways that were uniquely his. His design had style—an amalgamation of styles, which, in his characteristic manner, became a style of its own.

Despite its idiosyncrasies, the Irene studio and, for that matter, Peters's other designs of the early 1930s, including Bullock's downtown, his house for Lingenbrink, and the Skinner shop, were at the forefront of Los Angeles modernism. After years of hard work and struggle, he was now one of the leaders of the new movement. Over the next two years, his work would change once more, and what he designed would ultimately advance an even more individual vision for Southern California.

---

216. Jock Peters, three-part chaise lounge for the 1931 Cologne international exhibition. Made by the Schürmann Company, Cologne. Pencil and watercolor on paper. UCSB.

217. Jock Peters, smoking table for an unknown client, c. 1931. Pencil on paper. UCSB.

218. Jock Peters, Irene Ltd., Hollywood, 1931. Exterior. Charles E. Young Research Library, Department of Special Collections, University of California, Los Angeles (hereafter UCLA).

219. Jock Peters, Irene Ltd., Hollywood, 1931. Reception room. UCLA.

220. Jock Peters, Irene Ltd., Hollywood, 1931. Corner sitting area. UCLA.

221. Jock Peters, Irene Ltd., Hollywood, 1931. Desk nook. UCLA.

222. Jock Peters Irene Ltd., Hollywood, 1931.
Telephone bench. UCLA.

PARK MODERNE

A NEW IDEA IN LODGE SITES

PHONE: HEmpstead 0244

OFFICE OF WILLIAM LINGENBRINK
ROOM 714 · 215 WEST SIXTH STREET
LOS ANGELES, CALIF. · TUCKER 9784

ROOM 500
HOLLYWOOD SECURITY BLDG.
HOLLYWOOD, CALIF.

Chapter 10 |
CALIFORNIA MODERN

By the early months of 1931, Jock Peters, like nearly everyone in the nation, was feeling the full force of the ever-deepening Depression. He was earning a good salary at Paramount, but little new work was coming in. After ending his partnership with Ruck, he was effectively operating a one-man studio, with only a single assistant to help him with correspondence and drawings. Peters also had broken with F. K. Ferenz at the Academy of Modern Art. Enrollments at the school had declined sharply in the aftermath of the stock market collapse, and Peters saw no purpose in continuing there. In a bid to save money, he left the Fine Arts Building, moving to a smaller, less expensive office space in the First National Bank Building on Colorado Boulevard, in downtown Pasadena.[326] One promising job, however, had appeared some months earlier, while he was still working with Ruck. It was for a residential development called Park Moderne, in Calabasas, on the other side of the coastal range from Malibu.

Park Moderne was the brainchild of developer William Lingenbrink. Ever active, Lingenbrink continued to have his hand in the making of much of Southern California modernism. Park Moderne was yet another of his visionary—and risky—developments.

Around 1927, while still working on Silver Strand Beach, Lingenbrink had acquired a 140-acre tract with two partners; by 1930, they decided to develop it—even in the face of what looked to be a disastrous financial headwind. Lingenbrink envisioned the new development, which he christened Park Moderne, as an artists' colony and rural getaway for himself and his bohemian friends (fig. 223). His plan was to build a series of small detached cottages designed by some of Los Angeles's leading progressive architects.

One of Lingenbrink's partners, Samuel Cooper Jr., initially served as site manager. The two men subdivided the land into 174 lots. Cooper laid out a network of streets, and his crew poured oil on the unpaved surfaces to hold down the dust.[327] Lingenbrink then hired Peters, R. M. Schindler, and a few others to design the first houses. Peters was also tasked with creating a pump house, clubhouse, swimming pool, and fountain for the "village center."

He quickly came up with concepts for all four; they were among the earliest structures to be completed. Of these, only the pump house and the fountain still exist. They reveal that Peters employed a more or less standard version of the

223. William Lingenbrink's letterhead for Park Moderne, 1933. Collection Jock de Swart.

popular "modernistic style," with speed lines, chevrons, and stair-step massing. One side of the fountain even has an undulating inset panel of colored glass. The clubhouse and pool were probably similar. The drawings for all these designs unfortunately have been lost. But they must all have been in accord with Lingenbrink's wishes, because by this time Peters had already moved on to a more condensed and refined look.

Before he and Ruck dissolved their partnership, they also worked on at least two prototype cottages for Park Moderne. The sole surviving drawing in Peters's papers is labeled "Lodge Type B," suggesting there must have also been a Type A.

The carefully executed rendering shows a small, single-story structure with stucco walls, nautical metal railings, and a flat roof (fig. 224). Vertical pylons and prominent surrounds extend along and around the windows and doors. The overall scheme resembles Schindler's aesthetic of the time, especially his recently completed R. F. Elliot House in Los Angeles. And there are suggestions of other influences: Frank Lloyd Wright's Prairie Style in the projecting window on the left and the large stack, and Kem Weber's contemporary designs in the window mullions. The coloristic effects—red and green highlights along the "edges"—on the other hand, seems to have been uniquely Peters's.

Whether this house—or any others from his hand—was realized at Park Moderne is unknown. In the end, because of the financial downturn, only a small number of dwellings were built. Lingenbrink lost a healthy portion of his investment, and the area remained mostly undeveloped until the 1960s. Almost all the original cottages have long since been demolished or drastically altered. There have been suggestions that Peters designed some of the houses shown on the Park Moderne brochure that Lingenbrink had made (fig. 225). At least one, shown on the upper left, is clearly from Schindler. It is very unlikely that any of the others were Peters's work.[328]

Peters was involved with the Park Moderne project throughout 1930, even while he was working on the Hollander store. Lingenbrink paid him little for the Park Moderne designs, but the income he subsequently earned from other sources, including Paramount, more than made up for it. In fact, he earned more in 1931 than he had in the previous year—a rare feat at the time. In 1930, his reported total earnings on his federal tax forms were $7,346; in 1931, he earned $10,534 (more than $150,000 today), a comfortable income, especially in view of the fact that nearly a third of the workers in the Los Angeles area were jobless.[329]

Nonetheless, Peters still felt the need to trim his expenses. He feared—correctly, as it would turn out—that the Depression would go on for some time, and he sensed that his position at Paramount was far from secure—a belief that would also prove accurate. By the end of March 1931, he had terminated the lease for his office in the First National Bank Building and begun looking for even less expensive office space. When his search proved fruitless, he rented a larger house at 1651 Hill Drive in Eagle Rock, moved his family there, and began working out of one of the bedrooms.[330]

Peters saw the move as a temporary solution. He was intent upon building his own freestanding studio and house on a lot he had recently purchased nearby, at 5333 College View Avenue, at the corner of Hill Drive. Peters reasoned, as he wrote to LeMaire, that he would "probably pay in interest just about half for [the] house and studio" what he had been paying "on rent for the residence and the downtown studio."[331]

Peters worked on the design of the new house and studio in every spare moment. He first made a simple clay-massing model of a two-story house, which had a prominent balcony and an impressively sized round window (fig. 226). He soon expanded the structure, increasing the square footage and adding larger terraces. He also made drawings for a separate studio and garage on the lower portion of the steeply sloping site (figs. 227, 228).

In stylistic terms, the studio and garage, especially its cubic form and pronounced horizontality, owed something to Frank Lloyd Wright's language of the early 1930s. The house, by contrast, was a more purified exercise, a tightly composed, extended cubic volume, with planar surfaces, large expanses of glass, and clean lines—more akin to Neutra's designs of the time (figs. 229, 230).

What was true of the outside was not carried through in the interior. Peters prepared a lovely and unusual axonometric rendering of the ground floor (fig. 231). It shows that his planned disposition of the rooms was conventional: the spaces were large, but they were delimited in standard ways, with walls or narrow thresholds set between them. Some of the formal features of the ground floor—for instance, the framed hearth and bench set into an inglenook in the living room—appear as if they could have come from the prewar era, carried over from old bungalow plans. The second floor is scarcely any different. The bedrooms are connected by means of a hall running nearly the full length of the house (fig. 232). It is only the large surfaces given over to glazing and the direct access to the terraces that even suggest that it was to be built in California and not in a less benign climate.

224. Jock Peters with W. F. Ruck, cottage (Lodge Type B) for Park Moderne (unrealized), 1930. Pencil and colored pencil on board. UCSB.

PARK MODERNE
HOLLYWOODS' MOST UNIQUE SUBURBAN SUBDIVISION

 Ideal climatic conditions. Raise your own garden products and live independently away from congestion. No lot under 5000 square feet in size. Restrictions are reasonable and protective.

BIG LOTS $100 TO $350

Garden soil, water, electricity, roads, some trees. Improvements in and paid for. Charming location in foothills with views. Suitable for small estates, week end or suburban residence. 21 miles or ½ hour drive to center of Hollywood over broad highway with 30 ft. of cement paving.

How To Go

From Hollywood over Cahuenga Pass follow the Ventura Highway to a mile beyond Girard (where the Mulholland Drive meets the Ventura Highway), go south one mile to PARK MODERNE.

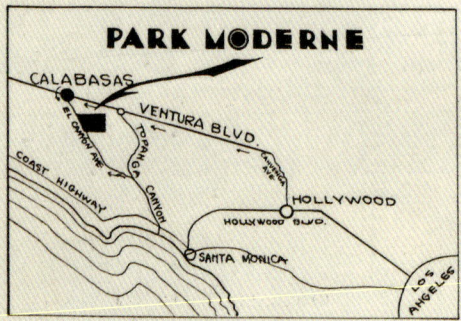

PARK MODERNE is owned by the American Holding Corporation.

Wm. Lingenbrink, General Manager

C. Henry Taylor, Tract Manager

OFFICE

Room 500, Hollywood Security Building, Hollywood Blvd. at Cahuenga Blvd.

Phone HE 0244

226. Jock Peters, project for Peters House on College View Avenue, c. 1931. Photograph of a clay model. UCSB.

Following pages:
227. Jock Peters, project for Peters House on College View Avenue, c. 1931. Perspective of the studio and garage. Pencil and watercolor on board. UCSB.

225. Brochure for Park Moderne, c. 1932. UCSB.

STUDIO & GARAGE
RESIDENCE of Mr. & Mrs. JOCK D. PETERS
LOS ANGELES · CALIFORNIA

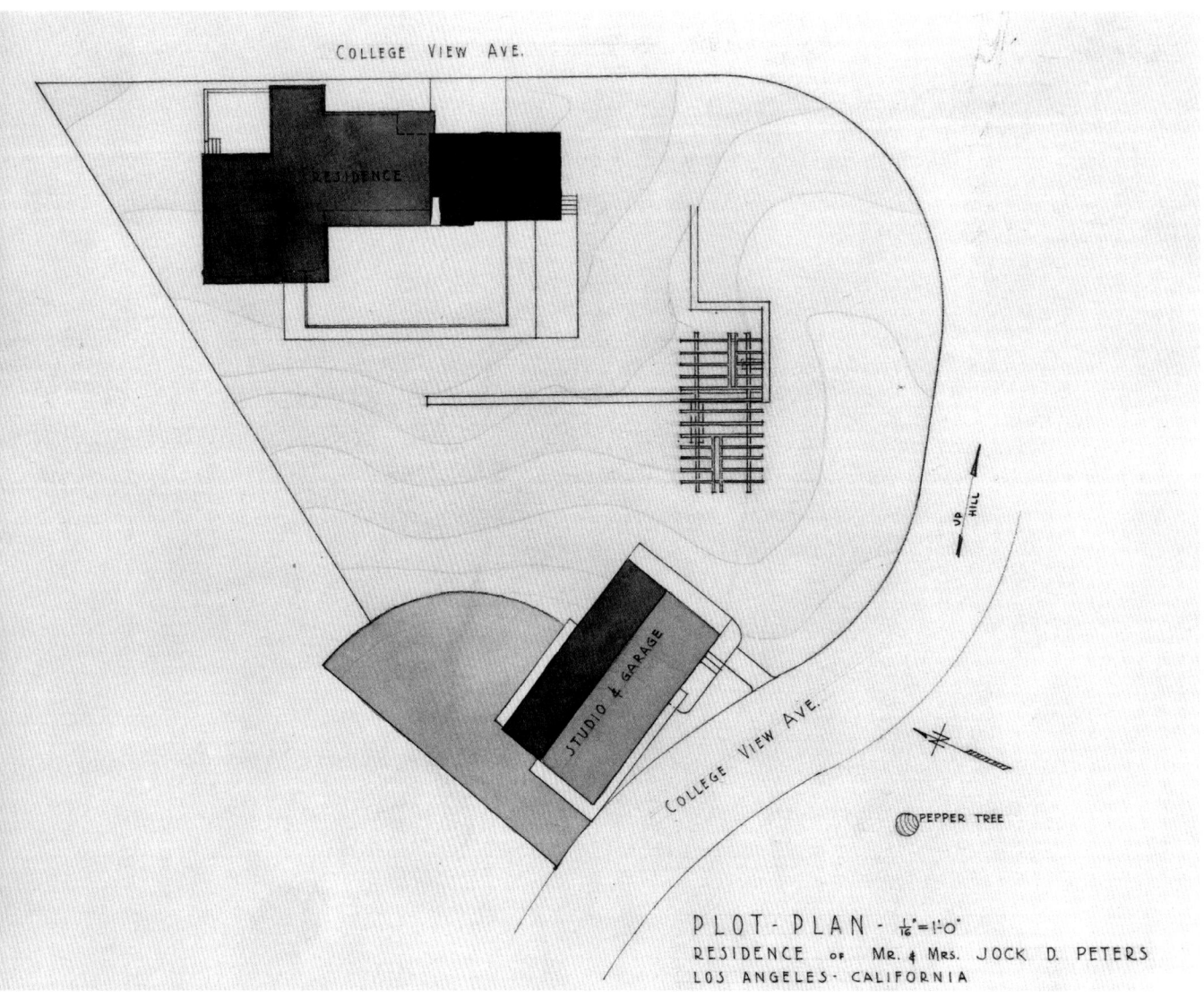

228. Jock Peters, project for Peters House on College View Avenue, c. 1931. Plot plan. Pencil on paper UCSB.

229. Jock Peters, project for Peters House on College View Avenue, c. 1931. Perspective. Pencil and watercolor on board. UCSB.

230. Jock Peters, project for Peters House on College View Avenue, c. 1931. Elevation of rear.
Pencil and watercolor on board. UCSB.

231–232. Jock Peters, project for Peters House on College View Avenue, c. 1931. Axonometric plans of ground floor and second floor. Pencil on paper. UCSB.

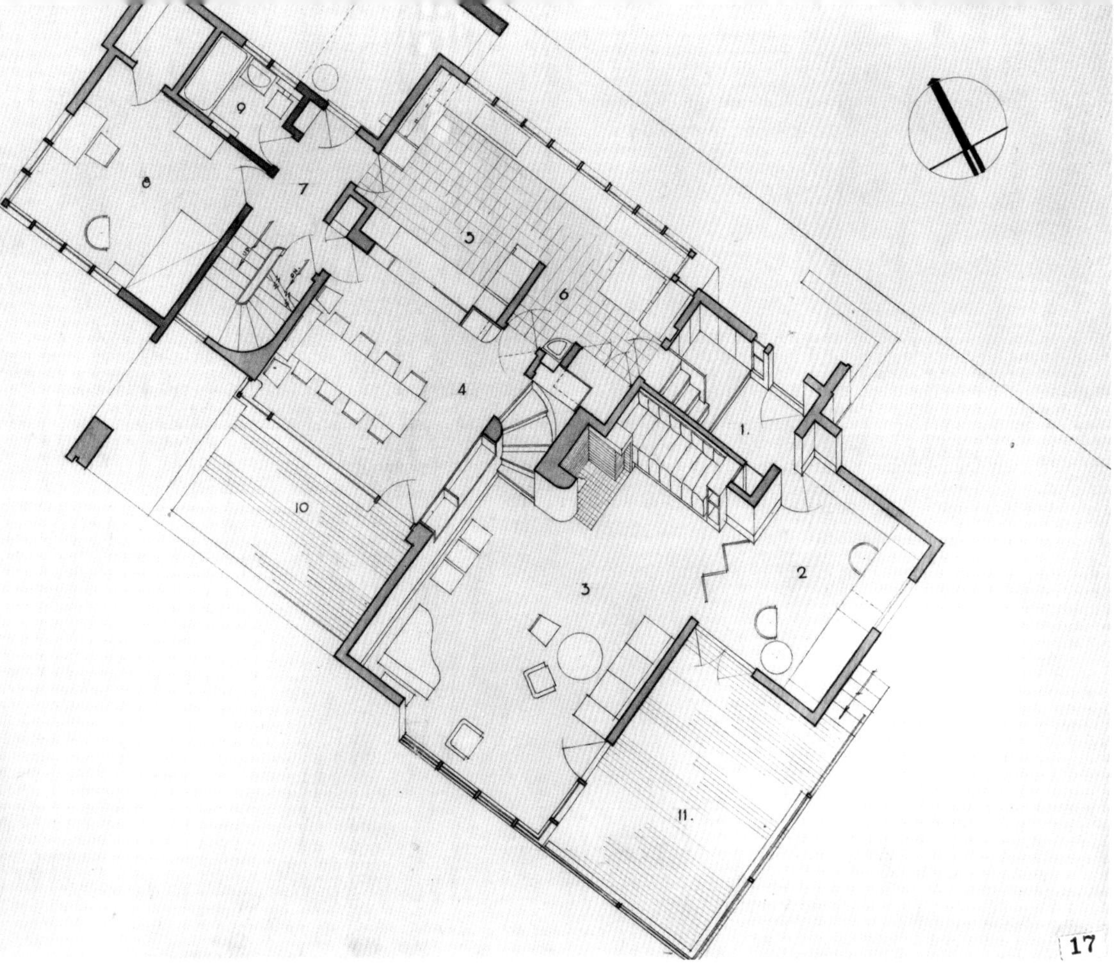

1	entrance hall
2	den
3	living room
4	dining room
5	kitchen
6	breakfast r'm
7	rear entr. hall
8	bedroom
9	bathroom
10	dining r'm. terrace
11	living r'm. terrace

17

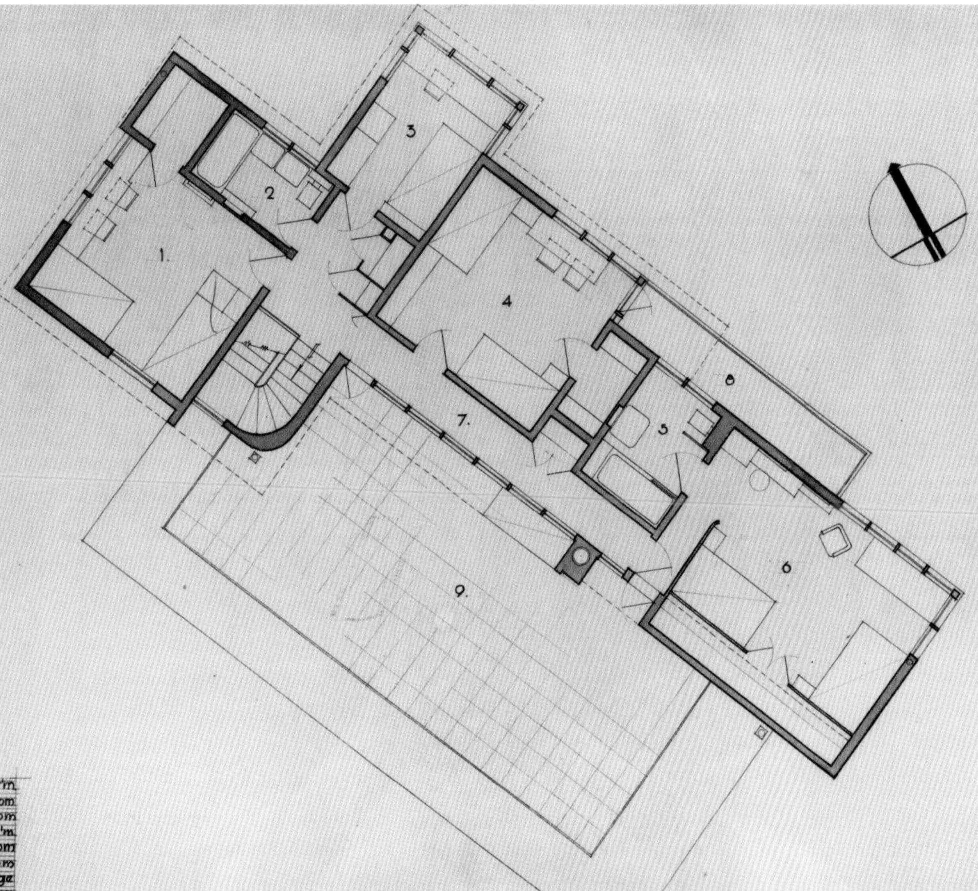

1	daughters' r'm
2	bathroom
3	son's room
4	daughters' r'm.
5	bathroom
6	master bed room
7	passage
8	balcony
9	roof deck

Peters applied for financing to build the house and studio. But even with his hefty income from Paramount, the bank refused the loan, because his personal net worth was too small.[332] He decided to put the project on hold and stay in the rented house on Hill Drive—at least until his financial circumstances improved.

With the end of the Park Moderne work and his few other projects (including the Bullock's remodeling commission), Peters found himself idle for a time. But by March 1931, he was again fully engaged, producing set designs for Paramount.

He was first assigned to produce the backdrops for *Confessions of a Co-Ed*, directed by David Burton and Dudley Murphy. It was a drama about a young woman, played by Sylvia Sidney, who becomes pregnant by the man she loves but is unable to marry him and marries a classmate of his instead. Peters's set designs drew from his now well-developed vocabulary of modernist forms, unadorned yet vibrant, with sharp geometries and dramatic lighting effects. Some of the furniture pieces he used were identical to those he had ordered from the Vernon Fixtures and Cabinet Company for the Hollander store; others he acquired from leading New York modernist designers, and a few pieces came from local Los Angeles makers. In one scene, in which the heroine is chatting with her friends (most scantily dressed, as was still possible in pre-code Hollywood), Peters makes use of tubular steel chairs—among the earliest examples of tubular steel furniture in a Hollywood film (fig. 233).

His next film, *The Road to Reno*, was another melodrama, directed by Richard Wallace and starring Lilyan Tashman and Charles "Buddy" Rogers. It was about a twice-divorced woman whose son shoots husband number three on their wedding day and then kills himself. Peters gave these sets a different look: traditional interiors, in which he combined classically inspired and oversized pieces with modernist touches. The bedroom set mixes upholstered furnishings with a mirrored wall (fig. 234). For another scene, Peters devised an elegant streamlined bar cart, a harbinger of the many similar designs that would appear in Hollywood movies over the coming decade (fig. 235). Sam Jaffe, then the executive head of production for Paramount, was so pleased with the look of the film that he dictated a memo to Peters congratulating him on the sets (fig. 236).

While *The Road to Reno* was filming, Peters was already at work on his next project, the romantic comedy *Girls about Town*. Directed by George Cukor and starring Kay Francis, Joel McCrea, and Lilyan Tashman, it is the story of two gold-digging women who prey on rich men. Peters lavished attention on the project, producing his most elaborate set designs since his work for *The City of the Future*. Every scene abounds with his distinctive interpretation of modernist glamour (fig. 237). Peters developed a backdrop of lush surfaces and textures, and he filled the spaces with an array of modern seating and case pieces. The result was a fantasy world—in a way, not so different from his science fiction designs of the previous decade—a world the average moviegoer of those years could only dream of inhabiting.

When Peters started working for Paramount, he had openly dreaded the move. He found, to his happy surprise, as his assistant, Walter Holscher, wrote to LeMaire, that he was "getting quite some satisfaction, more than we all expected."[333] The fact that his base pay was $325 a week—a very healthy income—only added to his contentment.

Peters found the entire process of devising modern make-believe sets absorbing. By the time he had finished his third film for Paramount, he was thinking about more efficient and less costly ways to make sets. He wrote a memo to Hans Dreier (who continued to head the art direction department for the studio), suggesting a new approach:

> I am very glad to have had an opportunity of doing some designs of modern settings for your department. The work was exceedingly interesting, and I could not help thinking about ways and means of obtaining the best possible results in such work. Permit me to submit a few proposals to this effect. In order to arrive at this perfect result, there are two ways:
>
> The more costly one is to have everything, stationary and movable parts alike, made up especially for every single set. The other way is to buy or rent all movable parts outside of the studio and to have the stationary elements constructed on the lot. But considering things as they are, how can an architect be expected to get any outstanding result, if he does not know beforehand what type of furniture, hangings, carpets, etc., are going to be used for this setting? It is only natural that he will try to have his ideas dominate; and it is inevitable that his design will clash with the rented props when they are placed in the setting.
>
> The consequence of the ideas set forth above seems to be that the Studio should have its own modern furniture and props made and built. The architect, before starting on his design, would merely have to make his selection of the pieces to be used. PARAMOUNT has its own recognized standard for actors and stories. It would, in addition, acquire its own standard in modern settings if furniture and props were used that cannot berented [*sic*]

233. Jock Peters, set for *Confessions of a Co-Ed*. Paramount Pictures (directors: David Burton and Dudley Murphy; released 11 July 1931). JT Vintage/glasshouseimages.com.

Following pages:
234. Jock Peters, set for *The Road to Reno*. Paramount Pictures (director: Richard Wallace; released 26 September 1931). Pencil and watercolor on board. UCSB.

ROAD TO RENO

235. Jock Peters, set for *The Road to Reno*. Paramount Pictures
(director: Richard Wallace; released 26 September 1931).
Private collection.

```
                              Form 405—G-39
            PARAMOUNT PUBLIX CORPORATION
                        WEST COAST STUDIOS

                    INTER-OFFICE COMMUNICATION
                                Date    August 21, 1931.



    JOCK PETERS:

              I want to take this means of commending you
    upon the fine and distinguished sets in ROAD TO RENO.
    The general background of the picture will be a very
    important feature in its success.

                                       SAM JAFFE
```

236. Memo from Sam Jaffe to Jock Peters, 1931. Collection Jock de Swart.

237. Jock Peters, sets for *Girls about Town*. Paramount Pictures (director: George Cukor; released 7 November 1931). Private collection.

from or by any other studio. It might as well be the PARAMOUNT chair, table or door as it is now the PARAMOUNT star.[334]

It all made eminently good sense, but the studio's higher-ups immediately rejected the idea, insisting that it would be too costly. Disappointed, Peters continued to work as he had before, designing purpose-made sets for each new production and acquiring furniture as needed—a practice that was almost certainly more, not less, expensive than what he had proposed.

After the completion of *Girls about Town*, Peters was assigned to another production. The film was dropped, and in mid-October, he finally had the opportunity to take a short vacation. He and Herta went to Palm Springs. But within a week and a half, he was called back to work on a new project, a comedy directed by Ernst Lubitsch and starring Maurice Chevalier.[335] It was titled *One Hour with You*.

The film was a convoluted story about an unhappily married couple that interferes in the relationship of another couple. The most spectacular of the sets Peters created was an elegant, cascading staircase with a minimalist rod-and-sphere balustrade. Fronting it is another signature Peters design, a sideboard featuring a shieldlike inset panel (figs. 238, 239).

Almost immediately after wrapping the film, Peters began working on yet another production, a comedy titled *This Is the Night*. Starring Roland Young and Thelma Todd, with Cary Grant in a supporting role, and directed by Frank Tuttle, it was a trifling tale about a woman played by Todd who is having an affair while her husband is off at the Summer Olympics. Peters's sets (which in the end were not used) were as sophisticated and debonair as any he produced for Paramount, bringing together pared-down classical columns with modernist details and open, expansive interiors (fig. 240).

What Peters produced for Paramount in the early 1930s, in keeping with Dreier's effort to promote cutting-edge design, amounted to a summing up of his own ideas about modernism. The sets were current and stylish and ever manifold. They were far more about the possibilities of modern life and new modes of inhabiting spaces than they were statements of any dogmatic position on design.

Despite Peters's successes, his time at Paramount was coming to an end. He continued to work for the studio for some months after *This Is the Night* premiered, in April 1932. He produced sketches for at least one more project—an unnamed adventure film about aviators set in the Middle East during and after the Great War—which was never produced (figs. 241–243). The company by then was in deep financial difficulties as a result of poor management and diminished box office receipts. Production slowed and then nearly halted when the studio was forced into receivership. Peters and many others were let go.

Remarkably, Peters was able to stay busy and even find income with two new commissions for single-family residences. One of the designs, for the Lawrence Shepard House in San Marino, California, was an essay on the possibility of combining cubic volumes with an unusual selection of modernist details. Peters inserted another of his round windows into the front façade, and he applied a patterned stucco texture to the wall adjacent to the front door (fig. 244). He even toyed with the idea of using pink paint on the underside of the eaves and the side vertical pylon (fig. 245).

The rear of the house, at first glance, was rather more standard for Southern California modernism. Peters inserted a partially enclosed terrace, with a trellis extending along one side to enhance the possibilities for outdoor living (fig. 246). The interiors were open and mostly underfurnished—focused, like the exterior spaces, on comfort and leisure (fig. 247).

In spite of the almost minimalist quality of the spaces, they were very much Peters's. If one looks carefully at the detailing of the furniture and fixtures—in the dining room, for instance—what stands out is the extent to which his individual hand is ever present; the objects retain a separateness from what other designers in Southern California were doing at the time. They displayed a way of making surfaces and textures that were distinctively his own (fig. 248).

This is true of another of Peters's commissions of 1932, the interiors for the very upscale Cavanaugh & Stebins women's shop on Wilshire Boulevard.

The space was light and airy, but most impressive is the range of forms and ideas he infused into the built-in and free-standing furnishings (fig. 249). Peters had them fabricated by the Vernon Fixtures and Cabinet Company, which, starting with the Hollander store, had made many of the pieces he used in his interiors. Everything at first glance looks as if it might belong squarely to the vocabulary of early-1930s American modernism. On closer inspection, it becomes apparent that many of the objects are unique—eccentric, even for the time. The suspended lighting fixtures, which look like satellites from a later age, are based on the language of pure geometries. Yet they are shaped and scaled in such a way as to make them quite singular. They seem at once oversized and too small for the space. The various furniture pieces, including, most dramatically, the color-blocked sofa, are just as peculiar and distinctive.

238. Jock Peters, set for *One Hour with You*. Paramount Pictures (directors: George Cukor [uncredited] and Ernst Lubitsch; released 25 March 1932). Elevations of a staircase. Pencil on paper. UCSB.

239. Jock Peters, staircase for *One Hour with You*. Paramount Pictures (directors: George Cukor [uncredited] and Ernst Lubitsch; released 25 March 1932). Private collection.

240. Jock Peters, set for *This Is the Night*. Paramount Pictures (director: Frank Tuttle; released 8 April 1932). Elevation of living room. Print with pencil captions. UCSB.

241. Jock Peters, sketch for an unnamed film, 1932. "Fliegerstaffel" (airplane squadron), perspective. Pencil on notebook paper. Collection Jock de Swart.

242. Jock Peters, sketch for an unnamed film, 1932. "Lazarette u. d. Weise" (military hospital and the wise one), perspective. Pencil on notebook paper. Collection Jock de Swart.

243. Jock Peters, sketch for an unnamed film, 1932. "Jerusalem," perspective. Pencil on notebook paper. Collection Jock de Swart.

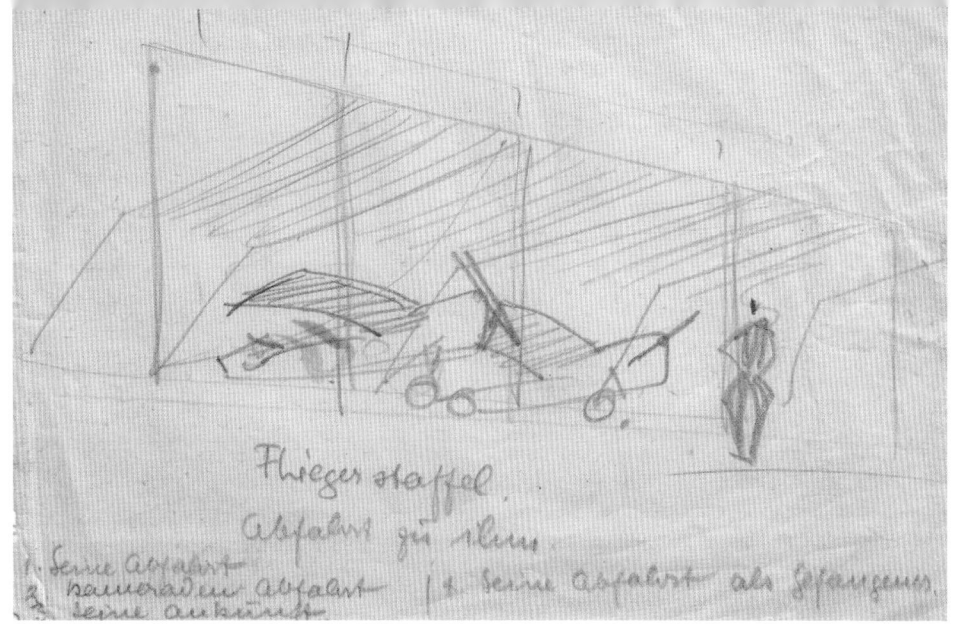

Fliegerstaffel.
Abfahrt zu ihm.
1. Seine Abfahrt
2. Kameraden Abfahrt | 4. seine Abfahrt als Gefangener.
3. seine Ankunft

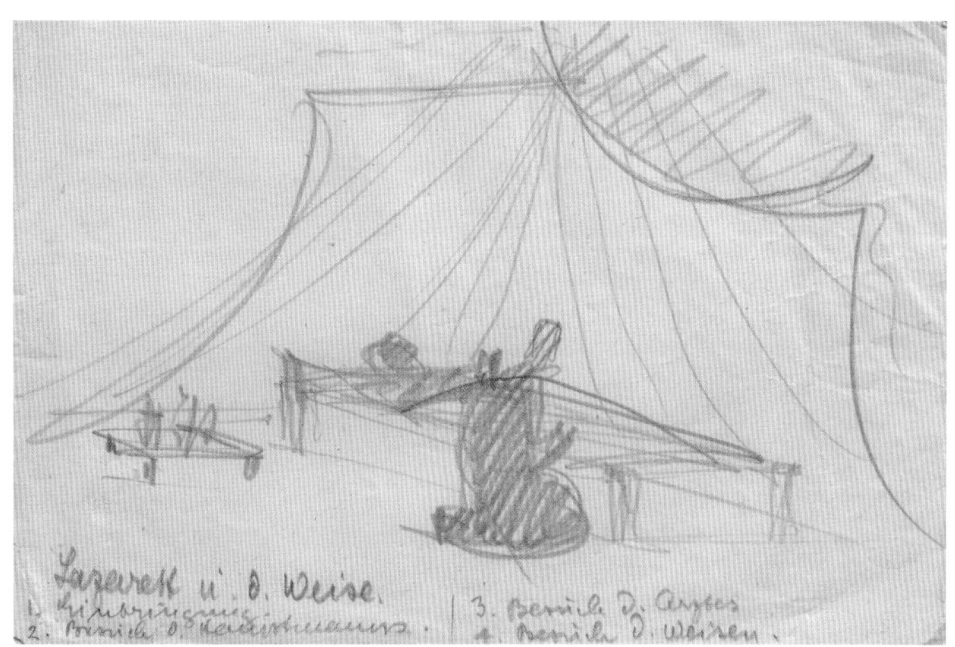

Lazarett u. d. Weise.
1. Hinbringung.   3. Besuch d. Arztes
2. Besuch d. Verrichtmanns.   4. Besuch d. Weisen.

Jerusalem.

244. Jock Peters, Lawrence Shepard House, San Marino, California, 1933. UCSB.

245. Jock Peters, Lawrence Shepard House,
San Marino, California, 1933. Perspective.
Pencil and colored pencil on paper. Collection Jock de Swart.

246. Jock Peters, Lawrence Shepard House, San Marino, California, 1933. Rear patio. UCSB.

247. Jock Peters, Lawrence Shepard House,
San Marino, California, 1933. Living room. UCSB.

248. Jock Peters, Lawrence Shepard House, San Marino, California, 1933. Dining room. UCSB.

249. Jock Peters, Cavanaugh & Stebins women's shop, Los Angeles, 1932. Mott-Merge Collection, California State Library, Sacramento.

250. Jock Peters, A. L. Gilks House, Los Angeles, 1934. UCSB.

251. Jock Peters, A. L. Gilks House, Los Angeles, 1934.
Rear patio and upper-floor deck. UCSB.

In 1933, Peters received another house commission, in the Los Feliz neighborhood near Griffith Park. The client was Alfred Gilks, a cinematographer who was employed by Famous Players-Lasky and, later, Paramount; much later, in 1951, he would win an Oscar for his work on *An American in Paris*.

The Gilks House speaks in a variant of modernism that is sure and accomplished but also decidedly personal. The massing and the fenestration of the house, which was completed in 1934, are once more unusual (fig. 250). Peters's two slender front piers, which extend the full length of both stories and support the upstairs balcony, and the porte cochere, to the right, are vestiges late-nineteenth-century design presented in a modern way. Perhaps Peters intended them to evoke the past, or perhaps they were merely another of his formal experiments. From the rear, the side patio and terrace project a more standard modernist image—sharp and vibrant, framed by bold and assertive lines (figs. 251, 252). The difference between the two elevations is stark. The house's plan is a hybrid in the same way, a mix of relatively large unencumbered spaces that are conjoined with narrow, even cramped, openings (fig. 253).

What again stands out in Peters's architectural works of the 1930s—and his film sets of the period, for that matter—is their insistent variety. If one regards them as a group, they look as if they could have come from different makers—perhaps even intended for different locales. Peters's design for his own house on Hill Drive is vaguely European, the Shepard House could readily be in Florida, and the Gilks House (from the rear) in California, albeit a bit later. Formally, they speak in surprisingly divergent languages.

The differences, however, are not only superficial. The houses seemingly represent distinct and separate concepts of modern living: open versus closed, inside versus outside, intimate versus exposed. Some of these differences were probably the result of his clients' wishes; Peters was an unusually obliging architect for an early modernist (in marked contrast, say, to Neutra, who gave his clients what *he* thought they needed, despite requiring them to fill out an extensive questionnaire about their desires and lifestyles). Many of the special features of Peters's houses, however, must have been his.

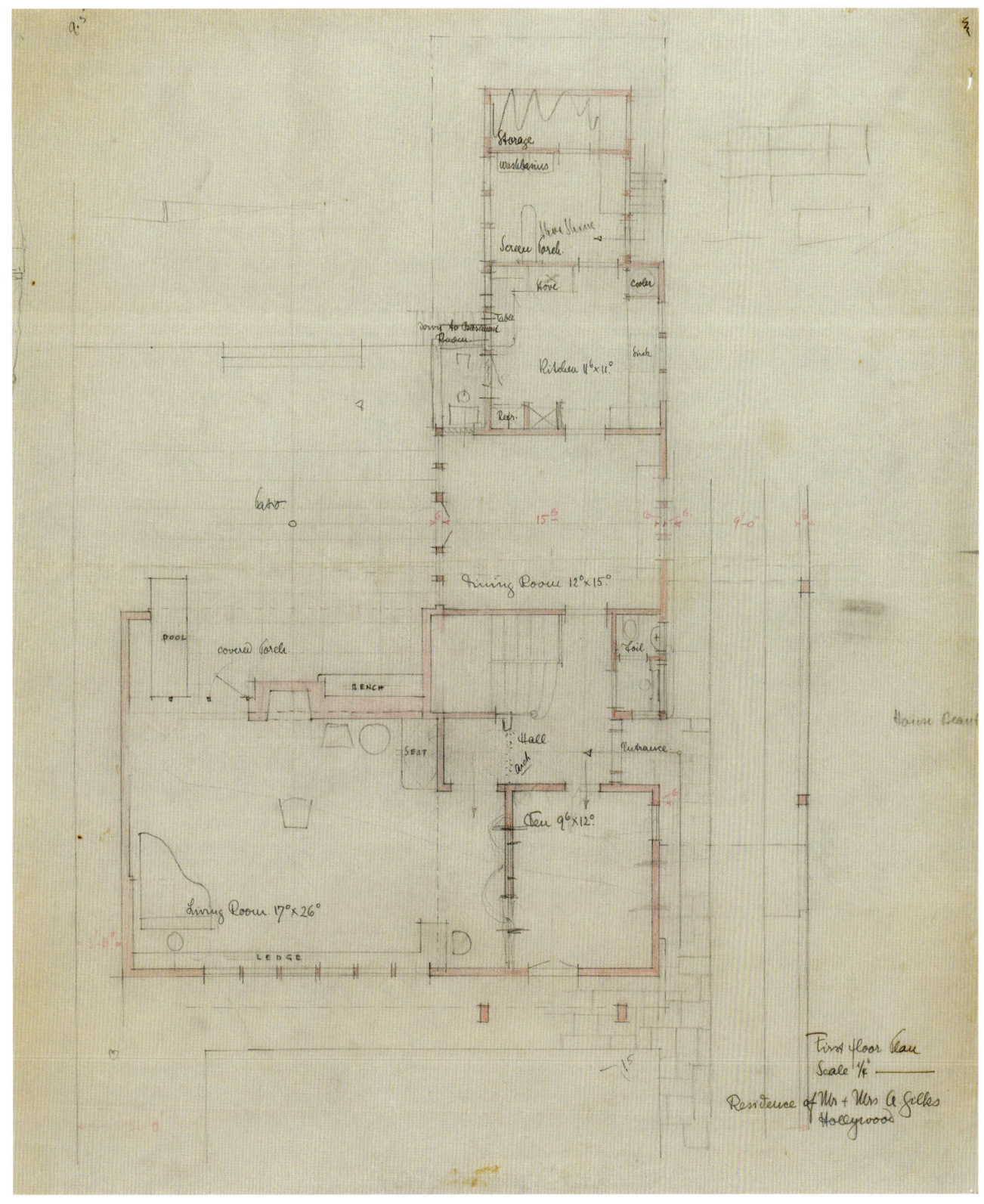

253. Jock Peters, A. L. Gilks House, Los Angeles, 1934.
Ground floor plan. Pencil, colored pencil, and ink on paper. UCSB.

252. Jock Peters, A. L. Gilks House, Los Angeles, 1934.
Elevation of rear patio and upper-floor deck.
Pencil on paper. UCSB.

By 1933, Peters's health was deteriorating rapidly. A photograph taken of him at the time sitting on a rock next to an ancient bristlecone pine tree shows just how slight and drawn he had become (fig. 254). His clothes hang on his frame; his body is seemingly made up of desiccated skin and bones; the lines on his face are deeply incised. It is the image of an old man, not one still in his mid-forties. In the period after World War I, he had experienced serious health crises from time to time, but he had always bounced back. This time his disease kept diminishing him. He continued working, just as he had for years, but it became ever more challenging for him.

What might have come next for Peters we can never know. He died suddenly on March 29, 1934, not even two weeks after his forty-fifth birthday. The death certificate lists the cause as heart failure. The poor functioning of his lungs doubtless contributed to his passing.

Many of Peters's former friends, clients, and colleagues wrote heartfelt letters of condolence to Herta.[336] The newspapers and professional journals, however, paid scant notice. Even the *Los Angeles Times*, which had followed his work closely over the previous half decade, ran only a brief, seven-line tribute.[337] Peters, it seems, had died too soon, before he had a chance to secure his place in the story of modernism in Southern California.

Peters's insistence on going it alone, on holding himself mostly apart from the other Los Angeles modernists and staying out of the politics and squabbles that defined the local scene, also had much to do with his rapid eclipse. Within a short time, he had become a forgotten figure. Three decades later, when the first histories of California modernism were being written, no one among the local historians or critics sought to promote or preserve his legacy. That task fell almost entirely to Herta—and, later, to Ursel—who did what they could, though always from the outside.[338]

If Peters was undervalued in later years, it was in some part because he could not be readily defined. He never developed a signature style. No one copied him; no one took direct inspiration from his designs, because it was not possible to do so. He was a one-off. Not only was his output small, but also much of what he had achieved was not publicly accessible. Peters never had the chance to design a major public work in Southern California. And the store designs he made were essentially transitory, ever prone to adjustment or removal as the needs of the retail establishments changed.

Peters's death came at a time of transition for modernism in Southern California—and for the country more generally. By 1934, the first refugee architects and designers fleeing the rise of fascism in Europe were arriving, bringing with them very different ideas about design. Within a few years, tastes in America would change dramatically. The indigenous modernism—or, at least, the variant of the new style that had developed in the United States, very often the work of foreign-born designers—would give way to an aesthetic of ever-greater simplicity and purism.

It is possible that Peters might have embraced the new trend, just as he had embraced other modernist styles before. Yet it is just as likely that he would have gone his own way, merging the new look of austerity with other modernist variants. The question is an interesting one but, of course, unanswerable. What is telling is that up to the moment of his death he had remained true to his own understanding of the new aesthetic, one that left room for a full miscellany of stylistic possibilities.

254. Jock Peters, c. 1934. Collection Jock de Swart.

EPILOGUE |

Jock Peters was one of the small number of visionaries who first conceived of Southern California modernism, shaped it, and rendered it tangible and real. He also made it accessible and consumable, the two most important attributes of what was uniquely American in the American design of those years. By the mid-1930s, American modernism—even before it was mass-produced and displayed for sale on every downtown main street and, later, in every shopping mall—was already a commodity: less applied art in the European sense (as had been the case for Art Nouveau or the early Bauhaus) than art applied to commerce.

Nearly everything Peters designed and made after he arrived in Southern California, whether it was a custom product or an article intended for the broader public, was about selling. He first retailed an image of suspense and glamour for the movies; then he sold furnishings and interiors that put into the marketplace messages about new ways of living. His brief fame, around 1930, came as a result of his great store designs: Bullock's in Los Angeles and the Hollander store in New York City. Both were palaces of commerce and engines for the powering of free enterprise.

Jock Peters, c. 1933. UCSB.

Yet if Peters often surrendered willingly to the exigencies of the retail world, his designs were much more about the fostering of images. They were visual devices for inducing shoppers to look and buy, while serving, equally, as fantasies of refinement and sophistication. Later, during the early years of the Great Depression, when the sales machine that was America sputtered and nearly stopped running altogether, Peters made houses and movie set designs—places in which to reside and scenes of entertainment—that were at their core about trying to renew enthusiasm for modern times. He sold a set of pictorial metaphors—about progress, happiness, prosperity, and a gleaming future.

At least one judgment can be issued about Peters without equivocation: he did what he did with a special emphasis on style. He was far less preoccupied than most of his fellow modernists with issues of materiality or construction. He spoke rarely of functionality, and when he did, he usually interpreted the idea prosaically: the function of a store for him was to sell products; the function of a film set was to amaze and entertain—and to compel us to dream. He was gripped by how things looked, the play of their surfaces, their colors and forms, the ways in which they might yield a statement about modern times. He was relentless in his experimentation with style and stylistic dress in his designs. Often, he would seize one idea, one formal solution, then ponder how to elaborate it, in that way laboring more like a couturier who crafts the same dress in an assortment of colorways, with multiple and varied appliqués. Throughout his working life, Peters designed nearly the identical building or interior in sundry styles, seeing which one fit best, which one looked the part. He was not the least troubled by what might have appeared from the outside as indecisiveness or a lack of commitment. In truth, he was simply not interested in finding a single, "unified" expression. He was a restless changeling whose imagery and color sense were forever shifting.

Peters encapsulated the freewheeling spirit of Southern California in those years. If modernism was fundamentally about liberation—and California modernism even more so—then he was a consummate modernist, unfettered by strictures, untethered to an aesthetic rule book. Such an approach does not fit neatly into the modernist canon. Still, anyone examining Peters's collective designs with care will come away with a sense of a figure with real talent and a powerful and original voice. His hand more often than not was sure, his designs invested with grace and vitality. His best works are as compelling as those of almost any of his contemporaries.

What Peters gave us, more than anything else, was a consistent celebration of *all* that was new. He embraced the spirit of a new and modern world precisely by exploring its full array of possibilities. He never gave up on his belief that modernity itself, and modern life with it, were manifold and alive. To pore over Peters's entire oeuvre is to see nearly everything in those years that constituted a new way of being, making, and living.

An examination of Peters's life and work also provides us with an object lesson in the shortcomings of how we conventionally read the past. What emerges from his story is a different view of the early modern design scene in Southern California. Seen through the lens of his life and work, it looks more variegated, less sure. It seems more vulnerable and ad hoc. And the way forward seems less clear. It is only in hindsight that we construct that sense of inevitability that now permeates so much of the history of modernism.

Even now—despite a heightened tolerance for the difficult and the motley in design—the unevenness of Peters's work remains unfashionable and somehow marginal. Too often—even today—do we look only to the leading lights of the past, to those whose efforts were most obviously prophetic and transformative. Too often do we search for the most conspicuous narrative, the one that speaks most directly to our contemporary interests and biases. And too often do we ignore those whose work is awkward and untidy, those movements or ideas that were peripheral or failed to pan out.

But history comes to us in the form that it does: confused and capricious, at times opaque, tangled, unruly, or anomalous. The task for the historian is to try to render the whole, the complete scene, as closely as possible to what it was, and to make meaning out of all of it.

Jock Peters, kitchen table, c. 1919. Collection Jock de Swart.

WORKS BY JOCK PETERS |

All works were realized unless designated as project, sketch, or competition design.

1912
| Project: Düsseldorf Kunstakademie
| Competition design: Department store in Nuremberg (with Carl Gustav Bensel)

c. 1912
| Architectural sketch of a temple

1913
| Project: Department store in Düsseldorf (with Carl Gustav Bensel)
| Levantehaus (with Carl Gustav Bensel) Mönckebergstraße 7, Hamburg
| Project: Bugenhagenhaus, Hamburg (with Carl Gustav Bensel)

c.1913
| Project: Design for a villa

1914
| Project: Building for the block of the Mönckebergstraße between Lange Mühren and Barkhof, Hamburg (with Carl Gustav Bensel)
| Project: War memorials in the cemetery in Hamburg-Ohlsdorf (with Carl Gustav Bensel)
| Wohldorf-Ohlstedt housing development, Hamburg (with Carl Gustav Bensel)
| Competition design: art exhibition building, Hamburg, motto: "gez. Säule," awarded first prize (with Carl Gustav Bensel)
| Competition design: Tiefstack Electrical Power Plant, Hamburg, motto: "Industria," awarded first prize (with Carl Gustav Bensel)

c.1914
| Project: *Großstadt*

1915
| Competition design: War monument in Hamburg-Ohlsdorf
| Project: Festival hall and gymnastics building, in Hamburg
| Project: Suburban house
| Electrical Power Plant (with Carl Gustav Bensel) Tiefstack-Hamburg

1916
| Project: Suburban house with columns
| Project: War memorial sarcaphagi
| Competition design: War memorial church

1916–17
| Project: Landhaus I

1915–18
| Competition design: War memorial exhibition tower, awarded first prize in 1918

1918
| Project: Landhaus II, house for Dr. Paulsen

c. 1918
| Competition design: Electrical power plant in Rendsburg, motto: "Schaubild," awarded first prize

1919
| Dining room of the Peters house, Hamburg
| Project: Renovation of the pavilion on Alster Lake, Jungfernsteig, Hamburg
| Competition design: Lyceum at the corner of Breitenfeld-

erstraße and Curschmannstraße, Hamburg, motto: "Durchgeistiger Raum," awarded first prize

c. 1919
| Gravestone for Emil Born (location unknown; executed?)

1920
| Competition design: Decorated war graves for the Hamburg-Ohlsdorf Cemetery, awarded third prize
| Project: Farmhouse in Holstein

c. 1920
| Project: City hall for Gadebusch, Germany
| Project: Tall, stair-stepped building
| Project: Skyscraper
| Project: Landhaus II, streamlined version

1921
| Project: Country house with a thatched roof
| Project: Art education center, Altona

1921–22
| Haus Schluck (with Karl Schneider and Karl Witte) Mellenbergweg 83, Hamburg-Volksdorf
| Villa Eber, renovation and addition (with Karl Schneider and Karl Witte) Schenefelder Landstraße 5, Hamburg-Blankenese

1922
| Competition design: Commercial building in Königsberg, now Kaliningrad, Russia (with Knud Lönberg-Holm)
| Competition design: Cultural center, possibly for Stuttgart (with Knud Lönberg-Holm)
| Competition design: *Chicago Tribune* competition, not submitted (with Knud Lönberg-Holm)
| Project: Dormitory for ten girls at the Loheland Settlement, near Fulda, Germany
| Project: Community center for the Loheland Settlement, near Fulda, Germany

c. 1922
| Project: Skyscraper façade for downtown Los Angeles (with Otto Neher)

1922–23
| Project: Plans for multiple houses for unnamed builders or developers

| Plans for various unidentified small houses in the Los Angeles area (realized?)

c. 1923
| Project: Mission Revival–style house, two versions
| Project: House in the style of Frank Lloyd Wright and Lloyd Wright
| Furnishings for the Peters House in Eagle Rock (with George Peters)
| Project: Motion picture sets for an unknown film (or films)

1924
| Project: Festival hall for the Loheland Settlement, near Fulda, Germany (two versions)
| Project: Sets for an unknown film
| Motion picture set for *The City of the Future* for Famous Players-Lasky (not produced; project dropped after the release of Fritz Lang's *Metropolis*)

1925–27
| Project: Various unrealized motion picture sets

1926
| Motion picture set for *What Price Glory*, Fox Film Company, director: Raoul Walsh; released 23 November 1926
| Project: Living space and library for *Hi-Hat Magazine*

c. 1926
| Project: Motion picture set for *Mars* for Famous Players-Lasky (not produced)
| Sidewalk for Silver Strand Beach, California, for William Lingenbrink

1927
| Project: Reception room for *Hi-Hat Magazine*
| Project: House for *Hi-Hat Magazine*
| Alcove for playing cards
| Competition design for furniture for S. Karpen & Brothers Company, Chicago, awarded first prize

c. 1927
| Project: House for Mrs. C. O. Blachley in Hollywood
| Dining room for H. Hofmann, Beverly Hills, California
| Watson and Son tailor shop 6605 Hollywood Boulevard, Los Angeles
| Furniture for Harry Blaine
| Blaine Studio Building

6605 Hollywood Boulevard, Los Angeles
| Lighting fixture designs
| Project: Dining room
| Project: Brick fireplace
| Project: Library reading room
| Project: Living room
| Project: Grand foyer
| Various furniture designs (with George Peters)
| Store buildings, Silver Strand Beach, California, for William Lingenbrink

1928

| Desmond's, storefront remodeling and interiors (with Feil and Paradise)
  717 Seventh Street, Los Angeles
| Competition design: Rug for Mohawk Carpet Mills, awarded first prize
| Interiors for Jock D. Peters office
  Studio of Contemporary Design
  507 Fine Arts Building, Los Angeles
| Maddux Air Lines ticket office, façade and interiors
  636 South Olive Street, Los Angeles
| Table and chairs for Mabel Skinner
  811 W. Seventh Street, Los Angeles
| Universal Assembling Furniture, US copyright number 15464, not executed

1929

| Bullock's Wilshire, interiors for floors one, two, and three (with Eleanor LeMaire, John Weber, and Feil and Paradise)
  3050 Wilshire Boulevard, Los Angeles
| Solar Lighting Fixtures Company, façade and interiors
  444 North Western Avenue, Los Angeles

1930

| Harbor Chevrolet automobile dealership (with W. F. Ruck)
  304 East Anaheim Street, Wilmington, California
| L. P. Hollander Company store, interiors, furnishings, packaging, and other designs
  (with Eleanor LeMaire and John Weber)
  3 East Fifty-Seventh Street, New York City
| House for William Lingenbrink (with W. F. Ruck)
  2000 Grace Avenue, Whitley Heights, Los Angeles
| Project: "Lodge Type B" for Park Moderne (with W. F. Ruck)

c. 1931

| Project: Peters residence and studio
  5333 College View Avenue, Los Angeles

1931

| Project: Bullock's department store remodel of main sales floor and exterior of downtown store
  Broadway Hill and West Seventh Street, Los Angeles
| Clubhouse for Park Moderne (altered)
  23031 Blue Bird Drive, Calabasas, California
| Fountain, pump house, swimming pool for Park Moderne
  Calabasas, California
| Mary Sachs department store, interiors
  (with Eleanor LeMaire)
  208 North Third Street, Harrisburg, Pennsylvania
| Irene Ltd.
  9000 Sunset Boulevard, now West Hollywood
| Motion picture sets for *Confessions of a Co-Ed*, Paramount Pictures, directors: David Burton and Dudley Murphy; released 11 July 1931
| Motion picture sets for *The Road to Reno*, Paramount Pictures, director: Richard Wallace; released 26 September 1931
| Motion picture sets for *Girls about Town*, Paramount Pictures, director: George Cukor; released 7 November 1931
| Room for a Young Lady, at the 1931 Cologne international exhibition, crafted by the Schürmann Company, Cologne
| Monogram for Mabel Skinner Cosmetics
| Showroom for Mabel Skinner
  811 W. Seventh Street, Los Angeles

1932

| Cavanaugh & Stebins women's shop
  3043 Wilshire Boulevard, Los Angeles
| Motion picture set for *One Hour with You*, Paramount Pictures, directors: George Cukor (uncredited) and Ernst Lubitsch; released 23 March 1932
| Motion picture set for *This Is the Night*, Paramount Pictures, director: Frank Tuttle (not used)
| Project: Various unrealized motion picture sets

1933

| Lawrence Shepard House
  1390 Lorain Road, San Marino, California

1934

| A. L. Gilks House (George F. Peters, builder)
  4600 Gainsborough Avenue, Los Angeles

Jock Peters, unidentified motion picture set, c. 1926.
Chalk and watercolor on board. UCSB.

NOTES

Chapter 1
JARRENWISCH AND HAMBURG

1| "Geburtsurkunde [birth certificate], Jakob Detlef Peters," Collection Jock de Swart (hereafter JdS).

2| As a girl, Anna Kruse lived only a few hundred meters from the Peters farm, in the nearby settlement of Poppenwurth. Annotated map of the Wesselburen district, Peters family papers, JdS.

3| Peters family tree drawn by Ursula (Ursel) de Swart, c. 1970, JdS.

4| The name Dithmarschen is said to derive from the old Saxon words "thiad," or people, and "marschen," or marshlands—together "people of the marshlands." Some etymologists have suggested, however, that "dith" may merely have denoted "large." The name thus may have meant "the great marshland." It was first recorded as "Theitmaresgano"–the district of great marshes or marsh people–in the ninth century. Anton Veith, B*eschreibung des Landes Dithmarschen, oder Geographische, Politische und Historische Nachricht vom bemeldten Lande: Aus bewehrten gedruckten und ungedruckten Urkunden verfasset, nebst einer Vorrede von Jo. Albert Fabricius* (Hamburg: Wierings Erben, 1733); J. Hanssen and H. Wolf, *Chronik des Landes Dithmarschen* (Hamburg: Langhoff, 1833); Willi Birker et al., *Dithmarschen: Land und Leistung* (Hamburg: Christian Wegner, 1946); Alfred Kamphausen, *Dithmarschen: Geschichte und Bild einer Landschaft* (Heide: Boysens, 1968).

5| "Als Sohn einer alt ansässigen Hofbesitzerfamilie bin ich ... in Norderdithmarschen gebornen." "Lebenslauf des Architekten J. D. Peters, Lehrer an der Kunstgewerbeschule Altona," 10 July 1920, JdS. Unless otherwise noted, all translations are my own.

6| For the history of the region, see Rudolph Nehlsen, *Geschichte von Dithmarschen* (Tübingen: H. Laupp, 1908); Ernst Sauermann, ed., *Dithmarschen: Ein Heimatbuch* (Hamburg: Paul Hartung, 1920); William Lawrence Urban, *Dithmarschen: A Medieval Peasant Republic* (Lewiston, NY: Edwin Mellen Press, 1991); Angela Lüdtke, *Zur Chronik des Landes Dithmarschen von Johann Adolph Köster, gen. Neocorus. Eine historiographische Analyse* (Heide: Boyens, 1992); Martin Geitzelt, *Geschichte Dithmarschens, 1559–1918* (Heide: Boyens, 2014).

7| Happy [pseud.], "Who's Who in Eagle Rock: Jock D. Peters," *Eagle Rock Sentinel*, 9 November 1930.

8| Ursula (Ursel) de Swart, "The Golden Chain," n.d., 1, JdS.

9| Happy, "Who's Who in Eagle Rock."

10| Ibid.

11| Swart, "Golden Chain," 1.

12| Quoted in Happy, "Who's Who in Eagle Rock."

13| "Lebenslauf des Architekten J. D. Peters."

14| On the development of Hamburg in the nineteenth and early twentieth centuries, see Eckart Klessmann, *Geschichte der Stadt Hamburg* (Hamburg: Die Hanse in der Europäische Verlagsanstalt, 2002); and Werner Jochmann and Hans-Dieter Loose, *Hamburg*,

Geschichte der Stadt und ihrer Bewohner, 2 vols. (Hamburg: Hoffmann und Campe, 1982).

15| Interview with Dierk Peters, 17 March 2014.

16| Happy, "Who's Who in Eagle Rock."

17| George [Georg] Peters to Herta Peters, n.d. [c. 1950], JdS. He added, "Das war ja die Tragik in der Peters Familie: in den jungen, empfindlichen Jahren mussten wir auseinander." (That was the tragedy of the Peters family: in our young, sensitive years we were scattered apart.)

18| Hella Häussler, "Eine Grabmal-Patenschaft für Johann Reimer (1847–1917), den engagierten Steinmetz aus dem Karolinenviertel," accessed 11 April 2016, http://www.fof-ohlsdorf.de/aktuell/2010/108s35_reimer.

19| Happy, "Who's Who in Eagle Rock."

20| Häussler, "Eine Grabmal-Patenschaft für Johann Reimer."

21| "Mein Meister schenkte mir zwei Winterhalbjahre der Lehrzeit." "Lebenslauf des Architekten J. D. Peters."

22| Ibid. Peters was duly registered in the school records as student number 1035. [Karl] B[ernhard] Thiele, ed., *Staatliche Baugewerkschule für Hochbau und Tiefbau zu Hamburg. Denkschrift die Geschichte der Gründung und der Entwicklung der Schule bis zum 50. Schuljahr 1915—Beiliegend: Bericht über das Schuljahr 1915/1916* (Hamburg, 1915), 55.

23| Jürgen Lecour, "Bauschulen, Baugewerkschulen, Polytechniken," in *Entwerfen–Architektenausbildung in Europa von Vitruv bis Mitte des 20. Jahrhunderts: Geschichte, Theorie, Praxis*, ed. Ralph Johannes (Hamburg: Junius, 2009), 482–83. The 1909 annual report from the school–at the time Peters was enrolled there–spells out its mission. *Staatliche Baugewerkschule für Hochbau und Tiefbau zu Hamburg: Bericht über das Schuljahr 1908/1909* (Hamburg, 1909), 4.

24| Ibid., 483–88.

25| On the history of the school, see Thiele, *Staatliche Baugewerkschule für Hochbau und Tiefbau zu Hamburg*, 5–25.

26| "Lebenslauf des Architekten J. D. Peters"; *Staatliche Baugewerkschule für Hochbau und Tiefbau zu Hamburg: Bericht über das Schuljahr 1908/1909*, 19.

27| Happy, "Who's Who in Eagle Rock."

28| Ibid.

Chapter 2 |
AN ARCHITECTURAL APPRENTICESHIP

29| "Lebenslauf des Architekten J. D. Peters." In his personnel file at the Handwerker- und Kunstgewerbeschule Altona, Peters noted that he worked for Jacob and Ameis from 1909 to 1911. Peters, Personalbogen, n.d. [c. 1920], Handwerker- und Kunstgewerbeschule Altona. Alfred Ernst Paul Jacob (1880–1945) and Otto Heinrich Ameis (1881–1958) were the principals of the firm. They had founded the partnership a few years before, and it would continue successfully for many years, well into the interwar period. See, for example, Gert Kähler and Hans Bunge, eds., *Der Architekt als Bauherr: Hamburger Baumeister und ihr Wohnhaus* (Munich: Dölling und Galitz, 2016), 56.

30| "Lebenslauf des Architekten J. D. Peters."

31| Born in Hamburg in 1848, Wilhelm Daniel Vivié served for a time as the director of the Kunstgewerbemuseum (Museum of Arts and Crafts) in Reichenberg (now Liberec, Czech Republic). After his return to Hamburg, he emerged as an influential figure in the local architectural scene.

32| Vivié's father, Ernst Gottfried Vivié, was a noted sculptor in the city. He aided Lichtwark early in his career, and the younger Vivié and Lichtwark as a result became close friends. For years, they and their families lived in the same apartment building. Carl Schnellenberg, ed., *Alfred Lichtwark: Briefe an Wolf Mannhardt* (Hamburg: Johann Trautmann, 1952), 69.

33| Lovis Corinth, Max Slevogt, Adolph Menzel, Pierre Bonnard, and Édouard Vuillard were among the artists whose works he acquired. Carsten von Meyer-Tönnesmann, "Imperator der Kunst: Bildungsreformer und Museumsvisionär; Der Hamburger Alfred Lichtwark war der bedeutendste Kunstvermittler des Kaiserreichs. Ein Porträt zum 100. Todestag," *Die Zeit*, 13 January 2014.

34| Meyer-Tönnesmann, "Imperator der Kunst."

35| "Lebenslauf des Architekten J. D. Peters."

36| Happy, "Who's Who in Eagle Rock."

37| Bensel had married Wilhelm Daniel Vivié's youngest daughter, Marianne, in 1906. "Carl Gustav Bensel, 24 Apr. 1878," in "Deutschland, Geburten und Taufen 1558–1898," index, *Family Search*, FHL microfilm 595583, accessed 9 February 2016, https://familysearch.org/pal:/MM9.1.1/NZ4J-1P8; Karl H. Hoffmann, "Bensel & Kamps," accessed 9 February 2016, http://www.architekturarchiv-web.de/portraets/a-d/bensel/index.html; "Carl Gustav Bensel," in *Hamburgische Biografie: Personenlexikon*, vol 4., ed. Franklin Kopitzsch and Dirk Brietzke (Göttingen: Wallstein Verlag, 2008), 45–46; Schnellenberg, *Alfred Lichtwark*, 54.

38| On Bensel and his career, see Jan Lubitz, "Carl Gustav Bensel: Eine Quintessenz der Idee vom geformten Raum," in Kähler and Bunge, *Der Architekt als Bauherr*, 168; and idem, *Geformter Raum: Die Hamburger Architekten Bensel, Kamps & Amsinck* (Munich: Dölling und Galitz, 2016), esp. 29–54. See also the portfolio of Bensel's early work, "C. G. Bensel, Regierungsbaumeister a. D., Architekt, Hamburg," Sonderheft *Bau-Rundschau* (Hamburg: Konrad Hanf, 1914).

39| Jan Lubitz, "Carl Gustav Bensel 1878–1949," May 2004, http://architekten-portrait.de/carl_gustav_bensel/index.html.

40| Happy, "Who's Who in Eagle Rock."

41| Peters's sketchbooks, c. 1912–13, Jock Peters Archive, Architectural Drawings Collection, Art, Design, and Architecture Museum, University of California, Santa Barbara (hereafter UCSB).

42| "Lebenslauf des Architekten J. D. Peters."

43| See, for example, the related discussion of the Werkbund and its aims in Frederic Schwartz, *The Werkbund: Design Theory and Mass Culture before the First World War* (New Haven, CT: Yale University Press, 1996).

44| On the Düsseldorf school's prominence, see John V. Maciuika, *Before the Bauhaus: Architecture, Politics, and the German State, 1890–1920* (Cambridge: Cambridge University Press, 2008), 149–52.

45| "Lebenslauf des Architekten J. D. Peters."

46| Lubitz, *Geformter Raum*, 55–56.

47| M. W. Herbert Eulenberg, "Architekt Fritz August Breuhaus," *Deutsche Kunst und Dekoration* 34 (September 1914): 191–204; M. W. Herbert Eulenberg and Max Osborn, eds., *Fritz August Breuhaus de Groot* (Berlin: Neue Werkkunst, 1929); "Fritz August Breuhaus," accessed 22 February 2016, http://fritz-august-breuhaus.com/home_en.html.

48| On the redevelopment of Hamburg in this period, see, for example, Dieter Schädel, *Wie das Kunstwerk Hamburg entstand: Von Wimmel bis Schumacher—Hamburger Stadtbaumeister von 1841–1933* (Hamburg: Dölling und Galitz, 2006); Pablo de la Riestra, *Hamburg: Architektur einer weltoffenen Stadt* (Hamburg: Michael Imhof, 2008); and Frank Pieter Hesse, ed., *Stadtentwicklung zur Moderne: Die Entstehung großstädtischer Hafen- und Bürohausquartiere* (Berlin: Hendrik Bäßler, 2011).

49| Lubitz, *Geformter Raum*, 60.

50| Ibid.

51| Ibid.

52| Peters evidently spent some time in Hamburg, because he was briefly enrolled in the Hamburg Kunstgewerbeschule. In the early 1920s, in his personnel file at the Altona Handwerker- und Kunstgewerbeschule, Peters notes that he attended the school in 1911 but does not list which term or terms he was there. Peters, Personalbogen, n.d. [c. 1920], Handwerker- und Kunstgewerbeschule Altona.

53| Ursula (Ursel) de Swart, "Who Is Moving My Hand: My Life with Jan de Swart, Sculptor," n.d. [c. 1970], 28, JdS; Swart, "Golden Chain," 3.

54| Herta was born on March 17, 1889. Boeger family tree, c. 1936, JdS.

55| De Swart, "Who Is Moving My Hand: My Life with Jan de Swart, Sculptor," 28–29.

56| Herta Boeger, certificate from the "Anstalt für Kunststickerei und Frauenerwerb zu Düsseldorf," 11 April 1906, JdS.

57| The letters, some two dozen in all, are preserved in the archive at UCSB and in the former collection of Jock de Swart.

58| Alfred Fischer studied with Theodor Fischer at the Technical University in Stuttgart just after the turn of the century. The elder Fischer, who, along with Peter Behrens, would emerge as one of the most important German architectural educators of the era (his many students would include Richard Riemerschmid, Hugo Häring, Ernst May, Erich Mendelsohn, J. J. P. Oud, and Bruno Taut), fostered in his disciples a powerful sense of the need for the new. On the younger Fischer's training see, for example, Winfried Nerdinger, *Theodor Fischer: Architekt und Städtebauer 1862–1938*, exh. cat. (Berlin: Ernst & Sohn, 1988).

59| Telegram from Peters to Herta Boeger, 9 August 1913, JdS.

60| Peters, Personalbogen, n.d. [c. 1920], Handwerker- und Kunstgewerbeschule Altona.

61| Lubitz, "Carl Gustav Bensel 1878–1949"; idem, *Geformter Raum*, 62–68. On the history of the Levantehaus, see Michael Seufert, *Levantehaus: Tradition und Moderne* (Hamburg: Hoffmann und Campe, 2012), 6–19. See also Roland Jaeger, "Von Altona nach Los Angeles: Jakob Detlef Peters (1889–1934)—Ein Rekonstruktionsversuch," in *Architektur in Hamburg—Jahrbuch 1993*, ed. Dirk Meyhöfer and Ullrich Schwarz (Hamburg: Hamburg Architektenkammer / Junius, 1993), 138; and Hans Bahn, "Von Hamburger Großbauten und ihren Schöpfern," *Der Kries* 2, nos. 6–7 (1925): 10–29.

62| Peters to Herta Boeger, 20 August 1913, JdS.

63| Jaeger, "Von Altona nach Los Angeles," 138; Hermann Hipp, *Freie und Hansestadt Hamburg: Geschichte, Kultur und Stadtbaukunst an Elbe und Alster*, 2nd ed. (Cologne: DuMont, 1990), 176–78.

64| Peters to Herta Boeger, 19 September 1912, JdS.

65| See, for example, Stanford Anderson, "The Legacy of German Neoclassicism and Biedermeier: Behrens, Tessenow, Loos, and Mies," *Assemblage* 15 (August 1991): 63–87.

66| Peters family papers, JdS.

67| Lubitz, "Carl Gustav Bensel 1878–1949"; idem, *Geformter Raum*, 74–77. See also Jan Lubitz, "Hamburg, Mönckebergstraße—Zum denkmalpflegerischen Umgang mit den Kontorhäusern des Architekten Carl Bensel (1878–1949)," accessed 27 February 2016, http://baugeschichte.a.tu-berlin.de/hbf-msd/MSD-ab_2004-06/14_hamburg_MSD_2004-06_AB_web.pdf.

68| Peters, Personalbogen, n.d. [c. 1920], Handwerker- und Kunstgewerbeschule Altona.

69| "Bescheinigung der Eheschließung zwischen dem Architekten Jakob Peters und der Herta Boeger," 20 December 1913, JdS.

70| Carl Gustav Bensel, "Der Bebauungsplan Wohldorf-Ohlstedt," *Bau-Rundschau* 19 (1914): 165–72.

71| Hugo Koch, "Der Wettbewerb zur Erlangung von Entwürfen für die architektonische Gestaltung des neuen Kraftwerkes der Hamburgischen Elektrizitätswerke in Tiefstack," *Bau-Rundschau* 29 (1914): 273–82 and 30 (1914): 287–91; Jaeger, "Von Altona nach Los Angeles," 140; Lubitz, *Geformter Raum*, 83–86.

72| Lubitz, *Geformter Raum*, 79–81.

73| Hugo Koch, "Wettbewerb für ein Kunstausstellungsgebäude in Hamburg," *Bau-Rundschau* 24–25 (1914): 20.

Chapter 3 |
OF LIGHT AND DARKNESS

74| "Lebenslauf des Architekten J. D. Peters."

75| "Militärpaß des Jacob [sic] Detlef Peters."

76| Ibid.

77| Ursel Peters was born on 9 December 1914. Peters family papers, JdS.

78| Peters to Herta Boeger, 16 March 1915, JdS.
79| On the formation of the Hamburg Secession, see, for example, *Die Hamburgische Secession, 1919–1933*, exh. cat. (Hamburg: Galerie Herold Hamburg, 1992); Friederike Weimar, *Die Hamburgische Sezession 1919–1933* (Fischerhude: Atelier im Bauernhaus, 2003).
80| Interview with Dierk Peters, 17 March 2014.
81| Lubitz, *Geformter Raum*, 81.
82| It is likely that someone in Hamburg aided Peters in his move to Behrens's office. It may have been Bensel, or possibly Fritz Schumacher, who was then the director of the city building office and another of Peters's benefactors. Both men were highly respected; their word would have carried weight with Behrens. It is not known how or when Peters first came to Schumacher's attention. Beginning in 1909, Schumacher had served as the building director for the City of Hamburg. He eventually constructed a number of public buildings for the municipality. He certainly would have been acquainted with Vivié (since the latter also worked in the city building permits office, the so-called Baupolizei) and with Lichtwark (because of his prominence in the local art scene). From at least 1914, Schumacher appears to have also known Peters, and the two men remained on friendly terms until Peters left for Los Angeles. Schumacher supported Peters's career at several crucial turns, aiding him with contacts and letters of recommendation.
83| Peters, in any event, knew the significance of the move. In Peters's papers is a clipping of an article about Behrens from one of the local Hamburg newspapers: Karl Schaefer, "Peter Behrens als führender Meister in der modernen Architektur und in den angewandten Künsten," *Neue Hamburger Zeitung* (morning ed.), 26 November 1915, JdS. Peters also kept a letter he received from Fritz August Breuhaus congratulating him on landing the position with Behrens. Breuhaus writes, "Peter Behrens . . . was always the preeminent and most important of the Darmstadt masters." Fritz August Breuhaus to Peters, 20 October 1915, JdS.
84| Robert Koch and Eberhard Pook, eds., *Karl Schneider: Leben und Werk (1892–1945)* (Hamburg: Dölling und Galitz, 1992), 9–10.
85| Interview with Dierk Peters, 17 March 2014.
86| Alan Windsor, *Peter Behrens: Architect and Designer, 1868–1940* (London: Architectural Press, 1981), 142–43.
87| Peter Behrens, "Zeugnis [für Herrn Architekt Jakob Detlef Peters]," 12 September 1916, JdS.
88| "Lebenslauf des Architekten J. D. Peters."
89| "Kriegs-Beorderung des Ersatzreservist Architekt Jacob [sic] Peters," 12 October 1915, JdS.
90| Behrens writes in his "Zeugnis," his certification of employment, that Peters continued to work for him until 30 August 1916. In truth, Peters had departed more than a month before. Behrens, "Zeugnis [für Herrn Architekt Jakob Detlef Peters]."
91| Jock Peters to Herta Peters, 1 August 1916, JdS.
92| Ibid.
93| Jock Peters to Herta Peters, 10 September 1916, UCSB.
94| Jock Peters to Herta Peters, 9–10 September 1916, UCSB.
95| Ibid.
96| Jock Peters to Herta Peters, 16 September 1916, UCSB.
97| The official date of his reassignment was 18 September 1916. Heereswerkstätte West, affidavit certifying Peters's service with the unit, 7 October 1918, JdS.
98| "Lebenslauf des Architekten J. D. Peters."
99| Ibid.
100| Peters captured the moment in his poem "Streik!" (Strike!). Jock Peters, "Streik!" (1916), JdS.
101| Swart, "Golden Chain," 4.
102| "Lebenslauf des Architekten J. D. Peters."
103| Herta Peters to Jock Peters, 18 October 1916, JdS.
104| Jock Peters to Herta Peters, 28 December 1917, UCSB.
105| Ibid.
106| Jock Peters to Herta Peters, 24 November 1917, JdS.
107| In another of his letters to Herta from this period, Peters describes the joy he derived after receiving a response from a friend to whom he had sent two of his woodcuts. Jock Peters to Herta Peters, 13 December 1917, JdS.
108| It is unclear whether Peters actually submitted any of the designs. See [?] Arntz, "Der Wettbewerb um ein Grabdenkmal für die Kriegsbegräbnisstätte des Hamburger Zentralfriedhofes in Ohlsdorf," *Bau-Rundschau* 20–22 (1915): 77–80, plate 82.
109| After the war, in an article in the Hamburg architecture journal *Bau-Rundschau*, Peters explained some of the logic that lay behind the design. "Space," he writes,

> is the basis of architectural creation, our culture, the design of our settlements and cities. . . . It is not enough to set a four-sided cube on a base and then attempt to establish a connection with the surroundings with plantings. . . . [W]ith cutouts set into walls (windows, in other words), they provide these four-walled spaces with a linkage to the outer world! Our existing rooms have the effect of separating people from the outside world. Today, we as fully engaged human beings may demand that we be the masters of our spaces. [We] can experience space, even if the rooms only have three enclosing walls and the fourth one is divided up with glazing, in such a way that its presence is not only visible but that allows one to retain a sense of having a connection with the world outside.

Jakob Detlef [Jock] Peters, "Zu meinen Landhäusern," *Bau-Rundschau* 11, nos. 12–13 (25 March 1920): 46.
110| Frank Lloyd Wright, *Frank Lloyd Wright, Chicago. 8. Sonderheft der Architektur des XX. Jahrhunderts* (Berlin: Ernst Wasmuth, 1911).
111| Winfried Nerdinger, *The Architect Walter Gropius* (Berlin: Gebr. Mann, 1985), 48.
112| Iain Boyd Whyte, "Peters and Schneider: The Drawing Board as Home," in *Caught by Politics: Hitler Exiles and American Visual Culture*, eds. Sabine Eckmann and Lutz Koepnick (New York: Palgrave Macmillan, 2007), 142–44.
113| "Militärpaß des Jacob [sic] Detlef Peters."

114| Jock Peters to Herta Peters, 22 February 1918, UCSB.
115| Jock Peters to Herta Peters, 16 March 1918, JdS.
116| Ibid.
117| Letter of recommendation for Peters from Melchior von Hugo, 7 May 1920, JdS.
118| "Militärpaß des Jacob [sic] Detlef Peters."
119| Ibid.

Chapter 4 |
EXPERIMENTS IN STYLE

120| Interview with Dierk Peters, 17 March 2014.
121| "Lebenslauf des Architekten J. D. Peters."
122| Interview with Dierk Peters, 17 March 2014.
123| Jock Peters to Herta Peters, 17 April 1918, JdS.
124| Ibid.
125| Jock Peters to Herta Peters, 6 December 1922, UCSB.
126| Fritz Schumacher to Peters, 3 December 1918, JdS.
127| See, for example, Fritz Schumacher, *Das Wesen des neuzeitlichen Backsteinbaues* (Munich: Georg D. W. Callwey, 1917).
128| Wolfgang Voigt, Hartmut Frank, and Ulirch Höhns, *Hans und Oskar Gerson: Hanseatische Moderne—Bauten in Hamburg und im kalifornischen Exil 1907–1957* (Hamburg: Dölling und Galitz, 2000).
129| "Gadebusch," *Bau-Rundschau* 11, nos. 20–21 (27 May 1920): 88; "Wettbeweb für den Neubau des Rathauses in Gadebusch," *Bau-Rundschau* 11, nos. 42–43 (28 October 1920): 175–76.
130| Surviving among the Peters papers are two small blueprints of the first Landhaus design with pencil corrections, suggesting that he had actively pursued the project with his client. That it remained unbuilt very likely had to do with Germany's postwar economic problems.
131| It is worth noting that Peters's version evidently came first, several months before Feininger's.
132| Jakob Detlef Peters, "Architektonischer Götzendienst," *Bau-Rundschau* 10, nos. 45–46 (13 November 1919): 195.
133| Ibid., 194.
134| Jakob Detlef Peters, "Bauet Räume, keine Zellen!" *Bau-Rundschau* 11, nos. 9–10 (11 March 1920): 36.
135| Hugo Koch, "Jakob Detlef Peters," *Bau-Rundschau* 11, nos. 12–13 (25 March 1920): 45.
136| Peters was one of the early members; indeed, he was the first architect to join. Weimar, *Die Hamburgische Sezession*, 132.
137| Koch and Pook, *Karl Schneider*, 10.
138| Jaeger, "Von Altona nach Los Angeles," 143.
139| "Dienstvertrag zwischen dem Magistrat der Stadt Altona und dem Architekten Herrn Jacob [sic] Peters," 6 May 1922, JdS.
140| An early brochure described the institution as a place where future "masters are introduced to modern ideas and techniques in special courses and, in others, instructors are prepared to teach drawing in advanced trade schools." *Die Fachschulen für bildenden Künste und Kunstgewerbe Deutschlands: Kunstakademien, Mal- und Zeichenschulen, Kunstgewerbe- und Schnitzereischulen* (Berlin: Carl Molcomes, 1906), 1.
141| For a general overview of the goals and curricula of these schools throughout Prussia, see Rudolf Bosselt, Hugo Busch, and Hermann Muthesius, eds., *Kunstgewerbe: Ein Bericht über Entwicklung und Tätigkeit der Handwerker- u. Kunstgewerbeschulen in Preussen* (Berlin: Ernst Wasmuth, 1922).
142| *Ministerial-Blatt der Handels- und Gerwerbe-Verwaltung* (Berlin: Carl Heymanns, 1905), 101.
143| Peters's application and the documents recording the decision of the Altona authorities to hire him as director of the school are preserved in his personnel file, now housed in the Freie und Hansestadt Hamburg, Staatsarchiv.
144| Peter Behrens to the Gewerbeschule-Verwaltung, Altona, 17 July 1920, UCSB; Fritz Schumacher to Jock Peters, n.d. [c. July 1920], JdS.
145| Weimar, *Die Hamburgische Sezession*, 132.
146| Hans-Werner Engels, "Jakstein, Werner," in Franklin Kopitzsch and Dirk Brietzke, eds., *Hamburgische Biographie* (Göttingen: Wallstein Verlag, 2008), vol. 4., 175–76.
147| Adrian Täckman, email message to the author, 11 August 2020.
148| Steven Clarke, "The Invisible Architect: K. Lönberg-Holm and His Visible *Tribune* Project," unpublished senior thesis, Yale University, 1966, 36.
149| See H. de Fries, "Wettbewerb der Börsenhof A.G. Königsberg i. Pr.," *Wasmuth Monatshefte für Baukunst* 7, Heft 9/10 (1922–23): 258, 289–91; Jaeger, "Von Altona nach Los Angeles," 144.
150| Clarke, "The Invisible Architect," 36-37.
151| On Lönberg-Holm's final design, see Katherine Solomonson, *The Chicago Tribune Tower Competition: Skyscraper Design and Cultural Change in the 1920s* (Chicago: University of Chicago Press, 2003), 111–13. See also Arnold Lehman, "The New York Skyscraper: A History of Its Development 1870–1939" (PhD diss., Yale University, 1974), 236–42.
152| See, for example, J. J. P. Oud, "Bij een Deensch ontwerp voor de Chicago Tribune," *Bouwkundig Weekblad*, 10 November 1923, 456–58; Walter Gropius, *Internationale Architektur* (Munich: Albert Langen, 1925), 48; and Adolf Behne, *Der modern Zweckbau* (Munich: Drei Masken Verlag, 1926), plate 34. Erich Mendelsohn took notice of the design and showed it in his "Dynamik and Form" lectures in Amsterdam, Rotterdam, and Den Haag in November 1923. Around the same time, Lönberg-Holm received an invitation to teach at the University of Michigan, and he moved to the United States, eventually settling in Detroit. Later, he would make his career working mostly as a graphic designer, sometimes in concert with Czech-born Ladislav Sutnar. Michael Stöneberg, *Arthur Köster, Architekturfotografie, 1926–1933: Das Bild vom "Neuen Bauen"* (Berlin: Gebr. Mann, 2009), 340.
153| Preußische Minister für Handel und Gewerbe, "Verleihung die Amtsbezeichnung Professor," 11 September 1922, JdS.

154| "Einkommensteuerbescheid für das Rechnungsjahr 1921 an Jakob Detlef Peters," JdS.

155| The astrologer's name was Wilhelm Th. H. Wulff. Wulff appears to have prepared at least three full charts for Peters, one covering the last part of 1922 and another, prepared after Peters departed Hamburg, for 1923, which was mailed to him in California in two versions. These later two charts survive. Wilhelm Th. H. Wulff, astrological charts for J. D. Peters, 4 and 12 June 1923, JdS. Peters regularly read his and Herta's horoscopes in the newspapers and seems to have placed great stock in them. See, for example, Jock Peters to Herta Peters, 15 December 1922, JdS, in which he mentions that he thought he would receive a letter from Herta a few days earlier than he did, based on a horoscope entry he had seen.

156| Peters to the Magistrat-Gewerbeschulverwaltung, 25 August 1922, UCSB.

157| Peters to the Magistrat-Gewerbeschulverwaltung, 28 November 1922, JdS.

Chapter 5 |
AMERIKA

158| "List of Cabin Passengers of the Triple-Screw Mail Steamer *Reliance*," 15 November 1922, Ellis Island Foundation, New York; Jock Peters to Herta Peters, 26 November 1922, JdS.

159| "Sworn Statement Submitted by Relative of Prepaid Passengers," 11 October 1922, JdS.

160| Jock Peters to Herta Peters, 28 November 1922, UCSB.

161| "Declaration of Intention for George Fritz Peters," 16 October 1951, National Archives, Washington, DC; Peters family papers, JdS.

162| Jock Peters to Herta Peters, n.d. [early December 1922], JdS.

163| Ibid.

164| Peters's letter, dated 22 January 1923 and sent from Pasadena, only reached the authorities in Altona on 17 February. See the correspondence in Peters's personnel file of the Handwerker- und Kunstgewerbeschule Altona, now housed at the Staatsarchiv, Freie und Hansestadt Hamburg.

165| Correspondence of late 1922 and early 1923 in Peters's personnel file, Staatsarchiv, Freie und Hansestadt Hamburg.

166| Jock Peters to Herta Peters, n.d. [early December 1922], JdS.

167| Ibid.

168| Ibid.

169| Jock Peters to Herta Peters, 6 December 1922, UCSB.

170| Ibid.

171| "Petition for Naturalization: Otto Heinrich Neher," US Naturalization Records, National Archives, Washington, DC. Neher entered into the partnership with Whittlesey in 1905. "Otto Neher, New Architect," *Los Angeles Herald*, 25 June 1905, II, 3. His partnership with Skilling lasted from 1907 to 1914. See also "Otto Neher," Pacific Coast Architecture Database, accessed 10 August 2016, http://pcad.lib.washington.edu/person/1157/.

172| Jock Peters to Herta Peters, 6 December 1922.

173| Ibid.

174| Ibid.

175| Jock Peters to Herta Peters, 24 December 1922, UCSB.

176| Jock Peters to Herta Peters, n.d. [10 December 1922], UCSB.

177| Jock Peters to Herta Peters, 15 December 1922, JdS.

178| Jock Peters to Herta Peters, 24 December 1922, UCSB.

179| Jock Peters to Herta Peters, 12 January 1923, UCSB.

180| Jock Peters to Herta Peters, 2 January 1923, UCSB.

181| Jock Peters to Herta Peters, 1 January 1923, JdS.

182| Ibid.

183| Jock Peters to Herta Peters, n.d. [early January 1923], UCSB.

184| Jock Peters to Herta Peters, 12 January 1923, UCSB.

185| Twenty-eight-year-old Hans Otto Peters (1894–1980), who would later find renown as a film designer for Twentieth Century Fox and Metro-Goldwyn-Mayer, accompanied Herta and the children. He was eventually nominated for five Academy Awards for art direction. Among his important credits are the designs for *Rebecca of Sunnybrook Farm* (1937) and *The Hound of the Baskervilles* (1938).

186| The address was 5202 Mt. Helena Avenue, Eagle Rock.

187| Swart, "Golden Chain," 7.

188| Interview with Dierk Peters, 17 March 2014.

189| It may well have been an earlier version, since it exists only in the form of a less elaborated elevation drawing.

190| Michael Siebenbrodt, "Planung und Aufbau der Siedlung Loheland und ihrer Architektur 1917 bis 1935," in *Loheland 100: Gelebte Visionen für eine neue Welt*, eds. Elisabeth Mollenhauer-Klüber and Michael Siebenbrodt, exh. cat. (Fulda: Vonderau Museum Fulda; Petersburg: Michael Imhof, 2019), 169–74. The drawings for the two buildings and two further versions of a festival hall were discovered in an attic at Loheland several years ago.

Chapter 6 |
FAMOUS PLAYERS-LASKY

191| Peters to Mr. [?] Richmond, 5 May 1923, JdS. The recipient was likely John Richmond, a onetime actor who by then had made the transition to art direction. By the beginning of the next year, Peters was probably working more or less full-time for the movies, although still as a freelancer. Herta, in a letter from early January 1924 to her mother back in Germany, notes, "Jock is working very happily in the film industry" and that he was also "sometimes finding time to do freelance work and to paint." Herta Peters to Maria Boeger, 6 January 1924, JdS.

192| *The Story of the Famous Players-Lasky Corporation* (New York: Famous Players-Lasky, 1919); E. J. Stephens, Michael Christaldi, and

193| Marc Wanamaker, *Early Paramount Studios* (Charlestown, SC: Arcadia, 2013); Bernard F. Dick, *Engulfed: The Death of Paramount Pictures and the Birth of Corporate Hollywood* (Lexington: University Press of Kentucky, 2001).

193| Kgl. Technische Hochschule in München, "Anmeldebogen für das Sommer-Semester 1906" and "Zeugnis über die Diplom-Hauptprüfung für Architekten, 1911," Technische Universität München-Archiv.

194| Jaeger, "Von Altona nach Los Angeles," 145.

195| Donald Albrecht, *Designing Dreams: Modern Architecture in the Movies* (New York: Harper & Row, 1986), 79–84; Juan Antonio Ramírez, *Architecture for the Screen: A Critical Study of Set Design for Hollywood's Golden Age* (Jefferson, NC: McFarland, 2004), 38–39.

196| Herta Peters to Maria Boeger, 19 October 1924, JdS.

197| Iain Boyd Whyte has suggested that Peters might have also been inspired by the architectural fantasies of Berlin architect Otto Kohtz. Kohtz had published a book of designs in 1909 titled *Gedanken über Architektur* (Thoughts about architecture), and after the war he advocated the erection of skyscrapers in Berlin. Whyte, "Peters and Schneider," 156; Otto Kohtz, *Gedanken über Architektur* (Berlin: Baumgärtel, 1909); Otto Kohtz, *Büroturmhäuser in Berlin* (Berlin: Zirkel, 1921).

198| Jock Peters, notebook, c. 1924, JdS.

199| Ibid.

200| Corbett's scheme was widely reproduced, including on the front cover of the *New-York Tribune*. The associated article was titled "Costly Street Widenings, as Manhattan Crowds Increase, Might Be Obviated by Planning This Kind of Thoroughfare," *New-York Tribune*, 16 January 1910, 1. Moses King was a publisher of guidebooks of US cities. His visionary images of a New York of great skyscrapers and multiple tiers of traffic appeared in several of his guides. See, e.g., *King's Views of New York City and Brooklyn 1896–1915* (New York: Benjamin Blom, 1972).

201| "The Wonder City You May Live to See," *Popular Science Monthly*, August 1925, 40–41.

202| Interview with Dierk Peters, 17 March 2014.

203| "What Price Glory," Internet Movie Database, accessed 23 September 2018, https://www.imdb.com.

204| The work was first serialized as "Under the Moons of Mars," *All-Story* 22, no. 2 (February 1912). It appeared in book form five years later. Edgar Rice Burroughs, *A Princess of Mars* (Chicago: A. C. McClurg, 1917).

205| The drawing is in the same style, using the same board and materials, as the other *Mars* drawings, suggesting that he had indeed added the caption later.

206| Happy, "Who's Who in Eagle Rock."

Chapter 7 | PETERS BROTHERS

207| Peters later told his son, Dierk, that he had been deeply unhappy his last year at Famous Players-Lasky and had wanted to quit but did not have the financial means to do so. Interview with Dierk Peters, 17 March 2014.

208| One of Peters's designs published in *Hi-Hat Magazine* bears the date 1926, suggesting that he was already beginning to think about an independent career then. See the design he made for a sitting room and library in *Hi-Hat Magazine*, 15 December 1927, 28.

209| Adolphe Barreaux, "Art Alliance of America: The Karpen Competition," *Bulletin of the Art Center* (Chicago) 5 (April 1927): 144.

210| Ibid.

211| Ibid., 144–45.

212| Adolphe Barreaux, "Art Alliance of America: Year's End," *Bulletin of the Art Center* (Chicago) 5 (June 1927): 182–83.

213| Walter Rendell Storey, "Modern Ideas in Designs for Furniture: Our Cities Will See Novel Types by a Group of Craftsmen," *New York Times*, 22 May 1927.

214| Ibid.

215| Interview with Dierk Peters, 17 March 2014.

216| In a letter announcing the formation of Peters Brothers sent to the Architectural Group for Industry & Commerce (the firm of R. M. Schindler and Richard Neutra), Peters mentions the Hofmann and Watson commissions, but he makes no reference to other projects, suggesting that those two were the extent of what they had executed at the time. Jock Peters to the Architectural Group for Industry & Commerce [R. M. Schindler and Richard Neutra], 22 August 1927, UCSB.

217| *Hi-Hat Magazine*, 15 December 1927, 51.

218| "Nothing Old-Fashioned Here!" *Hi-Hat Magazine*, December 1927–January 1928, 25.

219| Interview with Erika Plack (Kem Weber's daughter), 21 October 2008.

220| Ibid. Plack remembered that those friendships went on for many years afterward—well into the 1940s, when she was in her later teens.

221| Christopher Long, *Kem Weber: Designer and Architect* (New Haven, CT: Yale University Press, 2014), 74.

222| Ibid.

223| William Lingenbrink (1870–1949) owned the land with his brother Francis and another couple from Los Angeles, William and Alma Dunn. The history and development of the area is described in San Buenaventura Research Associates, *Historic Resources Report, 2001 Ocean Drive, Silver Strand (Oxnard) CA* (25 August 2015), 4–5.

224| Ibid.

225| "W. Lingenbrink Starts Work on Beach Project," *Oxnard Daily Courier*, 25 September 1925. Progress on the project was slowed after Lingenbrink suffered what was reported in the newspapers as a "nervous breakdown" and was forced to spend time "in the East."

See "Lingenbrink Better," *Oxnard Daily Courier*, 8 November 1926.

226| William Lingenbrink, *Modern Art in Store Fronts* (Los Angeles, n.d. [1928 or 1929]). The work, now very rare, is a great document of its time, showing many early modernist works in Southern California that have long since disappeared or have been entirely altered.

227| Alice M. Sharkey (Art Alliance of America) to Jock Peters, 27 April 1928, JdS.

228| N. C. Sanford, "Modernistic Rugs Made in America: Belated Attempts to Meet Demands Bring Surprising Results," *Good Furniture*, July 1928, 38–39.

229| Quoted in "The Vestal Bill for the Copyright Registration of Designs," *Columbia Law Review* 31, no. 3 (March 1931): 477–93.

230| Thorwald Solberg, documents affirming copyright status for Universal Assembling Furniture, No. 15464, sent to Jock Peters, 27 August 1928, JdS.

231| See, for example, Marla C. Berns, ed., *The Furniture of R. M. Schindler*, catalogue of exhibition at the University Art Museum, University of California, Santa Barbara (Seattle: University of Washington Press, 1997).

232| In the Peters papers is a form letter from Leo Karpen, of S. Karpen & Bros., from early 1929. The company evidently sent out identical letters to designers across the country soliciting "new designs and new ideas in furniture." Peters apparently did not respond, probably because he hoped to find a manufacturer that would produce his designs on better terms. The letter from S. Karpen stated flatly that "in submitting designs, quote price for sketch only, also additional price for making detail drawings." There is no mention of royalties, and it was clearly Karpen's intention only to pay for the designs. The whole issue became moot at the end of the year, with the onset of the Great Depression. By December of that year, manufacturers, rocked by the financial crisis and wary of new ventures, were already backing away from signing any new contracts. Leo Karpen to Peters, 17 January 1929, JdS.

233| Louis Fremont, "All about Modernage," accessed 24 August 2016, http://www.artdecoresource.com/2013/10/all-about-modernage.html.

234| Long, *Kem Weber*, esp. chapter 5.

235| "What about Art?" *West Coaster*, 1 May 1928, 26.

236| John Crosse, "Foundation of Los Angeles Modernism: Richard Neutra's Mod Squad," accessed 12 September 2018, http://socalarchhistory.blogspot.com/2010/08/foundations-of-los-angeles-modernism.html.

237| Interview with Dierk Peters, 17 March 2014.

238| See the advertisement for the Academy of Modern Art in *The Argus*, February 1929, 16.

Chapter 8 |
BULLOCK'S WILSHIRE

239| Interview with Dierk Peters, 17 March 2014.

240| Joseph Feil was born in 1890 and died in 1979. "Feil, Joseph L.," obituary, *Los Angeles Times*, 13 July 1979, II, 4; United States census, 1920, 1930, 1940; United States Social Security Death Index, 1935–2014.

241| Bernard Robert Paradise (1881–1958) was born in Mariampol, Russia (now Marijampol, Lithuania). He moved to Southern California around 1916. United States census, 1900, 1920, 1930, 1940; *United States Naturalization Record Indexes*, vol. 4, 290, Racine County, Wisconsin; Los Angeles city and telephone directories from the 1930s through the 1950s.

242| Martin Eli Weil, "James Oviatt Building," United States Department of the Interior, National Register of Historic Places Inventory—Nomination Form, 8 November 1982, https://www.nps.gov/subjects/nationalregister/database-research.htm.

243| Desmond's was an old Los Angeles business, founded as a hat shop in 1862 and expanded later to carry men's and boys' clothing and women's fashions. In the late 1920s, Ralph R. Huesman, who had purchased the business from the Desmond family heirs in 1921, owned Desmond's. He rapidly expanded the company, adding a six-story flagship store on South Broadway in 1923 designed by architect Albert C. Martin. Huesman had a second location on South Spring Street. The new store was added to take advantage of the development of an upscale shopping district on the 700 block of Seventh Street. Myrna Oliver, "Fred B. Huesman, Former Owner of Desmond's, Dies," *Los Angeles Times*, 22 June 1990.

244| "Today . . . a Beautiful New Addition to the Desmond Institution," unidentified newspaper clipping of an advertisement for Desmond's, c. 1928, UCSB.

245| Lingenbrink, *Modern Art in Store Fronts*, folio A, plate 4.

246| Maddux Air Lines was formed 2 September 1927; its first flight was on 1 November 1928. On the company's founding and early operation, see "Big Passenger Air Line Planned in Southwest," *New York Times*, 16 June 1927; "Maddux Air Traffic in Sharp Gain: Passenger Revues for August Reported as 50 Per Cent Up over July," *Los Angeles Times*, 5 September 1928.

247| Lingenbrink, *Modern Art in Store Fronts*, folio A, plate 5.

248| Peters's original drawing for the mural (now lost) is reproduced in "Shop Design: One of a Number by J. D. Peters," *Los Angeles Times*, 23 December 1928. The large chandelier at the center of the room is similar to several of Kem Weber's lighting designs from this period, and it was very possibly one of his designs or, at least, derived from them.

249| Margaret Leslie Davis, *Bullocks Wilshire* (Los Angeles: Balcony Press 1996), 15–22. On Bullock's early history, see also Devin T. Frick, *Bullock's Department Store* (Charlestown, SC: Arcadia, 2015): 11–38.

250| Davis, *Bullocks Wilshire*, 25.

251| Ibid.

252| Eleni Silverman and Robert C. Giebner, *Bullocks-Wilshire* [sic] *Department Store, Historic Building Survey Report No. CA. 1941/19-Losan, 56* (Los Angeles, 1969/1984), 2.

253| Davis, *Bullocks Wilshire*, 31.

254| Ibid.

255| On John Parkinson and his partnership with his son Donald, see, e.g., "John Parkinson (Architect)," Pacific Coast Architecture Database, accessed 19 July 2016, http://pcad.lib.washington.edu/perosn/108/; "John Parkinson," Los Angeles Conservancy, accessed 19 July 2016, https://www.laconservancy.org/architects/john-parkinson.

256| For the specific dates of his travel, see "Donald Berthold Parkinson (Architect)," Pacific Coast Architect Database, http://pcad.lib.washington.edu/person/202/, accessed 19 July 2016.

257| Davis, *Bullocks Wilshire*, 36, 37.

258| Eleanor Le Maire's (1897–1970) long career is documented in her archive, now housed at the Smithsonian. See Eleanor LeMaire Associates records, 1928–70, Archives of American Art, Smithsonian Institution, Washington, DC.

259| Michael Windover, *Art Deco: A Mode of Mobility* (Montreal: Presses de l'Université du Quebec, 2012), esp. 133–40.

260| Davis, *Bullocks Wilshire*, 35.

261| Ibid.

262| Gjura Stojana (1885–1974), who created the mural in the Sportswear Department on the ground floor of Bullock's, was born in France and moved to the United States in 1901. He changed his name to George Curtin Stanson but reverted back to Stojana in the later 1920s. He studied at the San Francisco Institute of Art and worked in the art department of the *San Francisco Chronicle* before moving to Los Angeles in 1918. Herman Sachs (also Hermann Sachs, born Hermann Segal, 1883–1940), who painted the *Spirit of Transportation* mural in the Bullock's porte cochere, was born in Romania and immigrated to the United States at age seventeen, settling in Chicago. He soon went back to Europe and studied in Munich. For a time, after he returned to the United States, he served as the first director of the Dayton Museum of Fine Arts (now the Dayton Art Institute) before moving to Los Angeles in 1925. Eugene Maier-Krieg (1897–1986), who fashioned the plaster reliefs in the Riding Shop, was born in Germany and studied at the Stuttgart Art Academy. He moved to New York City in 1924 and shortly thereafter settled in Los Angeles, where he first worked in the film industry.

263| Davis, *Bullocks Wilshire*, 45.

264| Ibid., 49.

265| Ibid., 45.

266| Interview with Dierk Peters, 17 March 2014.

267| Pauline G. Schindler, "A Significant Contribution to Culture: The Interior of a Great California Store as an Interpretation of Modern Life," *California Arts and Architecture* 38, no. 1 (January 1930): 25.

268| Ibid.

269| Arthur Millier, "Beauty Seen in Building: Bullock's Wilshire Structure Held Contribution to Art in Southern California," *Los Angeles Times*, 6 October 1929.

270| Schindler, "Significant Contribution to Culture," 23.

Chapter 9 | HOLLANDER

271| See, for example, Edith Bristol, "So. Cal. Spirit in Wilshire Store of Bullock's: New Establishment, Marvel of Beauty and Design, Is Opened," *Illustrated Daily News*, 26 September 1929; "Bullock's Wilshire Department Store Los Angeles, John and Donald B. Parkinson, Architects," *Architectural Record* 67 (January 1930): 51–64; "The Bullock's Wilshire Store," *Through the Ages* 8 (June 1930): 19–24; "Bullock's Wilshire Store, Los Angeles," *Architectural Record* 70 (July 1931): 20–26; "Bullock's Wilshire to Open Today: Thousands Wait to Visit Mercantile 'Cathedral,'" *Illustrated Daily News*, 26 September 1929.

272| "Second in Series of Art Forums Opens Monday," *Los Angeles Times*, 6 October 1928; "Art in Religion Topic for Talks," *Los Angeles Times*, 9 December 1928; "Brief Reviews of Southland Art," *Los Angeles Times*, 16 December 1928.

273| "Bullock's Presents an Exhibit of the Decorative and Fine Arts of Today," advertisement, *Los Angeles Times*, 9 December 1928.

274| Arthur Millier, "More about Bullock's Exhibit: Beauty in Design and Craftsmanship Mark Modern French Rooms Shown Here for First Time; Bizarre Effects Conspicuous by Absence," *Los Angeles Times*, 16 December 1928. Millier also specially makes note of the work of local designers, including Peters.

275| Robert L. Sweeney and Judith Sheine, *Schindler, Kings Road, and Southern California Modernism* (Berkeley: University of California Press, 2012).

276| Interview with Dierk Peters, 17 March 2014.

277| Ruck was born Wilhelm Friedrich Ruck in the town of Swabisch Hall, in the state of Baden-Württemberg, in 1886. He later anglicized his name, changing it to William Frederick Ruck. After leaving the partnership with Peters, he practiced for many years in and around Los Angeles. At one point, he formed a partnership with Claud W. Beelman. Among his later works were the Washington Boulevard School for Crippled Children, the Aliso Apartments, and the Rose Hill Courts public housing complex. He died in Deming, New Mexico, in 1971. "Wilhelm Friedrich Ruck, Declaration of Intention for U.S. Citizenship," 27 August 1927, https://www.archives.gov/research/immigration/naturalization/microfilm; "William Frederick Ruck, World War II Draft Registration Card," 1942; California Death Records, https://www.cdph.ca.gov.

278| "Agreement made in duplicate between Jock D. Peters Studio of Contemporary Design and W. F. Ruck, Architect," 1 September 1930, JdS. Peters and Ruck signed the document after they had already decided to make the move.

279| Arthur Millier, "Art Center Outlined: Project for Artists' Culture Seen among Designer's Drawings at Bullock's Wilshire," *Los Angeles Times*, 27 October 1929.
280| Eleanor LeMaire to Peters, 13 January 1930, JdS.
281| Ibid.
282| "(Former) L. P. Hollander & Company Building," New York City Landmarks Preservation Commission, 17 June 2003, Designation List 347, LP-2124, https://www1.nyc.gov/site/lpc/designations/designation-reports.
283| Eleanor LeMaire to Peters, 13 January 1930, JdS.
284| Telegram from Eleanor LeMaire to Peters, 1 February 1930, JdS.
285| Peters to Eleanor LeMaire, 19 February 1930, JdS.
286| Ibid.
287| Eleanor LeMaire to Peters, 21 February 1930, JdS.
288| Telegram from Eleanor LeMaire to Peters, 24 February 1930, JdS.
289| W. F. Ruck to Peters, 15 March 1930, JdS.
290| Peters to Eleanor LeMaire, 28 March 1930, JdS.
291| W. F. Ruck to Peters, 4 March 1930, JdS.
292| Eleanor LeMaire to Paul Williams, 2 April 1930, JdS.
293| Eleanor LeMaire to Paul Williams, 15 April 1930, JdS.
294| Eleanor LeMaire to Peters, 25 April 1930, JdS.
295| Eleanor LeMaire to Peters, 5 May 1930, JdS.
296| Eleanor LeMaire to Peters, 14 April 1930, JdS.
297| A week and a half before, LeMaire had written to Peters:

Now I am going to pass along some literature on the Audac. Let me know what you think about it? Do you think we ought to join? I must tell you I saw a petition that was sent to the heads of the Chicago Exhibition [she is referring here to the coming 1933 Century of Progress exhibition] that said that they were going to make a movement to have the work of younger designers represented. Kem Weber signed this. Personally, I have always stayed away from organizations and I hesitate to get into them, and even now I feel the same way although we are going to be in the limelight when the Hollander store opens.

Eleanor LeMaire to Peters, 5 May 1930, JdS.
298| Peters to Eleanor LeMaire, 30 April 1930, JdS.
299| Peters to Eleanor LeMaire, 1 July 1930, JdS.
300| *A Folio of Pictures Showing the L. P. Hollander Co. in Its New Home at 3 East 57 Street* (New York: L. P. Hollander, 1930), n.p.
301| Peters had most of these pieces manufactured in Los Angeles at the Vernon Fixtures and Cabinet Company—along with many of the other installations for the store. They were shipped to New York by train and filled five rail cars. "Store Fixtures Shipped East in Five Carloads," *Los Angeles Times*, 28 September 1930, D3.
302| *A Folio of Pictures Showing the L. P. Hollander Co. in Its New Home at 3 East 57 Street*, n.p.
303| See, for example, "L. P. Hollander Company Store: Jock D. Peters, Designer, Collaborating with Eleanor LeMaire," *Architectural Record* 69, no. 1 (January 1931): 3–15. The building received the 1930 gold medal of the Fifth Avenue Association "as the best structure erected in the Fifth Avenue district during the past year." "Hollander Building Wins 5th Av. Award: Association Gives Medal to New Store Structure in Fifty-Seventh Street," *New York Times*, 8 March 1931, 156.
304| Alfred Auerbach, "New Hollander's Shows How Specialty Shop May Fuse Decorative and Commercial Needs: Store Remarkable for Color Treatment of Several Floors; Planning Designed to Give Specific Mental Effects," *Retailing* (New York), 11 October 1930.
305| Ralph Flint, "Jock Peters," *Creative Art* 11 (September 1932), 32.
306| Ibid., 31–32.
307| He was forced to take some time off to deal with a suit filed by a neighbor who had been run over by Peters's son, Dierk, on his bicycle. She suffered injuries to her chest and went to court lodging a complaint for an unspecified $12,740 in damages. "Bicycle Damages Suits Filed by Pedestrians," *Los Angeles Times*, 7 November 1930, A8. It is not clear whether Peters was able to settle the suit or whether he ended up paying the full amount.
308| Peters to Clarence G. Sheffield, 13 October 1930, JdS.
309| Peters to Eleanor LeMaire, n.d. [late 1930], JdS.
310| Eleanor LeMaire to Peters, 18 October 1930, JdS.
311| Long, *Kem Weber*, 126–28.
312| "Agreement made in duplicate," typescript from 1931, JdS.
313| Peters to Eleanor LeMaire, 30 January 1931, JdS.
314| Eleanor LeMaire to Peters, 9 December 1930, JdS.
315| Peters to Eleanor LeMaire, 13 February 1931, JdS.
316| LeMaire, who viewed the drawings, sent Peters a long letter critiquing what she thought were its shortcomings, particularly with regard to movement and merchandising. Eleanor LeMaire to Peters, 18 February 1931, JdS.
317| Copies of all these publications are among the Peters papers formerly owned by Jock de Swart.
318| "University Exhibition Concludes; Architectural Examples Illustrate Development of Modernism," *Los Angeles Times*, 27 April 1930, D6; Arthur Millier, "Building for Our Age: California's Designers of Modern Style Architecture Distinguished from Those Who Imitate," *Los Angeles Times*, 27 April 1930, B15.
319| In 1931, Peters also took part in the "Contemporary Art Decoration and Store Design Exhibition" at the Plaza Art Center, in Los Angeles. "News of the Art World," *Los Angeles Times*, 8 February 1931, 18; "Art and Artists: Peters Is Honored,;" *Los Angeles Times*, 1 March 1931, B16; "Current Art Exhibitions," *Los Angeles Times*, 17 May 1931, B13; "Roundabout the Galleries: Contemporary Architecture, Decoration and Store Design," *Los Angeles Times*, 11 October 1931, B8.
320| Peters to Eleanor LeMaire, 30 January 1931, JdS.
321| "Decorative Craftsmen Form Group; Western 'Audac' Chapter Organized by Artists and Architects of City," *Los Angeles Times*, 6 July 1930, A6.

322| Eleanor LeMaire to Peters, 23 March 1931, JdS. LeMaire added, "Ken [sic] Weber is going to show his new furniture, which, no doubt, you have seen. It is neither nailed or [sic] glued together but the joints are dovetailed. I understand he has made applications for several rooms for the show so no doubt he expects to blossom forth once again." Here LeMaire is alluding to Kem Weber's Bentlock furniture, which he premiered at the 1931 AUDAC exhibition.
323| Walter Holscher to Eleanor LeMaire, 15 October 1931, JdS.
324| Ibid.
325| Donald L. Scoggins and Jay Jorgensen, *Creating the Illusion (Turner Classic Movies): A Fashionable History of Hollywood Costume Designers* (Philadelphia: Running Press, 2015), 204–5.

Chapter 10 | CALIFORNIA MODERN

326| The new address is shown on the letterhead of a note he wrote to Herta and the children in the summer of 1931, while they were vacationing in Laguna Beach. Peters wrote the entire two-page letter in Plattdeutsch, the dialect of his youth in Dithmarschen, addressing it to "Mein Lüdd und dat Krabbeltüch"—"My dear little one and all the little crawlers." Jock Peters to Herta Peters, 24 July 1931, JdS.
327| Laura Vanaskie, Building, Structure, and Object Record, June 2010, Department of Parks and Recreation, State of California; Bob Pool, "Calabasas Colony, Once Mecca for Artists, Now a Cause for Historians," *Los Angeles Times*, 6 July 1986, WS4–5.
328| Further research would be necessary to try to determine the authorship of the other houses.
329| J. Detlef Peters, individual income tax returns, form 1040, for the years 1930 and 1931, JdS.
330| Russell Burns (First National Bank Building) to Peters, 26 March 1931, JdS.
331| Peters to Eleanor LeMaire, n.d. [fall 1931], JdS.
332| Application of Jock D. Peters to Union Bank & Trust Co., Los Angeles, 2 April 1931, JdS.
333| Walter Holscher to Eleanor LeMaire, 15 October 1931, JdS.
334| Memo from Peters to Hans Dreier, n.d. [c. fall 1931], JdS.
335| Walter Holscher to Eleanor LeMaire, 15 October and 28 October 1931, JdS.
336| Among the many condolence letters Herta preserved were ones from Dione Neutra, Greta Davidson, and William Lingenbrink, JdS.
337| "A Fine Designer," *Los Angeles Times*, 3 April 1934, 8.
338| Herta Peters never remarried and lived until 1957. Ursula, the couple's eldest daughter, married the noted Los Angeles sculptor Jan de Swart (1908–1987). They lived together for many years at Allegro, the de Swarts' hilltop home in Eagle Rock. Ursula made a substantial gift of papers and drawings from her father's archive to UCSB in 1986. She died in 1991, leaving behind a 500-page memoir of her life, including a substantial section on her father's life and work. In 2014, Ursula's son, Jock de Swart, made an additional gift of archival materials to the UCSB collection. The remaining papers and drawings are still in private hands.

Ursula was instrumental in mounting an exhibition of her father's work at the R. M. Schindler House in West Hollywood in 1984. See Bill Rollins, "Jock Peters Retrospective on Exhibit at West Hollywood's Schindler House," *Los Angeles Times*, 25 March 1984: AC2.

Jock Peters, unidentified interior, c. 1932. Pencil on paper. UCSB.

SELECTED BIBLIOGRAPHY |

Archival Collections

Architecture and Fine Arts Library and Photography Collection, University of Southern California

California State Library and Archives, Sacramento

Charles E. Young Research Library, Department of Special Collections, University of California, Los Angeles

Collection Jock de Swart

Eleanor Le Maire Associates Records, Archives of American Art, Smithsonian Institution, Washington, DC

Ellis Island Foundation, New York

Freie und Hansestadt Hamburg, Staatsarchiv

Hagley Museum and Library, Wilmington, Delaware

Jock Peters Archive, Architecture and Design Collection, University Art Museum, University of California, Santa Barbara

Karl Schneider Archiv, HafenCity Universität Hamburg

Karl Schneider Papers, Special Collections, Getty Research Institute, Los Angeles

Los Angeles County Museum of Art

Los Angeles City Archives

Margaret Herrick Library, Academy of Motion Picture Arts and Sciences, Los Angeles

The Mitchell Wolfson, Jr. Collection, Wolfsonian—Florida International University, Miami Beach, Florida

Photograph Collection, Los Angeles Public Library

Various private collections

Primary Sources

"Annual Award for Best Building in Fifth Avenue Section, New York, to L. P. Hollander Company, Inc." *American Architect* 139 (May 1931): 62.

"Architectural Genius Related: Life History of Jock E. [sic] Peters Told Members of Forum Club Here." *Monrovia News-Post*, 21 November 1929.

Arlen, David. "Fifty Thousand Architects Can Be Wrong." *Hi-Hat Magazine*, February 1928, 33–35.

Arntz, [?]. "Der Wettbewerb um ein Grabdenkmal für die Kriegsbegräbnisstätte des Hamburger Zentralfriedhofes in Ohlsdorf." *Bau-Rundschau* 20–22 (1915): 77–80, plate 82.

"Artists Working Together: Achievements in Architecture, Sculpture, Painting, Decoration Seen in This City." *Los Angeles Times*, 2 June 1929.

"The Arts and Artists: Jock Peters." *Los Angeles Times*, 5 November 1939.

"Associate of Noted Designer Forum Speaker." *Monrovia News-Post*, 16 November 1929.

Auerbach, Alfred. "New Hollander's Shows How Specialty Shop May Fuse Decorative and Commercial Needs: Store Remarkable for Color Treatment of Several Floors; Planning Designed to Give Specific Mental Effects." *Retailing* (New York), 11 October 1930.

Bahn, Hans. "Von Hamburger Großbauten und ihren Schöpfern." *Der Kries* 2, nos. 6–7 (1925): 10–29.

Barreaux, Adolphe. "Art Alliance of America: The Karpen Competition." *Bulletin of the Art Center* (Chicago) 5 (April 1927): 144–45.

———. "Art Alliance of America: Year's End." *Bulletin of the Art Center* (Chicago) 5 (June 1927): 182–83.

Behne, Adolf. *Der modern Zweckbau*. Munich: Drei Masken Verlag, 1926.

Bensel, Carl Gustav. "Der Bebauungsplan Wohldorf-Ohlstedt." *Bau-Rundschau* 19 (1914): 165–72.

"Big Passenger Air Line Planned in Southwest." *New York Times*, 16 June 1927.

Bosselt, Rudolf, Hugo Busch, and Hermann Muthesius, eds. *Kunstgewerbe: Ein Bericht über Entwicklung und Tätigkeit der Handwerker- u. Kunstgewerbeschulen in Preussen*. Berlin: Ernst Wasmuth, 1922.

Bristol, Edith. "So. Cal. Spirit in Wilshire Store of Bullock's: New Establishment, Marvel of Beauty and Design, Is Opened." *Illustrated Daily News*, 26 September 1929.

"Built-In Lighting Featured in Smart Women's Apparel Shop." *Lighting* (November 1930): 20–24.

"Bullock's Wilshire." *Der Klubbote: Mitteilungen des Deutschen Klubs zu Los Angeles* 1, no. 7 (October 1929): 2.

"Bullock's Wilshire Department Store Los Angeles, John and Donald B. Parkinson, Architects." *Architectural Record* 67 (January 1930): 51–64.

"The Bullock's Wilshire Store." *Through the Ages* 8 (June 1930): 19–24.

"Bullock's Wilshire Store, Los Angeles." *Architectural Record* 70 (July 1931): 20–26.

"Bullock's Wilshire to Open Today: Thousands Wait to Visit Mercantile 'Cathedral.'" *Illustrated Daily News*, 26 September 1929.

"C. G. Bensel, Regierungsbaumeister a. D., Architekt, Hamburg," Sonderheft *Bau-Rundschau*. Hamburg: Konrad Hanf, 1914.

"Carl Gustav Bensel, 24 Apr. 1878." In "Deutschland, Geburten und Taufen 1558–1898," index. *Family Search*. FHL microfilm 595583.https://familysearch.org/pal:/MM9.1.1/NZ4J-1P8.

"Decorative Scheme Carried Out in Lighting Equipment: Bullock's Wilshire, Los Angeles, Installs a Completely Modernistic Set of Lighting Fixtures in Their New Building." *Lighting Fixtures and Lighting* (December 1929): 19–22.

"Design for Bullock's Wilshire by Jock D. Peters." *Los Angeles Times*, 27 October 1929.

Douglas, George. "Bullock's Wilshire Store Delights City's Art Critics." *Los Angeles Examiner*, 26 September 1929.

Eulenberg, M. W. Herbert. "Fritz August Breuhaus." *Deutsche Kunst und Dekoration* 34 (September 1914): 191–204.

———, and Max Osborn, eds. *Fritz August Breuhaus de Groot*. Berlin: Neue Werkkunst, 1929.

Flint, Ralph. "Jock Peters." *Creative Art* 11 (September 1932): 30–33.

Fries, H. de. "Wettbewerb der Börsenhof A.G. Königsberg i. Pr.," *Wasmuth Monatshefte für Baukunst* (1922–23): 258, 289.

A Folio of Pictures Showing the L. P. Hollander Co. in Its New Home at 3 East 57 Street. New York: L. P. Hollander, 1930.

"Forum to Hear about Work of L.A. Architect." *Monrovia News-Post*, 15 November 1929.

Gray, Olive. "Store Weds Art to Beauty: Bullock's Tower Gleams Like Jewel on Wilshire; Daring Originality Shown in Lighting." *Los Angeles Times*, 26 September 1929.

Gropius, Walter. *Internationale Architektur*. Munich: Albert Langen, 1925.

"Hamburg: Ergebnis des Wettbewerbes zur Erlangung von Vorschlägen für die Ausschmückung der Kriegergräber auf Ohlsdorfer Friedhofe." *Bau-Rundschau* 34–35 (26 August 1920): 139.

"Hamburger Sezessions-Ausstellung." c. 1919. Unidentified clipping in Jock Peter's scrapbook. Collection Jock de Swart.

Handwerker- und Kunstgewerbeschule Altona 1901–1926. Altona, 1926.

Happy [pseud.]. "Who's Who in Eagle Rock: Jock D. Peters." *Eagle Rock Sentinel*, 7 November 1930.

Harris, Allen. "Bullock's Wilshire: A Building Designed for Today." *California Arts and Architecture* 37 (January 1930): 20–28.

"Hollander Building Wins 5th Av. Award: Association Gives Medal to New Store Structure in Fifty-Seventh Street." *New York Times*, 8 March 1931.

"Hollander Moves into New Store." *New York Sun*, 24 September 1930.

"Interiors and Decoration." *Building Supplement of the Literary Digest* (Spring 1930): 32–33.

Koch, Hugo. "Jakob Detlef Peters." *Bau-Rundschau* 11, nos. 12–13 (25 March 1920): 45–46.

———. "Wettbewerb für ein Kunstausstellungsgebäude in Hamburg." *Bau-Rundschau* 24–25 (1914): 209–39.

———. "Der Wettbewerb zur Erlangung von Entwürfen für die architektonische Gestaltung des neuen Kraftwerkes der Hamburgischen Elektrizitätswerke in Tiefstack." *Bau-Rundschau* 29 (1914): 273–82 and 30 (1914): 287–91.

"L. P. Hollander & Co. Bankrupt." *New York Times*, 20 February 1932.

"L. P. Hollander Company Building, New York City." *Architectural Record* 69 (May 1931): 366–70.

"L. P. Hollander Company Store." *Architectural Record* 69, no. 1 (January 1931): 3–15.

Lehrmittel der Handwerker- und Kunstgewerbeschule Altona, 1918–1922. Altona, 1922.

Lingenbrink, William. *Modern Art in Store Fronts*. Los Angeles, n.d. [1928 or 1929].

"Little Studio Gallery Shows New Trend of Art." *Monrovia News-Post*, 27 November 1929.

Millier, Arthur. "Art Center Outlined: Project for Artists' Culture Seen among Designer's Drawings at Bullock's Wilshire." *Los Angeles Times*, 27 October 1929.

———. "Arts Working Together: Achievements in Architecture, Sculpture, Painting Decoration Observed in This City." *Los Angeles Times*, 2 June 1929.

———. "Beauty Seen in Building: Bullock's Wilshire Structure Held Contribution to Art in Southern California." *Los Angeles Times*, 6 October 1929.

"Modern Attitude in Furniture Design." *Los Angeles Times*, [c. 1927]. Peters scrapbook. Collection Jock de Swart.

Oud, J. J. P. "Bij een Deensch ontwerp voor de Chicago Tribune." *Bouwkundig Weekblad*, 10 November 1923, 456–58.

Peters, Jakob Detlef. "Architektonischer Götzendienst." *Bau-Rundschau* 10, nos. 45–46 (13 November 1919): 194–95.

———. "Bauet Räume, keine Zellen!" *Bau-Rundschau* 11, nos. 9–10 (11 March 1920): 36.

———. "Das Baupflege-Gesetz." *Bau-Rundschau* 11, nos. 24–26 (24 June 1920): 102.

———. "Bürgermeister Mönckeberg-Denkmal und -Brunnen." *Bau-Rundschau* 11, nos. 30–31 (29 July 1920): 122.

———. "Chaos!" *Bau-Rundschau* 11, nos. 16–17 (29 April 1920): 61.

———. "Chaos II" *Bau-Rundschau* 11, nos. 20–21 (27 May 1920): 81.

———. "Chaos III" *Bau-Rundschau* 11, nos. 22–23 (10 June 1920): 89.

———. "Eine deutsche Stadt." *Bau-Rundschau* 11, nos. 34–35 (26 August 1920): n.p.

———. "Ehrentafel für die Gefallenen der Uhlenhorster Turngesellschaft." *Bau-Rundschau* 11, nos. 44–45 (11 November 1920): 200.

———. "Das erlebnis der Architektur." *Bau-Rundschau* 11, nos. 30–31 (29 July 1920): 122.

———. "Die Erziehung des Architekten an den technischen Hochschulen." *Bau-Rundschau* 11, nos. 36–37 (9 September 1920): 154.

———. "Fritz Schumacher." *Bau-Rundschau* 11, nos. 18–19 (13 May 1920): 73.

———. "Gartenschönheit." *Bau-Rundschau* 11, nos. 22–23 (10 June 1920): 89.

———. "Grundzüge der Stilentwicklung." *Bau-Rundschau* 11, nos. 48–49 (16 December 1920): 222.

———. "Hamburg: Förderung des heimischen Kunstlebens." *Bau-Rundschau* 11, nos. 16–17 (29 April 1920): 72.

———. "Josef Olbrich." *Bau-Rundschau* 11, nos. 34–35 (26 August 1920): 140.

———. "Josef Ruff." *Bau-Rundschau* 11, nos. 16–17 (29 April 1920): 62.

———. "Junge Kunst." *Bau-Rundschau* 11, nos. 34–35 (26 August 1920): 140.

———. "Kann ich auch jetzt noch ein Haus bauen?" *Bau-Rundschau* 11, nos. 20–21 (27 May 1920): 88.

———. "Kleinsiedlung in Lübeck." *Bau-Rundschau* 11, nos. 36–37 (9 September 1920): 141–50.

———. "Ländliches Bauwesen." *Bau-Rundschau* 11, nos. 22–23 (10 June 1920): 89.

———. "Lebenslauf des Architekten J. D. Peters, Lehrer an der Kunstgewerbeschule Altona." 10 July 1920. Collection Jock de Swart.

———. "Maschinen-, Hand- und Qualitätsarbeit." *Bau-Rundschau* 11, nos. 40–41 (14 October 1920): 169–70.

———. "Niederdeutsche Kunstausstellung in Hameln." *Bau-Rundschau* 11, nos. 30–31 (29 July 1920): 123.

———. "Norddeutsche Backsteingotik." *Bau-Rundschau* 11, nos. 30–31 (29 July 1920): 124.

———. "Öffentliche Architekten-Wettbewerbe." *Bau-Rundschau* 11, nos. 44–45 (11 November 1920): 189–90.

———. Personalbogen. N.d. [c. 1920]. Handwerker-und Kunstgewerbeschule Altona. Freie und Hansestadt Hamburg, Staatsarchiv.

———. "Das Reiterdenkmal von Hahn vor dem Kunsthallen-Neubau." *Bau-Rundschau* 11, nos. 30–31 (29 July 1920): 118.

———. "Staat, Stadt und Kunstgewerbeschulen." *Bau-Rundschau* 11, nos. 44–45 (11 November 1920): 190, 194, 197–98.

———. "Volkshaus." *Bau-Rundschau* 11, nos. 30–31 (29 July 1920): 118.

———. "Wasmuths Monatshefte für Baukunst." *Bau-Rundschau* 11, nos. 44–45 (11 November 1920): 201.

———. "Der Wiederaufbau Ostpreußens." *Bau-Rundschau* 11, nos. 22–23 (10 June 1920): 89.

———. "Wohnstätte für Menschen, Heute und Morgen." *Bau-Rundschau* 11, nos. 22–23 (10 June 1920): 96.

———. "Zu meinen Landhäusern." *Bau-Rundschau* 11, nos. 12–13 (25 March 1920): 46–52.

"Peters Goes East to Building Opening." *Eagle Rock Advertiser*, 12 September 1930.

"Peters to Decorate New York Building." *Eagle Rock Advertiser*, 7 March 1930.

Schaefer, Karl. "Peter Behrens als führender Meister in der modernen Architektur und in den angewandten Künsten." *Neue Hamburger Zeitung* (morning ed.), 26 November 1915.

Schindler, Pauline G. "A Significant Contribution to Culture: The Interior of a Great Californian Store as an Interpretation of Modern Life." *California Arts and Architecture* 38, no. 1 (January 1930): 23–25.

Schnellenberg, Carl, ed. *Alfred Lichtwark: Briefe an Wolf Mannhardt*. Hamburg: Johann Trautmann, 1952.

"School of Art Opens New Exhibit: Jock Peters' [sic] Paintings Week's Attraction." *Pasadena Star-News*, 11 May 1931.

"Shop Design: One of a Number by J. D. Peters." *Los Angeles Times*, 23 December 1928.

Storey, Walter Rendell. "Modern Ideas in Designs for Furniture: Our Cities Will See Novel Types by a Group of Craftsmen." *New York Times*, 22 May 1927.

Swart, Ursula (Ursel) de. "The Golden Chain." N.d. [c. 1980]. Collection Jock de Swart.

———. "Who Is Moving My Hand: My Life with Jan de Swart, Sculptor." N.d. [c. 1970]. Collection Jock de Swart.

"The Vestal Bill for the Copyright Registration of Designs," *Columbia Law Review* 31, no. 3 (March 1931): 477–93.

"Warenhaus Prunk in Amerika: Das modern Warenhaus der amerikanischen Vorstädte." *Illustrierte Zeitung*, 2 March 1933, 284–85.

"What about Art?" *West Coaster*, 1 May 1928, 26.

Whitaker, Alma. "Bullock's in Debut Today: New Wilshire Store, Marking Daring Experiment in Merchandising, Ready to Open Doors." *Los Angeles Times*, 26 September 1929.

Wright, Frank Lloyd. *Frank Lloyd Wright, Chicago. 8. Sonderheft der Architektur des XX. Jahrhunderts*. Berlin: Ernst Wasmuth, 1911.

"Wunderwerk eines deutschen Architekten." *California Staatszeitung*, 15 November 1929.

"Eine Würdigung von Jock Detlef Peters, dem bekannten deutschen Architekt." *California Staatszeitung*, 18 October 1929.

Secondary Literature

Albrecht, Donald. *Designing Dreams: Modern Architecture in the Movies*. New York: Harper & Row, 1986.

Anderson, Stanford. "The Legacy of German Neoclassicism and Biedermeier: Behrens, Tessenow, Loos, and Mies." *Assemblage* 15 (August 1991): 63–87.

Berns, Marla C. *The Furniture of R. M. Schindler*. Seattle: University of Washington Press, 1997. Catalogue of exhibition at the University Art Museum, University of California, Santa Barbara.

Buddensieg, Tilmann, ed. *Berlin 1900–1933: Architecture and Design*. New York: Cooper-Hewitt Museum; Berlin: Gebr. Mann, 1987. Exhibition catalogue.

Campbell, Joan. *The German Werkbund: The Politics of Reform in the Applied Arts*. Princeton, NJ: Princeton University Press, 1978.

"Carl Gustav Bensel." In *Hamburgische Biografie: Personenlexikon*. Vol 4., edited by Franklin Kopitzsch and Dirk Brietzke, 45–46. Göttingen: Wallstein Verlag, 2008.

Clarke, Steven. "The Invisible Architect: K. Lönberg-Holm and His Visible *Tribune* Project." Unpublished senior thesis, Yale University, 1966.

Daily, Victoria. *From Z to A: Jake Zeitlin, Merle Armitage & Los Angeles's Early Moderns*. Los Angeles: UCLA Library, 2006.

Daily, Victoria, Natalie Shivers, and Michael Dawson. *LA's Early Moderns: Art / Architecture / Photography*. Los Angeles: Balcony Press, 2003.

Davis, Margaret Leslie. *Bullocks Wilshire*. Los Angeles: Balcony Press, 1996.

Engels, Hans-Werner. "Jakstein, Werner." In *Hamburgische Biographie*, vol. 4, 175–76. Edited by Franklin Kopitzsch and Dirk Brietzke. Göttingen: Wallstein Verlag, 2008.

"Feil, Joseph L." Obituary. *Los Angeles Times*, 13 July 1979.

"Feldberg-Eber, Lore." In *Hamburgische Biografie: Personenlexikon*. Vol 5, edited by Franklin Kopitzsch and Dirk Brietzke, 114–15 (Göttingen: Wallstein Verlag, 2008).

Friedman, Marilyn F. *Selling Good Design: Promoting the Early Modern Interior*. New York: Rizzoli, 2003.

"Fritz August Breuhaus." November 2006. http://fritz-august-breuhaus.com/home_en.html.

Gebhard, David, and Harriette Von Breton. *L. A. in the Thirties, 1931–1941*. Layton, UT: Peregrine Smith, 1975. Exhibition catalogue.

Gordon, John Stuart. *A Modern World: American Design from the Yale University Art Gallery 1920–1950*. New Haven, CT: Yale University Press, 2011.

Hesse, Frank Pieter, ed., *Stadtentwicklung zur Moderne: Die Entstehung großstädtischer Hafen- und Bürohausquartiere*. Berlin: Hendrik Bäßler, 2011.

Hines, Thomas S. *Architecture of the Sun: Los Angeles Modernism 1900–1970*. New York: Rizzoli, 2010.

———. *Richard Neutra and the Search for Modern Architecture: A Biography and History*. New York: Oxford University Press, 1982.

Hipp, Hermann. *Freie und Hansestadt Hamburg: Geschichte, Kultur und Stadtbaukunst an Elbe und Alster*. 2nd ed. Cologne: DuMont, 1990.

Hoffmann, Karl H. "Bensel & Kamps." Accessed 9

February 2016. http://www.architekturarchiv-web.de/portraets/a-d/ben-sel/index.html.

Hughes, Edan Milton. *Artists in California, 1786–1940*. 3rd ed. Sacramento: Crocker Art Museum, 2002.

Jaeger, Roland. "Von Altona nach Los Angeles: Jakob Detlef Peters (1889–1934)—Ein Rekonstruktionsversuch." In *Architektur in Hamburg—Jahrbuch 1993*, edited by Dirk Meyhöfer and Ullrich Schwarz, 138–49. Hamburg: Hamburg Architektenkammer / Junius, 1993.

"Jock Peters at Schindler House." *Los Angeles Times*, 25 March 1984, Sunday Westside supplement, 1–2, 32–33.

"John Parkinson." Los Angeles Conservancy. Accessed 19 July 2016. https://www.laconservancy.org/architects/john-parkinson.

"John Parkinson (Architect)." Pacific Coast Architecture Database. Accessed 19 July 2016. http://pcad.lib.washington.edu/perosn/108/.

Johnson, J. Stewart. *American Modern, 1925–1940: Design for a New Age*. New York: Metropolitan Museum of Art / Harry N. Abrams, 2000. Exhibition catalogue.

Kähler, Gert, and Hans Bunge, eds. *Der Architekt als Bauherr: Hamburger Baumeister und ihr Wohnhaus*. Munich: Dölling und Galitz, 2016.

Kaplan, Wendy, ed. *Designing Modernity: The Arts of Reform and Persuasion, 1885–1945*. Miami Beach: Wolfsonian, 1995. Exhibition catalogue.

———. *Living in a Modern Way: California Design, 1930–1965*. Los Angeles: Los Angeles County Museum of Art; Cambridge, MA: MIT Press, 2011. Exhibition catalogue.

Karlstrom, Paul, and Susan Ehrlich, eds. *Turning the Tide: Early Los Angeles Modernists, 1920–1956*. Santa Barbara: Santa Barbara Museum of Art, 1990. Exhibition catalogue.

Koch, Robert, and Eberhard Pook, eds. *Karl Schneider: Leben und Werk (1892–1945)*. Hamburg: Dölling und Galitz, 1992.

Leach, William. *Land of Desire: Merchants, Power, and the Rise of a New American Culture*. New York: Pantheon, 1993.

Long, Christopher. *Kem Weber: Designer and Architect*. New Haven, CT: Yale University Press, 2014.

Lubitz, Jan. "Carl Gustav Bensel 1878–1949." May 2004. http://architekten-portrait.de/carl_gustav_bensel/index.html.

———. *Geformter Raum: Die Hamburger Architekten Bensel, Kamps & Amsinck*. Munich: Dölling und Galitz, 2016.

———. "Hamburg, Mönckebergstraße—Zum denkmalpflegerischen Umgang mit den Kontorhäusern des Architekten Carl Bensel (1878–1949)." Accessed 27 February 2016. http://baugeschichte.a.tu-berlin.de/hbf-msd/MSD-ab_2004-06/14_hamburg_MSD_2004-06_AB_web.pdf.

Maciuika, John V. *Before the Bauhaus: Architecture, Politics, and the German State, 1890–1920*. Cambridge: Cambridge University Press, 2008.

Meyer-Tönnesmann, Carsten von. "Imperator der Kunst: Bildungsreformer und Museumsvisionär; Der Hamburger Alfred Lichtwark war der bedeutendste Kunstvermittler des Kaiserreichs. Ein Porträt zum 100. Todestag." *Die Zeit*, 13 January 2014.

Moure, Nancy. *Dictionary of Art and Artists in Southern California before 1930*. Los Angeles, 1975.

"Mrs. Herta Peters." Obituary. *Eagle Rock Sentinel*, 16 May 1957.

Nerdinger, Winfried. *The Architect Walter Gropius*. Berlin: Gebr. Mann, 1985.

———. *Theodor Fischer: Architekt und Städtebauer 1862–1938*. Berlin: Ernst & Sohn, 1988. Exhibition catalogue.

Oliver, Myrna. "Fred B. Huesman, Former Owner of Desmond's, Dies." *Los Angeles Times*, 22 June 1990.

Riestra, Pablo de la. *Hamburg: Architektur einer weltoffenen Stadt*. Hamburg: Michael Imhof, 2008.

Rollins, Bill. "Jock Peters Retrospective on Exhibit at West Hollywood's Schindler House," *Los Angeles Times*, 25 March 1984.

Schädel, Dieter. *Wie das Kunstwerk Hamburg entstand: Von Wimmel bis Schumacher—Hamburger Stadtbaumeister von 1841–1933*. Hamburg: Dölling und Galitz, 2006.

Schwartz, Frederic. *The Werkbund: Design Theory and Mass Culture before the First World War*. New Haven, CT: Yale University Press, 1996.

Seufert, Michael. *Levantehaus: Tradition und Moderne*. Hamburg: Hoffmann und Campe, 2012.

Sheine, Judith. *R. M. Schindler*. London: Phaidon Press, 2001.

Siebenbrodt, Michael. "Planung und Aufbau der Siedlung Loheland und ihrer Architektur 1917 bis 1935." In *Loheland 100: Gelebte Visionen für eine neue Welt*, edited by Elisabeth Mollenhauer-Klüber and Michael Siebenbrodt, 167–74. Fulda: Vonderau Museum Fulda; Petersburg: Michael Imhof, 2019. Exhibition catalogue.

Silverman, Eleni, and Robert C. Giebner. *Bullocks-Wilshire Department Store, Historic Building Survey Report No. CA. 1941/19-Losan, 56*. Los Angeles, 1969/1984.

Solomonson, Katherine. *The Chicago Tribune Tower Competition: Skyscraper Design and Cultural Change in the 1920s*. Chicago: University of Chicago Press, 2003.

Starr, Kevin. *Endangered Dreams and the Great Depression in California*. New York: Oxford University Press, 1996.

———. *The Dream Endures: California Enters the 1940s*. New York: Oxford University Press, 1997.

Stern, Robert A. M., Gregory Gilmartin, and Thomas Mellins. *New York 1930: Architecture and Urbanism between the Two World Wars*. New York: Rizzoli, 1987.

Stöneberg, Michael. *Arthur Köster, Architekturfotografie 1926–1933: Das Bild vom "Neuen Bauen."* Berlin: Gebr. Mann, 2009.

Sweeney, Robert L., and Judith Sheine. *Schindler, Kings Road, and Southern California Modernism*. Berkeley: University of California Press, 2012.

Turtenwald, Claudia, ed. *Fritz Höger (1877–1949): Moderne Monumente*. Munich: Dölling und Galitz, 2003.

Voigt, Wolfgang, Hartmut Frank, and Ulirch Höhns. *Hans und Oskar Gerson: Hanseatische Moderne—Bauten in Hamburg und im kalifornischen Exil 1907–1957*. Hamburg: Dölling und Galitz, 2000.

Weil, Martin Eli. "James Oviatt Building." United States Department of the interior, National Register of Historic Places, Inventory—Nomination Form. 8 November 1982. https://www.nps.gov/subjects/nationalregister/database-research.htm.

Weimar, Friederike. *Die Hamburgische Sezession 1919–1933*. Fischerhufe: Atelier im Bauernhaus, 2003.

Whyte, Iain Boyd. "Peters and Schneider: The Drawing Board as Home." In *Caught by Politics: Hitler Exiles and American Visual Culture*, edited by Sabine Eckmann and Lutz Koepnick, 139–73. New York: Palgrave Macmillan, 2007.

Wilson, Richard Guy, Dianne H. Pilgrim, and Dickran Tashjian, eds. *The Machine Age in America, 1918–1941*. New York: Brooklyn Museum / Harry N. Abrams, 1986. Exhibition catalogue.

Windover, Michael. *Art Deco: A Mode of Mobility*. Montreal: Presses de l'Université du Quebec, 2012.

Winter, Robert, and Alexander Vertikoff. *The Architecture of Entertainment: LA in the 1920s*. Salt Lake City: Gibbs Smith, 2006.

Jock Peters, project for a war memorial and exhibition tower, c. 1915.
Pencil on board. UCSB.

INDEX

A. L. Gilks House, 264–265 figs. 250–251, 266, 266–267 figs. 252–253, 277
Academy of Modern Art, Los Angeles, 150, 151 fig. 132, 237, 286n238
Ain, Gregory, 150
Allgemeine Elektricitäts-Gesellschaft (AEG), 31, 48, 56
Ameis, Otto Heinrich, 280n29
American Union of Decorative Artists and Craftsmen (AUDAC), 199–200, 231, 288n297, 289n322
Architectural Group for Industry & Commerce, 285n216
Art Alliance of America, 123, 143
Art Deco, 102, 115, 125, 143, 145, 212, 231
art education center, plans for, 81, 82–83 figs. 61–64, 195, 196 fig. 174, 276
Art Nouveau, 124, 271
Asanger, Jacob, 125, 193, 231
AUDAC. *See* American Union of Decorative Artists and Craftsmen
Auerbach, Alfred, 212
August Van Horne Stuyvesant House, 197
Aztec Revival, 98

Bach, Franz, 30–31, 32–33 figs. 12–13
Baldwin, Maria Theresa. *See* Hollander, Mrs. Louis P.
Ballin, Albert, 18, 34, 68
Barker Brothers department store, 93, 138, 150
Barlach, Ernst, 48
Barnsdall, Aline, 93
Baugewerkschulen, 21–22
Baugewerkschule zu Hamburg, 21–22, 25, 280nn22–23
Bauhaus, 27, 73, 102, 115, 271
Bau-Rundschau, 37 figs. 20–21, 40 fig. 25, 76, 80
Behrens, Peter, 26–27, 31, 34, 48, 50, 50–51 figs. 33–34, 53, 56, 62, 70, 80, 199, 281n58, 282nn82–83, 282n90
Benedict nickel, 200
Bensel, Carl Gustav, 26–27, 27 fig. 7, 29 fig. 10, 30–31, 32–33 figs. 12–13, 34, 37 figs. 20–21, 39, 40–41 figs. 25–26, 44–45 fig. 30, 47, 48, 50, 53, 275, 280n37, 282n82
Bentlock furniture, 289n322
Berlage, Hendrik Petrus, 26, 73
Berlin Secession, 48
Biedermeier, 34
Blachley, Mrs. C. O., 138, 276
Blaine, Harry, 125, 133–134 figs. 114–115, 276
Boeger, Friedrich, 30
Boeger, Hertha. *See* Peters, Herta
Boegie, 31, 32 fig. 14. *See also* Peters, Herta
Bollman House, 93

Breuhaus, Fritz August, 27, 47, 282n83
Breuhaus de Groot. *See* Breuhaus, Fritz August
Bugenhagenhaus, Hamburg (H. & O. lumber), 34, 37 fig. 21, 275
Bullock, John G., 159
Bullock's downtown, 159, 227, 231; exhibition (*Decorative Arts of Today*), 193, 287n274; expansion, 159; renovation proposal, 226 fig. 212, 227, 228–229 fig. 213-215, 231, 248, 277
Bullock's Wilshire, 13–14, 15, 152 fig. 133, 159–191, 197, 198, 199, 200, 271, 277; artwork, 168, 170 fig. 147, 174, 176–177 figs. 152–153, 287n262; Collegienne Shoe Department, 179, 189–190 figs. 166–167; critical reception, 179; design concept, 159, 160, 168, 179; Doggery, 174; elevators, 166–167 figs. 144–145, 168, 169 fig. 146; exhibit of Peters's drawings, 195; first floor plan, 162 fig. 140; flooring, 168, 169 fig. 146, 179; furniture, 168, 174, 175 fig. 151, 178 fig. 154, 182–183 fig. 157, 184 fig. 158, 191 fig. 169; Gift Shop, 174, 178 fig. 154; lighting, 164–165 figs. 142–143, 168, 169 fig. 146, 171 fig. 148, 173 fig. 149, 174, 176–178 figs. 152–154, 180 fig. 155, 182–185 figs. 157–158; Lingerie Department, 179, 189 fig. 165; lobby concourse, 160, 163–166 figs. 141–144, 169 fig. 146, 200; Menswear Department, 174, 179, 180 fig. 155, 181–183 fig. 156–157, 184–186 figs. 158–160; Millinery Department, 189 fig. 166; motor court entrance, 160; opening, 193; Perfume Department, 160, 164–165 figs. 142–143, 168; project timetable, 168, 194; radiator covers, 174, 180–181 figs. 155–156; restoration of, 13–14; Riding Shop, 174, 175–177 figs. 151–153; Salon of Beauty, 179, 191 figs. 168–169; Shoe Department, 179, 188 fig. 164; Sportswear Department, 168, 169 fig. 146, 170–173 figs. 147–150, 174; Stationery Department, 174, 178 fig. 154; store displays, 164–165 figs. 142–143, 168, 174, 179, 170–173 figs. 147–150, 175–178 figs. 151–154, 180–190 figs. 155-167
Burroughs, Edgar Rice, 115, 285n204
Burton, David, 248, 249 fig. 233, 277

C. R. Blackburn Company, 143, 143 fig. 125, 145
California Arts and Architecture, 179
California Art Club, 193
California bungalow, 94, 238
Cavanaugh & Stebins, 254, 263 fig. 249, 277
Century of Progress International Exposition, 199–200, 288n297
Charleroi, Belgium (foundry), 52 fig. 36, 53, 62, 64
Charleville, Belgium, 64
Chevalier, Maurice, 254
Chevrolet automobile dealership, Wilmington, California, 198, 212, 222 figs. 207–208, 277
Chicago Tribune competition, 85 figs. 67–68, 86, 276
Chilehaus, Hamburg, 66 fig. 47, 68

city hall competition, Gadebusch, Germany, 73, 276
"City of 1950", 109, 111 fig. 92
City of the Future (Corbett), 109
City of the Future, The, 6, 102, 106–108 figs. 83–85, 109, 110–111 figs. 86–91, 195, 248, 276
Čižek, Franz, 27
Classicism, role of in emerging modernism, 34, 48, 50, 56
clinker bricks, 68
Collins, David, 168
Cologne Werkbund Exhibition (1914), 70
Cologne international exhibition, 227, 230 fig. 216, 277
commercial building competition, Königsberg, Prussia, 81, 84 fig. 66, 86, 276
Confessions of a Co-Ed, 248, 249 fig. 233, 277
Connell, Will, 231
Constructivism, Russian, 73
Contemporary Art Decoration and Store Design Exhibition (Plaza Art Center, L.A.), 288n319
Cooper, Samuel, Jr., 237
copyright, of Universal Assembling Furniture, 145
Corbett, Harvey Wiley, 109, 123, 285n200
Creative Art, 212
Cukor, George, 248, 253 fig 237, 255 figs. 238–239, 277
cultural center competition, Stuttgart, Germany, 81, 84 fig. 65, 276
Cuypers, Eduard, 26, 73

Davidson, J. R., 15, 93, 125, 193, 227, 231, 289n336
Day, Clarence P., 89
De Stijl, 73, 174
de Swart, Jock, 13, 289n338
de Swart, Ursel (Ursula), 13, 18, 30, 47, 53, 65 fig. 46, 91, 92 fig. 72, 224, 268, 279n3, 281n77, 289n338
Decorative Arts of Today, downtown Bullock's exhibition, 195
del Río, Dolores, 109
Delaunay, Sonia, 168
department store competition, Nuremberg, Germany, 29 fig. 10, 30, 275
Deskey, Donald, 174
Desmond's, Los Angeles, 154, 155–156 figs. 134–136, 277, 286n243
Die Brücke, 48
Dithmarschen, Germany, 17–18, 19 fig. 3, 67, 279n4, 289n326
Dodge House (Irving Gill), 98
Donner Schloss, 81, 86
Dreier, Hans, 102, 109, 115, 224, 248, 254
Dunn, Alma and William, 285n223

Eagle Rock, Los Angeles, 94, 123, 125, 224, 227, 238, 276, 284n186, 289n338
Eagle Rock Annual Art Exhibit, 227
Einstein Tower (Erich Mendelsohn), 81
Elliot, R. F., house by Schindler, Los Angeles, 238
Exposition des Arts Décoratifs et Industriels Modernes, Paris (1925), 123, 154, 159
Expressionism, 15, 39, 48, 54, 56, 68, 70, 73, 76, 80, 81, 101–102, 124–125, 143, 200

Fagus Factory, Alfeld an der Leine, Germany (Gropius and Meyer), 48
Famous Players-Lasky, 14, 101–122, 106–107 fig. 83, 108 figs. 84–85, 110–111 figs. 86–91, 116–120 figs. 98–101, 125, 224, 266, 276; annual film production, 109; hiring of Peters, 102; resignation of Peters, 115, 123–124, 138, 285n207

Feil and Paradise, 150, 153–154, 159, 160, 195, 199, 224, 277
Feil, Joseph L., 153, 154, 286n240
Feininger, Lyonel, 73, 283n131
Feinman, Martin H., 149
Feldberg-Eber, Lore, renovation of residence, 80, 276
Ferenz, F. K., 150, 237
festival hall and gymnasium, Alster Lake, Hamburg, 50, 52 fig. 35, 70, 275
festival hall, Loheland Settlement, Fulda, Germany, 98, 99 fig. 77, 276, 284n190
Fine Arts Building, Los Angeles, 143, 150, 154, 194, 231, 237, 277
First National Bank Building, Pasadena, 237, 238
Fischer, Alfred, 30, 281n58
Fischer, Theodor, 30, 64, 102, 281n58
Flint, Ralph, 212
Fox Film Company, 109, 112–114 figs. 93–95, 276
Fox, William Henry, 123
Francis, Kay, 248
Frankl, Paul T., 123, 125, 150, 159, 199, 231
furniture, designed by Peters, 68, 69 fig. 48, 94, 94 fig. 73, 123–125, 126–135 figs. 106–116, 137 figs. 118–119, 144 figs. 126–127, 145, 146–149 figs. 128–131, 150, 156 fig. 136, 158 fig. 138, 159, 168, 174, 175 fig. 151, 178 fig. 154, 182–183 fig. 157, 184 fig. 158, 191 fig. 169, 209–211 figs. 189–193, 213 fig. 194, 215–217 figs. 196–200, 227, 230 figs. 216–217, 231, 233–234 figs. 219–221, 235 fig. 222, 248, 250–252 fig. 234–235, 254, 262–263 figs. 248–249, 274 fig., 290 fig.
Futurists, Italian, 54

German Expressionism. *See* Expressionism
German Werkbund, 27, 70, 76, 80, 81 fig. 60
German-Turkish Union, Constantinople, meeting hall for, 50
Gesamtkunstwerk, 212
Gibbons, Cedric, 102, 231
Gibbons, Eliot, 231
Gibbons, Irene Maud, 231. *See also* Irene, studio for
Gilks, Alfred L., 266. *See also* A. L. Gilks House
Gill, Irving, 93, 98
Girls about Town, 248, 253 fig. 237, 254, 277
glass walls, in architecture, 62
Goetheanum projects (Rudolf Steiner), 98
Grant, Cary, 254
Great Depression, 13, 224, 231, 237, 238, 271, 286n232
Great Fire of 1842, Hamburg, 18
Greene, Charles Sumner, 93, 94, 98
Greene, Henry Mather, 93, 94, 98
Gropius, Walter, 48, 53, 62, 70
Großstadt (etching), 39, 43 fig. 29, 275

H. & O. lumber company, the Bugenhagenhaus for, 34, 37 fig. 21, 275
Haller, Martin, 68
Hamburg municipal rail office, 25
Hamburg Sezession, 80
Hamburg-Amerika Line (HAPAG), 18, 34, 36 fig. 17, 68
Handicrafts and Applied Arts School, Altona. *See* Handwerker- und Kunstgewerbeschule
Handwerker- und Kunstgewerbeschule, Altona, 9–10, 80–81, 82–83 figs. 61–64, 86, 89–90, 150, 195, 281n52, 283n14, 284n164
Hanf, Konrad, 76
Hanging Gardens of Babylon, 109
Hanseatic modernism, 68, 80

Häring, Hugo, 39, 281n58
Harris, Harwell Hamilton, 150
Haus der Freundschaft, competition design, 50
Haus Schluck, Volksdorf, Germany, 80, 276
Heckel, Erich, 48
Heereswerkstätte West, 53, 282n97
Heimatstil, 34
Heizkraftwerk, Tiefstack, Hamburg. See Tiefstack Electrical Power Plant
Hi-Hat Magazine, 125, 136–137 figs. 117–119, 276, 285n208
Hoch- und Untergrundbahn (Hamburg municipal rail office), 25
Hoffmann, Josef, 90
Höger, Fritz, 30, 66 fig. 47, 67–68, 70, 73, 76, 80, 91
Hollander department store. See L. P. Hollander store
Hollander, Mrs. Louis P., 196
Hollyhock House, 98, 193
Holscher, Walter, 231, 248
Hound of the Baskervilles, The, 284n185
house designs, for builders, 93–94, 95–97 figs. 75–77, 98, 276
housing estate, Berlin-Lichtenberg, 50
Hugo, Captain Melchior von, 64

I. Magnin department store, 159, 224
Irene, studio for, 13, 14, 231, 232–235 figs. 218–222, 277
Itten, Johannes, 27
J. & J. Kohn Company, 212
Jacob and Ameis, 25, 280n29
Jacob, Alfred Ernst Paul, 280n29
Jaffe, Sam, 248, 252 fig. 236
Jakstein, Werner, 81
Jallot, Léon, 168
Jallot, Maurice, 168
Jarrenwisch, Germany, 17, 19 fig. 2, 62
Jock D. Peters—Studio of Contemporary Design, 142 fig. 123, 143, 150, 194–195, 195 fig. 173, 237, 238, 277; letterhead, 195 fig. 172; office interior, 142, fig. 124, 143, 194 fig. 171
John and Donald B. Parkinson Architects, 152 fig. 133, 159, 160, 162 fig. 140, 227
Johnson, Philip, 13
Ju' Nice Avocado Skin Food, label for, 143, 143 fig. 125, 145
Jugendstil, 15, 27, 34, 40 fig. 24

Karpen, Leo, 286n232
Karpen & Brothers. See S. Karpen & Brothers Company
Karstadt department store, Hamburg, 31, 33 fig. 13
Kiesler, Frederick, 199
King, Moses, 109, 285n200
Kirchner, Ernst Ludwig, 48
Klöpperhaus (Fritz Höger), 67
Koch, Hugo, 76
Kohn Company. See J. & J. Kohn Company
Kohtz, Otto, 285n197
Kontorhausneubauten, Hamburg, Germany, 27, 30
Koues, Helen, 123
Kreis, Wilhelm, 26–27
Kroller-Müller House, 39
Kunstakademie, Düsseldorf, competition, 27, 29 fig. 9, 275
Kunstgewerbeschule, Düsseldorf, 26–27, 30, 48
Kunstgewerbeschule, Hamburg, 281n52
Kunstgewerbeschule, Essen, 30, 31, 34

Kunsthalle Hamburg, expansion of, 39, 44–45 fig. 30, 70
Künstlerkolonie, Darmstadt, Germany, 26

L. P. Hollander store, 13, 14, 15, 196–221; bankruptcy, 224; Boudoir Accessories Department, 200, 208 fig. 188; Central Hall, 200, 204 fig. 183; critical reception, 212; Debonair Shop, 212, 216–217 figs. 197–200; Decorative Arts Department, 200, 209 fig. 189; delivery car, 212, 220 fig. 203; design concept, 200, 212; elevators, 200, 206–208 figs. 185–187; entrance foyer, 200, 203–204 figs. 181–182; façade, display windows, 200, 201–202 figs 178–180; furniture designs for, 210–211 figs. 190–193; LeMaire and Peters hired, 198; lighting, 200, 212, 218–219 figs. 201–202; Lingerie Department, 200; Millinery and Fur Department, 200, 208 fig. 187, 212, 213–215 figs. 194–196; opening, 200; packaging design, 192 fig. 170, 220–221 figs. 204–206; perfume area, 200, 205 fig. 184; presentation drawings, 197–199 figs. 175–177; project schedule, 197, 200; retail furniture line, 200, 209 fig. 189; store displays, 197–199 figs. 175–177, 198–199, 200, 212, 202 figs. 179–180, 204–205 figs. 183–184, 208–210 figs. 187–190, 213 fig. 194, 215–217 figs. 196–200
Landhaus projects: Landhaus I, 62, 63 figs. 44–45, 73, 275, 283n130; Landhaus II, 73, 74–75 figs. 52–54, 76, 79 figs. 58–59, 275, 276
Lang, Fritz, 109, 276
Langgaard, Louise, 98
Lasky, Jesse L., 102
Last Judgment, 102, 105 fig. 82
Lawrence Shepard House, San Marino, California, 254, 258–262 figs. 244–248, 266, 277
Le Corbusier, 48, 53
LeMaire, Eleanor H., 160, 191 fig. 168, 195, 224, 238, 248,288n316; AUDAC, thoughts on, 199, 231, 288n297; Bullock's Wilshire, 160, 168, 174, 191 fig. 168; Hollander, 196–200, 202 figs. 179–180, 212; Mary Sachs department store, 224, 225 figs. 210–211, 227
Lentz, Irene Maud. See Irene
Levantehaus, Hamburg, 30, 31, 32 fig. 12, 275
Lichtwark, Alfred, 25, 30, 34, 39, 280nn32–33, 282n82
lighting, designed by Peters, 126 figs. 106–107, 130 fig. 111, 131 fig. 112, 132 fig. 113, 134 fig. 115, 137 fig. 118, 156 fig. 136, 158 fig. 138, 164–165 figs. 142–143, 168, 169 fig. 146, 171 fig. 148, 173 fig. 149, 174, 176–178 figs. 152–154, 179, 180 fig. 155, 182–185 figs. 157–158, 204 fig. 183, 208–210 figs. 187–190, 212, 214–219 figs. 195–202, 222 fig. 208, 226 fig. 212, 254, 263 fig. 249, 286n248
Lille, France, bombing, 54, 55 fig. 37
Lingenbrink, William, 13, 138, 154, 155 fig. 135, 212, 223 fig. 209, 231, 236 fig. 223, 237–238, 240 fig. 225, 276, 277, 285n223, 286n226, 289n336
Little Studio-Gallery exhibition, Monrovia, California, 227
Lissitzky, El, 227
Loheland Settlement, Fulda, Germany, 98, 99 fig. 77, 276, 284n190
Lönberg-Holm, Knud, 81, 84 figs. 65–66, 85 fig. 68, 86, 276, 283n152
Los Angeles Times, 179, 195, 268
Los Feliz, Los Angeles, 93, 98, 266
Lowe, Edmund, 109
Lubitsch, Ernst, 102, 254, 255 figs. 238–239, 277

Maddux Air Lines, 13, 14, 154, 157–158 figs. 137–138, 159, 161 fig. 139, 277, 286n246
Maddux, Jack L., 154, 159
Magnin, Joseph, 224
Magnin department store. See I. Magnin department store
Maier-Krieg, Eugene, 125, 168, 174, 287n262
Mars, 115, 116–121 figs. 98–102, 123, 125, 195, 276, 285n205

INDEX 301

Mary Sachs department store, 224, 225 figs. 210–211, 227, 277
Mayan Revival, 98
Mendelsohn, Erich, 14, 76, 81, 86, 101, 115, 195, 281n58, 283n152
Messel, Alfred, 31
Metro-Goldwyn-Mayer, 102, 184n185
Metropolis, 109, 115, 276
Meyer, Adolf, 48, 62, 70
Mies van der Rohe, Ludwig, 39, 48, 62, 73
Millier, Arthur, 179, 195, 287n274
Mission Revival, 94, 95–96 figs. 74–75, 98, 276
Modernage Furniture Company, 150
modernism, early California, 13, 15, 93, 138, 231, 237, 238, 254, 268
modernism, German, 15, 48, 53, 67, 73, 212
Mohawk Carpet Mills, 141 fig. 122, 143, 154, 193, 277
Mönckebergstraße, Hamburg, 30, 33 fig. 13, 34, 39, 40 figs. 25, 67, 275
Murphy, Dudley, 248, 249 fig. 233, 277
Muschenheim, William, 199

Nationale Automobil-Gesellschaft, Berlin-Oberschöneweide, 50
Neher, Otto H., 90–91, 93, 98, 101, 153, 276, 284n171
neo-Biedermeier, 27, 76
Neo-Renaissance style, 67
neoclassicism, Nordic, 143
Nerdinger, Winfried, 62
Neutra, Dione, 193, 289n336
Neutra, Richard, 15, 93, 109, 125, 150, 193, 227, 231, 238, 266, 285n216
New York Times, 123–124

Olbrich, Joseph Maria, 26, 70
One Hour with You, 254, 255 figs. 238–239, 277
Oviatt Building, Los Angeles, 154, 159
Oviatt, James Zera, 154

packaging, designed by Peters,143, 143 fig. 125, 145, 192 fig. 170, 212, 220–221 figs. 204–206, 277
Pan-Pacific Auditorium, Los Angeles, 115
Paradise, Bernard R., 153–154, 286n241
Paramount Pictures, 14, 102, 224, 227, 231, 237, 238, 248, 249–253 figs. 233–237, 254, 255–256 figs. 238–240, 266, 277
Park Moderne, Calabasas, California, 236 fig. 223, 237–238, 239–240 figs. 224–225, 277
Parkinson, Donald, 159
Parkinson, John, 159
Parkinson and Parkinson. *See* John and Donald B. Parkinson Architects
Pasadena, California, 86, 89–91, 93, 94, 138, 196, 227, 237
Paul Cassirer Gallery, Berlin, 76
Paul, Bruno, 62, 125
Paulsen, Dr., house for, 73, 74–75 figs. 52–54, 275. *See also* Landhaus II
Peters Brothers Modern American Furniture, 122 fig. 103, 124–125, 124 figs. 104–105, 126–135 figs. 106–116, 153, 285n216
Peters family house, Eagle Rock, 224, 238, 241–247 fig. 226–232, 248, 277
Peters, Anna Marie Friederike (née Kruse), 16 fig. 1, 17, 279n2
Peters, Annemarie (daughter), 86
Peters, Annemarie (sister), 16 fig. 1, 17
Peters, Detlef, 16 fig. 1, 17, 21
Peters, Dierk, 62, 64, 65 fig. 46, 285n207, 288n307
Peters, Eva, 86
Peters, Fritz, 16 fig. 1, 17, 21, 62
Peters, Georg (George), 16 fig. 1, 17, 21, 86, 89–91, 93, 94, 94 fig. 73, 122 fig. 103, 123–124, 124 figs. 104–105, 125, 126 figs. 106–107, 128–129 figs. 109–110, 131 fig. 112, 135 fig. 116, 138, 143, 200, 276, 277, 280n17
Peters, Georg Fritz, 16 fig. 1, 17, 18, 21, 25
Peters, Hans Otto, 94, 284n185
Peters, Herta (daughter), 86
Peters, Herta (wife), 30, 31, 31 fig. 11, 34, 40 fig. 24, 47, 48, 53, 54, 62, 64, 65 fig. 46, 67, 68, 86, 89, 90, 91, 93–94, 102, 138, 254, 268, 281n54, 284n155, 284n185, 284n191, 289n336, 289n338; relationship with Peters, 30, 31, 32 fig. 14, 35 fig. 15, 193–194
Peters, Jakob Detlef. *See* Peters, Jock
Peters, Jock, 16 fig. 1, 12 fig., 17–18, 24 fig. 6, 36 fig. 18, 49 fig. 32, 65 fig. 46, 87 fig. 69, 88 fig. 70, 269 fig. 254, 270 fig.; apprentice to stonemason, 21; architectural apprenticeship, in Carl Bensel's office, 26, 27, 30–31, 32 fig. 12, 34, 37 figs. 20–21, 39; articles by, 76, 282n109; artist, desire to be, 18, 21, 31, 34, 67; assistant art director in Hollywood, hired as, 102, 248; collaboration with Eleanor LeMaire, 160, 168, 179, 191 fig. 168, 196, 197–200, 202 figs. 179–180, 212, 224, 225 figs. 210–211, 227, 277, 288n316; death, 268; design competitions, independent, 70, 72 fig. 51, 73, 123–124, 141 fig. 122, 143; director of school in Altona, 80–81, 86, 89–90; director of school in Los Angeles, 150, 237; education at Baugewerkschulen, 21–22, 280nn22–23; family move to Hamburg, 18; grenade explosion, Lille, 54, 55 fig. 37; illness, 53, 64, 86, 89, 91, 194, 268; immigration to America, 89; in Dithmarschen, 17–18, 19 fig. 3; in Fritz Höger's office, 30, 67–68, 70, 73, 80, 91; in Otto Neher's office, 90–91, 93, 98, 101, 153, 276; in Peter Behrens's office, 48, 50, 51 fig. 34, 53, 62, 282nn82–83, 282n90; military service, 9, 47, 53–54, 62, 64; name change (to Jock), 93; opens own design/architecture firm, 142 figs. 123–124, 143; reaction to war, 54, 62, 64; reading architectural journals, 227; relationship with Herta, 30, 31, 32 fig. 14, 35 fig. 15, 194; resignation from Famous Players-Lasky, 115, 123–124, 138, 285n207; resigns as director of school in Altona, 90; signet, 115, 116 figs. 96–97; teaching in Essen, 30, 34; teaching in Los Angeles, 150; trip to the Netherlands, 26; work for Feil and Paradise, 150, 153, 154, 159, 160, 195, 199, 224
Peters, Karl, 16 fig. 1, 17
Peters, Matilda, 16 fig. 1, 17
Plattdeutsch, 17, 189n326
Plaza Art Center exhibition, Los Angeles, 288n319
Poelzig, Hans, 39, 62
power plant competition, Rendsburg, Germany, 73, 275
Prairie Style, 238
Princess of Mars, A, 115, 285n204

R. F. Elliot House, Los Angeles (Schindler), 238
Rappolthaus, Hamburg, 30
Realgymnasium competition, Duisburg, Germany, 34, 37 fig. 20
Reimer, Johann, 21, 22, 54, 73
Renaissance revival, 68
Richards, Charles R., 123
Richmond, John, 284n191
Rietveld, Gerrit, 125, 145
Road to Reno, The, 248, 250–252 figs. 234–236, 277
Robie House, Chicago, Illinois, 73
Rogers, Charles "Buddy", 248
Rohden, Hedwig von, 98
Rolandhaus, Hamburg, 30
Rosenthal, Rena, 231
Ruck, Wilhelm Frederich, 194, 195 fig. 172, 198, 200, 222–223 figs. 207–209, 224, 237, 239 fig. 224, 277, 287nn277–278
Ruhlmann, Émile-Jacques, 174

Ruhr crisis, 91
S. Karpen & Brothers Company, 123–124, 193, 276, 286n232
S. S. *Reliance,* 88 fig. 71, 89
Sachlichkeit, 15, 50
Sachs, Herman, 168, 287n262
Sanford, N. C., 143
Sant'Elia, Antonio, 109
Schindler, Pauline, 168, 179
Schindler, R. M., 15, 93, 125, 138, 145, 150, 168, 193, 227, 231, 237, 238, 285n216
Schlemmer, Oskar, 115
Schluck, Haus, Volksdorf, Germany, 80, 276
Schneider, Karl, 48, 62, 80, 276
Schoen, Eugene, 150, 174
School of Applied Arts, Altona. *See* Handwerker- und Kunstgewerbeschule
Schumacher, Fritz, 68, 76, 80, 282n82
Schürmann Company, 230 fig. 216, 277
Segal, Hermann. *See* Sachs, Herman
set designs, by Peters: *City of the Future, The,* 6 fig., 102, 106–108 fig 83–85, 109, 110–111 figs. 86–91, 195, 248, 276; *Confessions of a Co-Ed,* 248, 249 fig. 233, 277; *Girls about Town,* 248, 253 fig. 237, 254, 277; *Last Judgment,* 102, 105 fig. 82; *Mars,* 115, 116–121 figs. 98–102, 123, 195, 276, 285n205; *One Hour with You,* 254, 255 figs. 238–239, 277; *Road to Reno, The,* 248, 250–252 figs. 234–236, 277; *This Is the Night,* 254, 256 fig. 240, 277; unidentified, 100 fig. 78, 103–105 figs. 79–82, 121 fig. 102, 257 figs. 241–243, 278 fig.; *What Price Glory,* 109, 112–114 figs. 93–95, 115, 276
Sheffield, Clarence G., 196–198, 224
Shepard, Lawrence, house for. *See* Lawrence Shepard House, San Marino, California
Shreve, Lamb & Harmon, 197, 199, 200
Sidney, Sylvia, 248
Silver Strand Beach, Ventura County, California, 13, 14, 138, 139–140 figs 120–121, 154, 237, 276, 277, 285n223
Skilling, Chauncey F., 90, 284n171
Skinner, Mabel, 231, 277
Skyscraper furniture, Paul T. Frankl, 124, 150
Southwestern Law School, Los Angeles, 13–14
Spanish Colonial Revival, 93, 212, 227
Spirit of Sports, The (mural), 168, 170 figs. 147, 174, 287n262
Spirit of Transportation (mural), 287n262
St. Genevieve Rose marble, 168
Stanson, George Curtin. *See* Stojana, Gjura
Steiner, Rudolf, 98
Sternberg, Josef von, 102
Stickney Memorial School of Fine Arts exhibition, Pasadena, 227
Stiller, Hermann, 26
Stojana, Gjura, 168, 170 fig. 147, 174, 287n262
store displays, designed by Peters, 8 fig., 14, 156 fig. 136, 164–165 figs. 142–143, 168, 174, 170–173 figs. 147–150, 151–154 figs. 175–178, 180–190 figs. 155–157, 197–199 figs. 175–177, 198–199, 200, 212, 202 figs. 179–180, 204–205 figs. 183–184, 208–210 figs. 187–190, 213 fig. 194, 215–217 figs. 196–200, 263 fig. 249
Storey, Walter Rendell, 123–124
Straumer, Heinrich, 80
Südseehaus, Hamburg, 30
Sullivan, Louis, 90, 93
Sutnar, Ladislav, 283n152

Taggart House, Los Feliz, Los Angeles (Lloyd Wright), 98

Tashman, Lilyann, 248
Taut, Bruno, 62, 281n58
This Is the Night, 254, 256 fig. 240, 277
Tiefstack Electrical Power Plant, Hamburg, Germany, 39, 41–42 figs. 26–28, 47, 275
Todd, Thelma, 254
tuberculosis, 9, 53, 62, 64, 268
tubular steel furniture, 171 fig. 148, 174, 179, 182–184 fig. 157–158, 190, fig. 167, 191 fig. 168, 216 figs. 197–198, 217 fig. 200, 248, 249 fig. 233
Tuttle, Frank, 254, 256 fig. 240, 277
Twentieth Century Fox, 284n185. *See also* Fox Film Company

UFA. *See* Universum Film-Aktien Gesellschaft
Unit Furniture, 145
Universal Assembling Furniture, 144 fig. 127, 145, 146–149 figs. 128–131, 277
Universum Film-Aktien Gesellschaft (UFA), 102, 109

Valentino, Rudolph, 102, 138
Vernon Fixtures and Cabinet Company, 198–199, 200, 248, 254, 288n301
Vestal Bill, 145
Vivié, Marianne, 280n37
Vivié, Wilhelm Daniel, 25–26, 30, 34, 39, 280nn31–32, 280n37, 282n82

Wallace, Richard, 248, 250–252 figs. 234–235, 277
Walsh, Raoul, 109, 112–114 figs. 93–95, 276
war memorial church, 56, 58–59 figs. 40–41, 275
war memorial sarcophagi, 56, 56–57 figs. 38–39, 275
war memorial tower/exhibition hall, Ferdinandstor, Hamburg, 70, 71 fig. 50, 80, 275
Wasmuth Portfolio (Frank Lloyd Wright), 62
Watson and Son tailor shop, Hollywood Boulevard, 125, 135 fig. 116, 276, 285n216
Weber, John, 168, 179, 191 fig. 168, 198, 200, 277
Weber, Kem, 9, 15, 93, 123, 125, 138, 150, 153, 193, 224, 227, 231, 238, 286n248, 288n297, 289n322
Wedding Tower, Darmstadt, Germany (Maria Olbrich), 70
Werkbund, 27, 70, 76, 80, 81 fig. 60
Wertheim department store, Berlin (Alfred Messel), 31
Westermann Company, 227
What Price Glory, 109, 112–114 figs. 93–95, 115, 276
Whittlesey, Charles F., 90, 284n171
Williams, Paul R., 199
Wilshire Boulevard, development, 159
Winnett, P. G., 159–160, 200, 227
Witte, Karl, 80, 276
Wohldorf-Ohlstedt housing development plan, Hamburg, Germany, 39, 275
World War I, 15, 39, 47, 48, 53–54, 55 fig. 37, 56, 62, 64, 67–68
Wright, Frank Lloyd, 14, 62, 73, 93, 97 fig. 76, 98, 174, 193, 238
Wright, Lloyd, 93, 97 fig. 76, 98, 125, 193, 231
Wurdeman & Becket, 115

Young, Roland, 254

Zeitlin, Jake, bookstore, 193–194
Zukor, Adolph, 102

JOCK PETERS | *Architecture and Design*
The Varieties of Modernism

Editor: **Beth Daugherty**
Cover and book design: **Jiří Příhoda**
Copyediting: **Florence Grant**
Proofreading: **Leslie Kazanjian**

Typeset in Gill, Etelka
Printed on 128 gsm Gold East Matt Art

Copyright 2021 Christopher Long

All rights reserved. No part of this publication may be reproduced, stored in a retrieval system, or transmitted, in any form or by any means, electronic, mechanical, photocopying, recording, or otherwise without the prior written permission of publisher.

First edition

Printed and bound in China by Pimlico Book International

ISBN-13: 978-1-7356001-1-6 (hardcover)

Library of Congress Control Number: 2021909843

Published by Bauer and Dean Publishers, Inc.
P.O. Box 98, Times Square Station
New York, NY 10108
www.baueranddean.com

Distribution by ACC Art Books
(orders processed by National Book Network)
6 West 18th Street, Suite 4B
New York, NY 10011
Tel (212) 645-1111
ussales@accartbooks.com

Front cover: Detail of Sportswear Department, Bullock's Wilshire, Los Angeles, 1929.

Back cover: "Palace entrance," set for an unknown film, 1923. Pen and ink and watercolor on paper. UCSB.

Front endpaper: Elevator station, set for *Mars*, Famous Players-Lasky (not produced), c. 1926. Pencil, pen and ink, and watercolor on paper. UCSB.

Back endpaper: Radio station, set for *Mars*, Famous Players-Lasky (not produced), 1926. Pencil, pen and ink, and watercolor on paper. UCSB.

Frontispiece: Maddux Air Lines ticket office, 1928. Mott-Merge Collection, California State Library, Sacramento.

Image opposite Contents: Unidentified motion picture set, possibly for *The City of the Future*, Famous Players-Lasky (not produced), c. 1925. Pencil and watercolor on paper. UCSB.